Savvy *in the* City:

SAN FRANCISCO

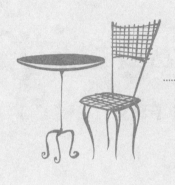

Jayne Young

and

Sheridan Becker

 St. Martin's Griffin ✖ New York

Savvy in the City:

SAN FRANCISCO

A "See Jane Go" Guide to City Living

For Mary Frances Young,

"The Original Jane Girl"

www.stmartins.com

BOOK DESIGN BY VICTORIA KUSKOWSKI

MAPS BY JEFFREY L. WARD
ARTWORK © 2001 BY JORDI LABANDA

Library of Congress Cataloging-in-Publication Data
    Young, Jayne
        Savvy in the city—San Francisco / Jayne Young and Sheridan Becker.—1st ed.
            p.   cm. (A "see Jane go" guide to city living)
        ISBN 0-312-25278-1
            1. San Francisco (Calif.)—Guidebooks. 2. Women—Travel—California—
    San Francisco—Guidebooks. 3. City and town life—California—San Francisco.
    I. Title: San Francisco. II. Becker, Sheridan. III. Title.

F869.S33 Y69 2001
917.94'610454—dc21   2001041947

First Edition: December 2001

10   9   8   7   6   5   4   3   2   1

Contents

Anything and everything your heart, mind, body, soul, and mother desire all over the city in every nook and cranny . . . Big or small, outrageous or simple, luxurious or bargain . . . If you can't find what you need, we suggest you contact NASA for a shuttle ticket.

Twilight *149*

"Twinkle twinkle little star, how I wonder what cute boy we might trip over on our adventures into the night . . ." Take advantage of all these opportunities for entertainment and wild abandon. Little black dress not provided!

Tripping *179*

We're not talking acid, we're talking adventure. You've hit the City by the Bay with a bang . . . What's fun, unique, free, freeing, shocking, educational, trendy, playful, creative, exotic, adventurous, athletic, and artistic this side of the Golden Gate Bridge (and beyond!)? Fasten your seat belts.

Acknowledgments

This book would not have been a reality without

Mary Dorrian
&
Whitney Daane

Extra special thanks to: William Clark, agent extraordinaire; Adam Robinson, a genius man with a plan; Jordi Labanda, for making "Jane" come alive; Kelley Ragland, for belief and motivation; Sally Carnes, truly a visionary graphic artist; W&R Group, for patience and understanding; James Young, for his unwavering positive attitude and "clippings"; and last but not least, my loving siblings, Gary, Linda, Gilbert, Brian, Mary Ann, and Larry.

Jane would also like to thank: Stuart Allen, Siobhan Callahan, Stefano Eco, Amy Young, Parma Chaudhury, Pacy Wu, Claire Canavan, Michela Hill, Bob Doyle, Peter Imber, Pam Rousakis, Andy and Helga Fuhrmann, Alexandra Hannen Scott, Tracy Denton, Jennifer Paterino, Steve Prue, Ben Sevier, John Carley, the Dorrian family, Patrica Murphy, Dewey and Barbara "Bubbles" Daane, St. Martin's Press, Stephanie and the Art Department, and all of the cooperative establishments listed (you know who you are!).

Also, Sheridan would like to thank Catherine Perry and James Sanders.

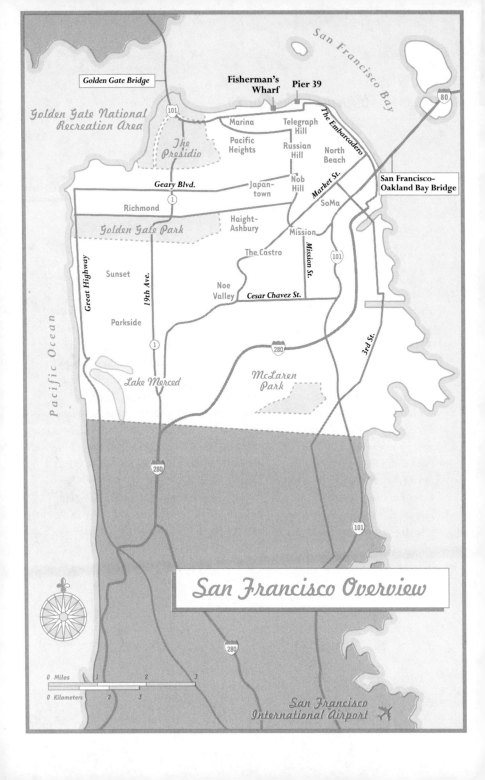

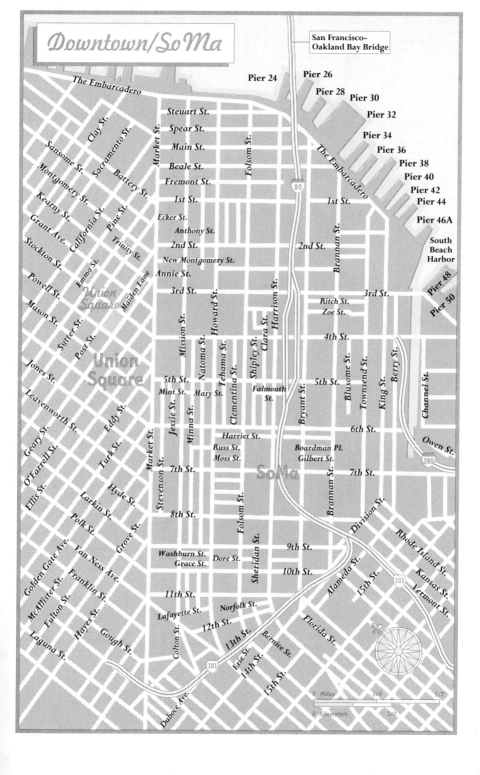

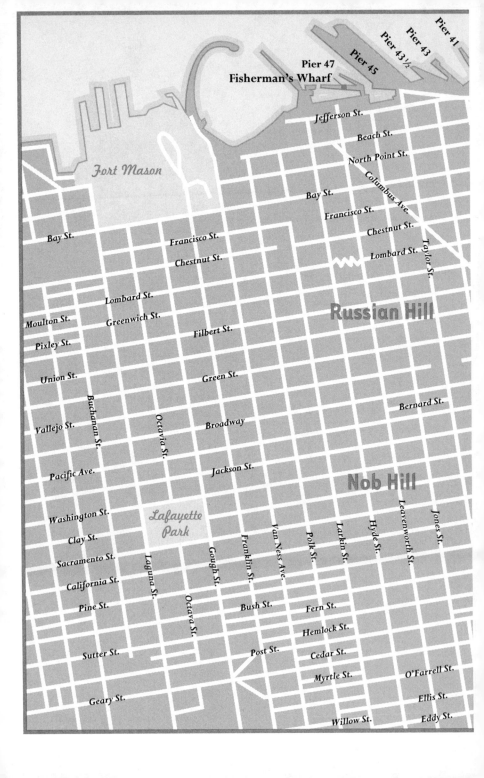

Nob Hill/North Beach/Chinatown

Pier 39

The Embarcadero

Pier 35

Pier 33

Pier 31

Pier 29

Pier 27

Stockton St.

Telegraph Hill

Coit Tower

Greenwich St.

Pier 23

Pier 19

Telegraph Hill Blvd.

Pier 17

Filbert St.

Pier 15

Union St.

Pier 9

North Beach

Green St.

Grant Ave.

Kearny St.

Pier 7

Vallejo St.

Montgomery St.

Sansome St.

Battery St.

Front St.

Davis St.

The Embarcadero

Pier 5

Pier 3

Pier 1

Powell St.

Chinatown

Washington St.

Drumm St.

Clay St.

Mason St.

Sacramento St.

California St.

Pine St.

Bush St.

Sutter St.

Market St.

SoMa

Post St.

Union Square

Geary St.

Union Square

San Francisco Bay

0 Miles   1/4   1/2

0 Kilometers   1/4   1/2

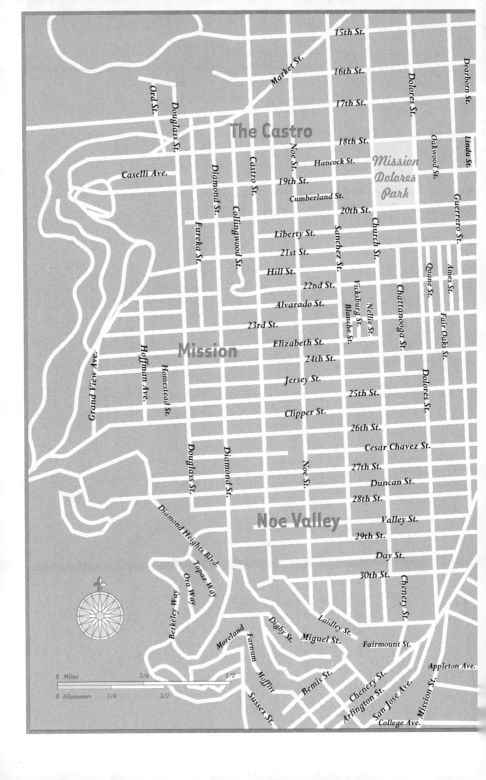

The Castro/Noe Valley/Mission

Hoff St.
Randall St.
Sycamore St.
San Carlos St.
Lapidge St.
Lexington St.

Mariposa St.
18th St.
19th St.
Mistral St.
20th St.
21st St.

Alabama St.
Bryant St.
Hampshire St.
101

Harrison St.
Florida St.
York St.
Potrero Ave.
Rhode Island St.

Hill St.
22nd St.

Valencia St.
Mission St.
South Van Ness Ave.
Folsom St.
Treat Ave.
Potrero
23rd St.
Vermont St.
Kansas St.
San Bruno St.
Utah St.

Capp St.
Shotwell St.
24th St.

Bartlett St.
San Jose Ave.
Lilac St.
Cypress St.
Virgil St.
Horace St.
Lucky St.
25th St.
26th St.

26th St.

Marin St.

Cesar Chavez St.
Army St.

Precita Ave.
Peralta St. Wright St.
York St.

Tiffany Ave.
Mirabel Ave.
Montezuma St.
Coso St.
Manchester St.
Franconia St.
Alabama St.
Jerrold Ave.

Powers Ave.
Fair Ave.
Esmeralda
Coleridge St.
Lundy's Ave.
Prospect Ave.
Winfield St.
Bonview St.
Elsie St.
Montcalm
Rutledge
Brewster St.
Faith
Joy St.
Bay Shore Blvd.
Loomis St.
Patterson St.
Barneveld Ave.

Virginia Ave.
Esmeralda Ave.

Eugenia St.
Kingston St.
Bocana St.
Bernal Heights
Mayflower St.
Oakdale Ave.
Palou St.

Santa Marina St.
Powhattan Ave.
Wool St.
Moultrie St.
Eugenia Ave.
Nevada St.
Nebraska St.
Bradford St.
Putnam St.
Bronte St.

Bennington St.
Cortland Ave.
101

Holly Park Circle
Newman St.
Highland Ave.
Andover St.
Ellsworth St.
Jarboe Ave.
Folsom St.
Banks St.
Prentiss St.
Tompkins Ave.
280

Holly Park
Park St.
Crescent Ave.
Anderson St.
Gates St.

Golden Gate Park (west end)

Cross Over Dr.

Portals of the Past

Lloyd Lake

Marx Meadow

Middle Drive West

Elk Glen Lake

Mallard Lake

25th Ave.

25th Ave.

Fulton St.

Barbecue Pits

Speedway Meadow

Metson Lake

30th Ave.

J. F. Kennedy Dr.

Lindley Meadow

Speckels Lake Dr.

Speckels Lake

Golden Gate Park Stadium and Polo Field

Metson Rd.

Martin Luther King Jr. Dr.

36th Ave.

Senior Citizens Center

Model Yacht Club

Anglers Lodge

Middle Drive West

Dog Training Area

Buffalo Paddock

Fly-casting Pools

Middle Lake

South Lake

1/2

J. F. Kennedy Dr.

Chain of Lakes Dr. E.

Bercut Equitation Field

41st Ave.

North Lake

Chain of Lakes Dr. W.

43rd Ave.

Lincoln Way

Lincoln Way

1/2

1/4

Fulton St.

Golden Gate Park Golf Course

J. F. Kennedy Dr.

1/4

Archery Field

47th Ave.

Queen Wilhelmina Tulip Garden

Soccer Fields

Martin Luther King Jr. Dr.

0 Miles

0 Kilometers

Beach Chalet (Visitor Information Center)

La Playa

La Playa

Great Highway

Golden Gate Park (east end)

Fell St.

Oak St.

Waller St.

Stanyan St.

Carl St.

Horseshoe Pits

McLaren Lodge

Kezar Pavilion

Mothers' Meadow

Conservatory Dr. W.

Kezar Dr.

Kezar Stadium

Sharon Meadow

Arguello Blvd.

Conservatory of Flowers

J. F. Kennedy Dr.

Tennis Courts

Frederick St.

HANC Recycling Center

2nd Ave.

Bowling Green Dr.

National AIDS Memorial Grove

Lawn Bowling

Fulton St.

Lily Pond

Middle Drive East

Handball Courts

Big Rec Ball Field

Lincoln Way

Morrison Planetarium

Steinhart Aquarium

9th Ave.

10th Ave.

Music Concourse

Tea Garden Dr.

M. H. de Young Memorial Museum

Japanese Tea Garden

Shakespeare Garden

Strybing Arboretum and Botanical Gardens

Library of Horticulture and County Fair Building

Park Presidio Blvd.

Redwood Memorial Grove

Stow Lake

1/2

Fulton St.

Pioneer Log Cabin

Stow Lake Dr.

Strawberry Hill

Martin Luther King Jr. Dr.

Lincoln Way

Cabrillo St.

1/4

1/2

Rainbow Waterfall

Boat House

Park Presidio Bypass Dr.

19th Ave.

Irving St.

0 Miles

1/4

Transverse Dr.

Middle Drive West

0 Kilometers

Marina/"The Heights" (Pacific/Laurel/Presidio)

San Francisco Bay

Marina Small Craft Harbor

East Harbor

West Harbor

Yacht Rd.

Marina Blvd.

Casa Way
Rico Way
Cervantes Blvd.
Retiro Way

Mason St.

Jefferson St.

Marina

Beach St.

North Point St.

Scott St.

Capra Way

Mallorca Way

Bay St.

Alhambra St.

Toledo Way

Francisco St.

Chestnut St.

101

The Presidio

Halleck St.

Edie Rd.

Lincoln Blvd.

Kennedy Ave.

Palace Dr.

Lyon St.

Lombard St.

Magnolia St.

Cow Hollow

Presidio Blvd.

Sherman Rd.

Baker St.

Broderick St.

Divisadero St.

Greenwich St.

Filbert St.

Fillmore St.

Webster St.

Buchanan St.

Laguna St.

MacArthur Ave.

Union St.

Green St.

Vallejo St.

Morton St.

Rodriguez St.

Portola St.

Clark St.
Liggett St.
Sibley Rd.

Presidio Blvd.

Broadway

Pacific Ave.

Steiner St.

Jackson St.

Washington St.

Pacific Heights

Clay St.

Sacramento St.

Presidio Heights

Lyon St.

Presidio Ave.

Walnut St.

Laurel St.

Locust St.

Spruce St.

Pierce St.

Scott St.

California St.

Pine St.

Wilmot St.

Jackson St.

Washington St.

Clay St.

Sacramento St.

California St.

Laurel Heights

Lupine St.

Bush St.

Sutter St.

Post St.

Fillmore

Euclid Ave.

Emerson St.

Wood St.

Collins St.

Blake St.

Cook St.

Geary Blvd.

O'Farrell St.

Geary Blvd.

Terra Vista Ave.

Masonic Ave.

Turk St.

0 Miles   1/4   1/2

0 Kilometers   1/2

Hayes Valley/Civic Center/Haight-Ashbury

Civic Center

Leavenworth St.
Hyde St.
Larkin St.
Polk St.
Van Ness Ave.
Franklin St.
Gough St.
Geary Blvd.

Elm St.
Redwood St.
Grove St.
Lech Walesa St.
McAllister St.
Hickory St.
Lily St.
Rose St.
Market St.

Civic Center Complex

Western Addition

Jefferson Square
Octavia St.
Ivy St.
Laguna St.
Dolores St.
Waller St.
Germania St.
Herman St.
Webster St.
Fillmore St.
Steiner St.
Belcher St.

Hayes Valley

Golden Gate Ave.

Pierce St.
Alamo Square
Scott St.
Pierce St.
Duboce Park
Waller St.
Duboce Ave.

O'Farrell St.
Ellis St.
Eddy St.
Broderick St.
Josephs Ave.
Divisadero St.
Page St.
Broderick St.
14th St.
Henry St.
Noe St.
16th St.
Castro St.
15th St.
Beaver St.
Alpine Terrace
Buena Vista Terrace

Corona Heights

Terra Vista Ave.
Baker St.
Fortuna
Encanto
Barcelona
Anza Vista Ave.
Nido Ave.
Vega St.
Anza St.
Geary Blvd.

McAllister St.
Fulton St.
Grove St.
Hayes St.
Lyon St.
Baker St.
Central Ave.

Presidio Ave.
Masonic Ave.
Fell St.
Oak St.
Haight St.
Waller St.

University of San Francisco

Turk St.
Golden Gate Ave.
Ashbury St.
Clayton St.
Cole St.
Shrader St.
Stanyan St.

Panhandle

Haight-Ashbury

Delmar St.
Downey St.
Belvedere St.
Beulah St.
Frederick St.
Carl St.
Parnassus Ave.
Grattan St.
Alma St.

Buena Vista Park

Roosevelt Way
Museum Way
States St.
Java St.
Piedmont St.
Ashbury Terrace
Clifford Terrace
Loma Vista Terrace
Upper Terrace

101

0 Miles   1/4   1/2
0 Kilometers   1/4   1/2

Eats

Anjou, 44 Campton Place (bet. Post & Sutter Sts.), (415) 392-5373, *Quiet Lunch*

Tucked into an alleyway, this very French bistro is a delightful place to take a client for lunch. It is quiet, cozy and well off the beaten path. . . . There is no reason you can't do a little work and have a lovely lunch experience at the same time! Have steak au poivre and tarte tatin with vanilla ice cream. Or, go for a hearty pretheater bistro dinner.

Aqua, 252 California St. (bet. Battery & Front Sts.), (415) 956-9662, *Power Scene*

If you're having a good hair day and sporting the perfect Marc Jacobs suit, sit at the bar, enjoy a fabulous seafood lunch and take in the grandeur, or perhaps a peek at Sharon Stone. . . . Try the tuna tartare, lobster potpie, foie gras steak, or tapioca-crusted Thai snapper. Their flowers could pinch-hit for an impromptu wedding . . . The large bar area attracts the more financially solvent of the male species, so meet a potential investor in your new business or maybe a prospective suitor. Best seafood in the whole Bay Area. *Psst . . . California beauty Wynona Ryder recommends the tried-and-true root beer float! Delish!*

Campton Place, 380 Stockton St. (bet. Post & Sutter Sts.), (415) 955-5555, *Power Breakfast*

Breeding "ground zero" for many a famous chef who takes the fairy dust with them and becomes the top brass at other restaurants. It's about as close to perfection as you are able to find in San Francisco. Insiders go for the incomparable breakfasts, but don't limit yourself. . . . Go anytime you get an invitation or big spender's disease! It's French Provençal and worthy of our "Côte D'Azur" award of the year . . . meaning we'd rather eat here than sunbathe in Saint-Tropez with a gorgeous hunk . . . not! But almost!

Ciao Bella, 685 Harrison St. (@ 3rd St.), (415) 541-4940, *www.ciaobella-gelato.com, Best Desserts*

There is ice cream, and then there is gelato, the dense, intense ambrosia that is so readily available in Firenze and Roma and more or less nonexistent hereabouts (despite nominal imitations). The Ciao Bella version, however, is wonderful. The company started in New York's Little Italy in 1983, and currently manufactures its mind-altering product in two places—New Jersey and here, smack in the middle of Soma. At its adjacent café you can sample such varieties as Scharffen Berger chocolate, cinnamon caramel, fresh mint, rice (!), two kinds of green tea, three kinds of vanilla (bourbon, French and Tahitian), all of them 12 percent butterfat, 20 percent air (most ice creams are 60 percent air), and handmade in batches from "the family recipe from Torino, Italy." There are also sorbettos (which are 70 to 80 percent fruit juice) in flavors like grapefruit Campari, lemon ginger, and apricot chardonnay. Each season produces a specialty or two as well (pumpkin in October, champagne around New Year's). *Psst . . . you can even have the store develop a flavor you've come up with for $25 and the purchase of five gallons. Ciao Bella is on Ristorante Laghi's dessert menu, or you can purchase a pint at Whole Foods and a few other outlets.*

Dottie's True Blue Café, 522 Jones St. (bet. Geary & O'Farrell Sts.), (415) 885-2767, *American Breakfast*

Stand in line with the rest of the strange and unusual crowd at this popular early-morning café. Why wait? The ginger and cinnamon pancakes. Fifties-style décor sets the stage for the avant-garde crowd of Harley Davidson–riding boys and a few Junior League girls for good measure. Their other baked goods on hand are scrumptious. B.Y.O.H.: Bring Your Own Hangover.

Farallon, 450 Post St. (bet. Mason & Powell Sts.), (415) 956-6969, *Fish & More*

Poseidon's bride would feel right at home! Built in 1924, the domed ceiling in the main dining room is utterly gorgeous. The whole place is a bit over the top, but in the good sense of the word: the interior of this downtown seafood dream feels like an underwater fantasyland. The stairway covered with thousands of blue-black beads that resemble caviar is just the tip of the iceberg. Chef/Owner Mark Franz delivers refined dishes that will enthrall as well as fulfill your champagne wishes and caviar dreams. Don't miss the Dungeness crab gratin with truffle crème fraiche. Loud and rowdy but still manages to remain highly refined. Open for lunch Tues.–Sat., dinner daily. Valet parking $12 (at dinner).

Fina Estampa, 1100 Van Ness Ave. (@ Geary St.), (415) 440-6343, *Speciality Appetizer*

By now, almost everyone in San Francisco has tried seviche at least once, and though lime-cured seafood is hard to beat, it can, like anything else, get boring after a while. If you've reached this point, it's time you ordered the seviche mixto at the Peruvian-Spanish Fina Estampa—a heaping plate of whitefish, prawns, mussels, squid, and onions, marinated in lemon juice as opposed to lime, then touched with fiery aji chili sauce. Your taste buds have never felt so alive.

Frinagle, 570 4th St. (bet. Brannan & Bryant Sts.), (415) 543-0573, *Intimate French*

Reasonable prices and first-rate food are what keep die-hard patrons coming back to this small French bistro. Over the past ten years the neighborhood has been built up and competition is stiff, but Gerald Hiroigoyen blends his magical Basque roots with a California flare to keep the offerings fresh. If frisee salad with warm bacon dressing, mussels with fried garlic, rack of lamb and crème brulee light your fire, then this is your "meal ticket." Parking is difficult during business hours but easy at night. Entrées from $14 to $21.

Fuzio, One Embarcadero Center (bet. Clay & Front Sts.), (415) 392-7995, *Casual Fusion*

See details in Marina/Cow Hollow, other location in Castro/Noe Valley.

Hamburger Mary's, 1582 Folsom St. (@ 12th St.), (415) 626-5767, *Burger Joint*

A San Francisco fixture. Tourists have uncovered this destination for greasy burgers served in a kitschy atmosphere. Show up for a quick lunch with the on-the-go crowd, for brunch the morning after a big party or for a late-night "munchies" attack. You can't go wrong, darling!

John's Grill, 63 Ellis St. (bet. Powell & Stockton Sts.), (415) 986-0069, *Old World Institution*

Feels like a private men's club where you are the first girl allowed to dine! As of 1908 (before we voted, or had blow-dryers or Botox on our side), this Downtown standard was serving lunch to the multitudes. Some things never change. Lunch at the bar is a trip. The American food is less than exciting, yet we keep coming back for more.

Le Charm, 315 5th St. (bet. Folsom & Harrison Sts.), (415) 546-6128, *Quaint French*

Unlike most of its "pan-Asian, industrial chic, power-scene" neighbors, this place is a refreshing respite in the sea called Soma. Husband-and-wife team Alain and Lina serve simple but tasty French fare at this refreshingly charming little gem. Sit outside on beautiful nights and gloat on your freedom to choose when, where and how to dine in San Francisco! The prix fixe is a bargain for locals without expense accounts.

Lulu, 816 Folsom St. (bet. 4th & 5th Sts.), (415) 495-5775, *Parisian Landmark*

If French food is your passion, then this is your place . . . in ambiance and cuisine. A decade after its opening, Reed Hearon's ode to French cuisine is still ruling the Soma restaurant roost, mainly thanks to consistent excellence on the menu. Come into this noisy and festive environment to have your taste buds tantalized by melt-in-your-mouth breads and uniquely flavorful condiments and vinegars, all made on premises. Visit heaven in the fresh whole snapper à la nicoise deboned tableside, the wild boar sausage on a bed of goat cheese or our favorite, iron-skillet-roasted mussels. If you want to totally blow your daily caloric intake, head facedown into the bourbon-caramel pot-de-crème. . . . You may get a little attitude from the staff, but the food will blind you to any momentary lapses in hospitality.

Masa's, @ Hotel Vintage Court, 648 Bush St. (bet. Powell & Stockton Sts.), (415) 989-7154, *Fine Dining*

You won the lottery or maybe you have met Mr. Right, finally? This is the place to celebrate in opulence. For many years, this has been one of the best restaurants in the city, but the former chef left and it slid into obscurity for a couple of years. It's back in a big way. Chef Ron Siegel knows how to make scrumptious food that is never too overbearing for the taste buds. The sweetbreads are unique: They are crisp and melt in your mouth. Otherwise, we recommend the six or nine course tasting menu. Enlist the help of Michelle Kaseman, the female sommelier, to pair the perfect wine with each course. The cellar is beyond fab. It's romantic too!

Maya, 303 2nd St. (bet. Folsom & Harrison Sts.), (415) 543-2928, *Upscale Mexican*

The original location is in Manhattan, fabulous but just half the size of this Soma outpost. Located in the ground floor of an office building, the ambiance is much the same. Pale orange walls with

Mayan masks set the tone. The food is outstanding authentic Mexican with a slight nouvelle twist. The inviting, large bar is great for groups just looking to booze it up or waiting to be seated for a meal that will awaken the taste buds big time! Pitchers of margaritas as well as the innovative menu keep this place packed nightly.

One Market, 1 Market St. (@ Steuart St.), (415) 777-5577, *Original American*

This posh Embarcadero eatery has spawned a revolution. Yes, we are prone to exaggeration, but executive chef Bradley Ogden has won awards, penned cookbooks and opened other restaurants thanks to the success of this tried-and-true place. The cuisine is considered "haute Mid-western" which sounds like an oxymoron but it works in a big way! Jazz-inspired piano music fills the background air as you devour prime pork ribs. Lunch is hopping with movers and shakers in search of a hearty meal . . . with a bit of a scene to match! Valet parking available.

Plouf, 40 Belden Place (bet. Pine & Bush Sts.), (415) 986-6491, *Neighborhood Favorite*

Calling all sexy mermaids to this French translation of "splash!" And what a splash and a blast it is: cute waiters and yummy food! Mussels by the bucket-full for $10 can be ordered seven different ways thanks to their delicious sauces and broths: the sublime tomato, the simple garlic and white wine, or the more flavorful crayfish. And be sure to go all the way and order the crispy, delectable "frites," that are great to dip in the leftover sauce or just shove directly into your mouth by the handful. Our favorite lunchtime treat is the fresh seafood salad. Warm weather brings open windows with rows of tables lining the alley for open-air dining and flirting. The Gallic French waiters are almost as much fun as that afternoon in 1999 on the streets of Paris when France won the World Cup. *Psst . . . plan ahead— parking is scarce in this neighborhood.*

Postrio, 545 Post St. (bet. Mason & Taylor Sts.), (415) 776-7825, *Late Night*

Since opening over 12 years ago, this brainchild of Wolfgang Puck has held the city's attention. Step down the spacious staircase into the main dining room, where the vaulted ceiling bleeds down to an exposed kitchen that is set far enough apart to be intriguing instead of annoying. The clinking of the plates and the grilling sounds only add to the feel. The toque-wearing kitchen staff make you feel as if something exciting is about to happen. And it is! It's a lively place to eat after seeing a brilliant art film at the Embarcadero Center cinema (see Tripping, Downtown/Soma). Sunday brunch, our personal favorite, features lobster sandwiches with yellow tomato on homemade wholegrain bread. No rushing, just eating and drinking to your heart's content. . . . Life is good, no? *Psst . . . finish with the dessert sampler for two or a selection of European cheeses.*

Rubicon, 558 Sacramento St. (bet. Montgomery & Sansome Sts.), (415) 434-4100, *Power Scene*

Thanks to new chef Dennis Leary (not the comedian, thank God!), this downtown favorite is still securing its spot on the "best of" lists as well as your list of hot numbers in your Palm Pilot IV. Investors Robert De Niro, Francis Ford Coppola and Robin Williams obviously knew what they were doing when they brought this incredible California-inspired French menu to the neighborhood. The Mork-inspired wine list is otherworldly! Besides its stellar investors, many luminaries of stage and screen can be seen nibbling here, especially San Francisco's favorite romantic, Danielle Steel. Not for the budget-minded, but worth every last dime you have in your bank account. Valet parking available for $10.

Sear's Fine Food, 439 Powell St. (bet. Post & Sutter Sts.), (415) 986-1160, *Casual Breakfast*

Women in classic movie-style "bib" waitress outfits serve world-renowned Swedish pancakes as well as oodles of other traditional American favorites for those with hearty appetites . . . or just swollen heads from one too many margaritas last night at Maya (see above).

Shalimar, 532 Jones St. (@ Powell St.), (415) 928-6654, *Ethnic/Indian*

Set in the heart of the Tenderloin, this neighborhood dive dishes up superspicy Indian-Pakistani curry-infused dishes with plenty of nan. It's a bit chaotic during busy hours, which is most of the time. Festive, but be sure to arrange transportation in this less-than-desirable neighborhood for girls going solo, especially after dinner. Cheap: nothing on the menu is over nine dollars. Cash only.

South Park Café, 108 South Park (bet. 2nd & 3rd Sts.), (415) 495-7275, *Authentic French*

Located in the mellow South Park area, this quaint bistro could have been plucked out of the heart of France. Newspapers lined up on wooden bars entice you to catch up on the daily scoop while noshing on steak frites and cheap red wine. Great casual hang without a bunch of fuss.

Tadich Grill, 240 California St. (bet. Battery & Front Sts.), (415) 391-1849, *Historic Landmark*

The oldest restaurant in San Francisco, it was serving manly food before California was admitted to the union! Cute boys in suits line the bar for its authentic American fare—think steaks and chops. It's a bit noisy, and the tourists have discovered its charm. Worth a peek and a little nibble at the counter to feel a part of something bigger than yourself.

Tu Lan, 8 6th St. (@ Market St.), (415) 626-0927, *Ethnic / Vietnamese*

This place is on a sketchy block, so be sure to bring your bodyguard or Jeff Garcia from the San Francisco 49ers. One rumor says these are the best Imperial rolls this side of Vietnam, another that this is Julia Child's favorite restaurant in San Francisco. Atmosphere is negligent, but once you are munching on world-class food that costs a little more than McDonalds', you will hardly take note.

Working Girls' Café, 239 Kearny St. (bet. Sutter & Bush Sts.), (415) 398-1390; 100 Spear St., (@ Mission), (415) 495-8995, *On The Run*

See description in Marina/Cow Hollow.

✧ ***Not to Miss:***

Bizou, 598 4th St. (@ Brannan St.), (415) 543-2222, *Historic Building*
Boulevard, 1 Mission St. (@ Steuart St.), (415) 543-6084, *Show Stopper*
Fleur de Lys, 777 Sutter St. (@ Taylor St.), (415) 673-7779, *Grand Dame*
Hawthorne Lane, 22 Hawthorne St. (bet. 2nd & 3rd Sts.), (415) 777-9779, *Cal / Asian Standard*
Original Joe's, 144 Taylor St. (bet. Eddy & Turk Sts.), (415) 775-4877, *Gigantic Burgers*

Acquerello, 1722 Sacramento St. (@ Polk St.), (415) 567-5432, *Truffle Hunting*

Elegance abounds on Polk Street. High-end Italian food is served here in a romantic setting that was formerly a stately old church. They have stood the test of time, and the test of critics, by offering an award-winning list to match the world-class menu. A winning combination by our "Jane" standards! The rabbit pappardelle and parmesan budino are both notable, but anything on the menu will delight even the most die-hard food fairies.

Albona Restorante Istriano, 545 Francisco St. (@ Taylor St.), (415) 441-1040, *Alternative Cuisine*

Tired of traditional Italian fare? Host/Owner Bruno Viscovi welcomes patrons wtih the excitement of a long-lost family member. You'll be led graciously to your own "special" table, where the incredibly informed waiters, or Bruno himself, will steer you through a menu based on the cuisine of Istria (the peninsula in the north Adriatic Sea). Loosely related to classic Italian food, but with a Mediterranean twist. We loved trying something new for a change . . . it also sounded snazzy to say we had had "Istrian" food for dinner like it was our best-kept secret! Well, now it's yours. Open for dinner only.

Café Jacqueline, 1454 Grant Ave. (bet. Green & Union Sts.), (415) 981-5565, *Romantic Dinner*

For over 20 years charming owner Jacqueline has been quietly serving an all-soufflé menu to lovers and to the neighborhood "in" crowd. Linger over these masterpieces of raised perfection with your new crush, or get a baby-sitter and steal away with your hubby for a night of romance soufflé-style! She has the art of making the light-as-air concoctions down to a science, and if you've ever tried to make one at home, you know *exactly* what we mean. . . . Talk about infuriating! Don't be scared away by the sound of this single-minded menu, there is something for everyone. Rise to the occasion, girlfriend.

Eastern Bakery, 720 Grant Ave. (@ Clay St.), (415) 392-4497, *Snack To Go*

All black bean cakes come down to two elements—the black

bean filling and the surrounding crust—and the Eastern scores high marks on both counts. The filling is rich, smooth, and almost creamy, with a deep, earthy quality that transcends sweetness; the flaky, lard-enriched crust is its perfect complement. For those purist aficionados of the black bean purée, period, the Rose Black Bean Cake is the way to go. It has three times the amount of filling as the regular cakes, and its thin envelope of crust is just a platform for the purée. (You might want to avoid the Black Bean Golden Yolk Mooncake, though—it not only has a distracting hard-boiled yolk nestled inside of it, but its filling is dry and overcooked.)

The Gold Spike, 527 Columbus Ave. (bet. Green & Union Sts.), (415) 421-4591, *Family Style*

If these walls could talk. But they are covered with photos documenting the history of this place and its owners. The family started out with a candy store and then it turned into an "unofficial bar" (speakeasy) serving booze during Prohibition "to pay the bills." Since opening this version in 1960, they have been serving Crab Cioppino to devoted diners sitting comfortably in the cool, old-fashioned wood booths. Open for dinner only, starting at 5 P.M., closed on Wednesday.

Hyde Street Bistro, 1521 Hyde St. (@Jackson St.), (415) 292-4415, *Neighborhood Favorite*

Romantic in a cozy as opposed to sexy way. Opt to dine in the tiny alcove complete with a curtain that separates lovebirds from the rest of the diners. So sweet! Take our advice, order the goat cheese salad, Bouillabaisse, and the hot chocolate cake. We died and went to Heaven on that one . . . more than once! The waiting area is small, so bring your patience along with your appetite. Reservations are a must.

I Fratelli, 1896 Hyde St. (@ Green St.), (415) 474-8240, *Neighborhood Favorite*

This is a cozy, classic Americanized Italian restaurant complete with checkered tablecloths, a large bar and lots of locals wining and dining among friends. After a long day at the office, it's great to meet a gal pal here for a bite or two. Our meal of the hour: linguini with clam sauce (considered SF's best) with a side of bruschetta and a bottle of merlot! Home is where someone else cooks and you don't have to pay for it . . . hopefully your date will! Dinner only.

Kowloon, 909 Grant Ave. (bet. Jackson & Washington Sts.), (415) 362-9888, *Vegetarian Delight*

Overdosed on your boy-toy last night? Clear your mind and your body with healthy dim sum, the best in the city. Then head over to the convenient Green Door, an informal and funky neighborhood spa, for a massage. Now, don't you feel better? We do, if only for giving this scoop to other "Jane" girls.

La Folie, 2316 Polk St. (bet. Green & Union Sts.), (415) 776-5577, *Dining Experience*

Celebrate life here! In a city that boasts of the most important culinary institutions in America, this place raised the bar one more notch. Chef Roland Passot creates magic beyond our wildest expectations. All things we love: lobster, caviar, foie gras and pink Krug champagne. What more could a girl need to celebrate a new love, new job, new house, new attitude, new hairdo, new lease on life for just about anything that warrants a toast? Put on your favorite flirty Calypso skirt and pick a reason to party!

Liguria Bakery, 1700 Stockton St. (@ Filbert St.), (415) 421-3786, *Baked Goods*

Opened in 1911 by three brothers, this landmark business is still serving some of the best baked goods in the city. Mon. to Fri. from 7 A.M. to 4 P.M., or until they run out! And believe us, it is disappointing to arrive and see empty shelves behind glass . . . devastating, in fact! So get off your tush (it burns calories) and go early. They are baking while you sleep, but if you oversleep you'll miss what they've baked! Now that's a deep thought. . . .

L'Osteria del Forno, 519 Columbus Ave. (bet. Union & Green Sts.), (415) 982-1124, *Northern Italian*

Okay, Guidorella (our made-up Italian term for Cinderella!), missing the family back in the homeland? North Beach is a bona fide destination for anything and everything Italian to put in your mouth. . . . Never mind. . . . This place is the best *little* find. Known for the smallest kitchen and dining room ever created, nothing stops the throngs of devotees from coming for milk-braised pork, homemade focaccia sandwiches and the wildly popular pumpkin ravioli, a house specialty. We challenge any granny in Tuscany to beat the flavor. Open seven days, from 11 A.M. to 10:30 P.M. Cash only.

Mario's Bohemian Cigar Store Café, 566 Columbus Ave. (@ Union St.), (415) 362-0536, *Lunch On The Go*

Italy, Italy, everywhere and nothing in between! This is a funky North Beach coffee shop that sells delicious authentic Italian sandwiches on foccacia, with hot meatballs and melted Swiss cheese in homemade marinara sauce. On the lighter side, the eggplant version is just as delicious and slightly less of a lead bomb on the old tummy. Top it off with the scrumptious lemon ricotta cheesecake. Go for it, you can always work out at one of the city's many 24 Hour Fitness any time of the day or night!

MC², 470 Pacific Ave. (@ Montgomery St.), (415) 956-0666, *Trendy Fish*

No longer the "hip fish" it was made out to be during its heyday, this is still a fun favorite for the "Jane" in all of us. The hype has dwindled, but the sleek and chic industrial interior still holds fond memories for us, so we return again and again to the scene of the crime . . . namely to the groovy bar that makes the groovy Cosmopolitans. We usually cocktail ourselves into a stupor before heading to a table to literally nibble on the miniscule portions of over-priced delicacies. The wine list is still great, and all over the map in terms of price and selection. This has become one of those SF eateries you just love to hate . . . and then love it some more.

Oriental Pearl, 760 Clay St. (bet. Kearny & Grand Sts.), (415) 433-1817, *Dim Sum*

Jonesing for fresh dim sum in a neighborhood that is crawling with seemingly good Chinese food? Throw caution, and chopsticks, to the wind and trust us: this is the one-stop destination in Chinatown. Prepare to wait along with the rest of the world because everything is made fresh daily, and according to legend neither Rome nor dim sum can be "built" in a day!

Polker's American Cafe, 2226 Polk St. (Vallejo & Green Sts.), (415) 885-1000, *Cheap Grease*

In a wasteland of cheap eats, this is the place to go for your self-imposed culinary embargo. If the man of your dreams wants a burger and you want a salad, then this is the ideal compromise! And believe us, engagements have been broken over less. Didn't your mama tell you the way to a man's heart is through his stomach? Serving until 11 P.M. daily.

R&G Lounge, 631 Kearny St. (@ Clay St.), (415) 982-7877, *Long Live Seafood*

Rated the Best by *SF Weekly,* Jane of course had to check it out for herself—we'll be the judge of our own sesame noodles, thank you very much. Well, we were blown away! Select anything and everything from its centerpiece oceanic tanks, and you will not be disappointed! Fried prawns, roasted crab, steamed fish reeking of ginger . . . On a more earthly plane, the brisket is fantastic, along with the not-to-miss exotic Chinese veggies. The atmosphere is two-fold: the downstairs is festive and casual, the upstairs more uptight. Hang with your gal pals in the former or drag your "It Boy" up the staircase for a little quiet Kung Pao courting. Staff is friendly and helpful . . . in fact you might want to let them order for you!

Rose Pistola, 532 Columbus Ave. (bet. Green & Union Sts.), (415) 399-0499, *Citywide Favorite*

Local celebrity chef Reed Hearon, the "Bobby Flay" of San Francisco, rules the roost in this neighborhood with his hip and happening hot spot. There are several ways to enjoy your dining experience: Numero Uno is at the bar, where couples and solo diners casually chat with each other; Numero Due is the lively and *noisy* main dining room; Numero Tre is at one of the sidewalk tables on a warm afternoon. The food is light Cal-Med with plenty of fresh herbs for natural flavoring. The best dessert is Chocolate Budino with brandy-lized whipped cream. Some say it's better than sex, but we'll leave that for you to decide. Success breeds attitude, so be patient if you are not getting the all-star attention that you feel you deserve. . . .

Swan Oyster Depot, 1517 Polk St. (bet. California & Sacramento Sts.), (415) 673-1101, *Historical Fixture*

In a history book of San Francisco eating, this place would have its own chapter. Since the doors opened in 1912, generations have passed through its portals to get a taste of *real* seafood. Oysters are shucked with fervor and crabs are cracked in a hurry for tourists and locals alike. It is obvious that these guys will be here for years to come, and crowds will continue to line up for a seat at the counter long after we're dead and gone. On that happy note: no credit cards accepted, here or in Heaven. *Psst . . . in a rush? They stop serving at 5:30 P.M. which means get in and get out on time.*

Swenson's Ice Cream, 1999 Hyde St. (bet. Union & Hyde Sts.), (415) 775-6818, *Sweets on the Run*

Where all chains begin. This adorable corner ice-cream shop boasts of being the oldest in the city. Since 1948, these guys have been scooping out yummy single- and double-dip cones. What was once a mere quarter will now set you back about $2.10, but inflation will never keep us away from these cones! Try our personal "Jane" fave—the refreshing yet rich Peppermint! Good for the breath too, Mwa, Mwa, Mwa!

The Terrace, @ The Ritz-Carlton, 600 Stockton St. (bet. California & Pine Sts.), (415) 296-7465, *Sunday Brunch*
   Calling all "ladies-who-brunch." This is perhaps one of the most civilized dining experiences Stateside; it is sheer perfection on every level. On a sunny day, wear your Sunday best with a big floppy straw hat, sip chardonnay and browse huge buffet tables for favorites: a raw bar (including beluga caviar), pasta bar, filet mignon and lamb chops, cheese tray, and an outrageous dessert spread with everything imaginable. We did the rounds three times. Ouch! Linger and chat for $50 per person without the booze or wine. Reservations strongly suggested.

Tommaso's, 1042 Kearny St. (bet. Broadway & Pacific Ave.), (415) 398-9696, *Old-World Italian*
   The boys from *Goodfellas* could be regulars while passing through San Fran on "family business." In a neighborhood wrought with Italian eateries, this standout is worthy of your attention. Its historic wood-fired oven has churned out the most authentic pies and lasagna in the Bay Area since the 1930s, when they first fired it up! A delicious blast from the past reinvented for the modern-day mama. So let your boyfriend out of the trunk and be nice!

Venticello, 1257 Taylor St. (@Washington St.), (415) 922-2545, *Neighborhood Favorite*
   Looking for a non-hotel-attached place to have a romantic dinner in your neighborhood? No problem. Book a table at this oh-so-romantic Tuscan-style bistro. It's intimate and fun to dine elbow to elbow in a Taylor Street apartment-style restaurant. Try it for a change of pace!

Yabbie's Coastal Kitchen, 2237 Polk St. (bet. Green & Vallejo Sts.), (415) 474-4088, *Fresh Seafood*
   We were nervous after the departure of chef Mark Lusardi, but he passed the baton, along with his magic wand, to world-renowned chef Max

Martinez of Aqua. The seafood is to die for, whether you're craving cray-fish, oysters, scallops or tuna. The freshness is unparalleled. We doubt you could find it this fresh if you dove to the bottom of the Bay yourself . . . and Lord knows what you would wear on that adventure! Don't be in a rush; just relax, flirt and be content that eating light can also be deliciously satis-fying.

Yuet Lee Seafood, 1300 Stockton St. (@ Broadway), (415) 982-6020, *Late Night*

When we were searching for a little late-night noodle action, this place came highly recommended to us by one of the city's top chefs, from Masa (see Eats). He did not lead us astray. Keep the night alive by dining until the wee hours of the morning on fresh bowls of noodles with shrimp. Just be sure to have your sunglasses while you pass the joggers when you leave . . . with a satisfied party-girl smile on your face! Open until 3 A.M., past most bars' hours.

Zarzuela, 2000 Hyde St. (@ Union St.), (415) 346-0800, *Ethnic / Spanish*

There's good news and bad news. The bad news is that there is zero parking; the good news is the traditional Castillian paella that we gobble up in a frighteningly short amount of time. The lowdown: when a light meal and sangria are worth a hunt for parking, which is scarce in the whole neighbor-hood, this is the place for girls on a mission! The dazzling tapas menu offers the opportunity to sample a little of everything. We are prone to change our minds mid-meal, right? Wash it back with some sangria, and hold onto your patience for the no-reservations policy.

✎ *Not to Miss:*

Café Niebaum Coppola, 916 Kearny St. (@ Columbus Ave.), (415) 291-1700, *Food / Emporium*

Caffe Greco, 423 Columbus Ave. (bet. Green & Vallejo Sts.), (415) 397-6261, *People Watching*

Caffe Trieste, 601 Vallejo St. (bet. Grant & Columbus Aves.), (415) 392-6739, *Sidewalk Coffee*

The Dining Room, @ The Ritz-Carlton, 600 Stockton St. (bet. California & Pine Sts.), (415) 296-7465, *Prix-Fixe Elegance*

Elan Vital Restaurant and Wine Bar, 1556 Hyde St. (bet. Jackson & Pacific Sts.), (415) 929-7309, *Cozy French*

Baker Street Bistro, 2953 Baker St. (bet. Greenwich & Lombard Sts.), (415) 931-1475, *Neighborhood Favorite*
 Paris, anyone? Save the cost of the airfare and head over to this little ultra-French bistro, just like what you would find on the Left Bank! Fall head over heels in love with this place . . . tiny and charming and oh so deliciously French in the food department. The owner, Jacques, is hands-on with his talented chef making sure they turn out the best: duck liver pate, coq au vin, and crème brulee are a few of the superb standards. *Psst . . . it's hard to beat the prix-fixe option, a mere $14.95 for four courses. Just say oui, oui, mademoiselle!*

Barney's Gourmet Hamburger, 3344 Steiner St. (@ Chestnut St.), (415) 563-0307, *Prime Beef*
 See details in Castro/Noe Valley.

Bonta, 2223 Union St. (bet. Fillmore & Steiner Sts.), (415) 929-0407, *Light Lunch*
 Feel like one of the family in this quaint Italian restaurant that is a real insiders' favorite. In a neighborhood with many options, this is a romantic spot with little twinkle lights, murals and delicious homemade pastas. If you are on a health kick or watching your waistline (and who isn't?), the vegetarian options are a bonanza. Going "dutch?" Prices are reasonable, so you can stash a little cash for that Louis Vuitton piece you've been craving. Prices range from $6.75 to $18.95.

Café Marimba, 2317 Chestnut St. (bet. Divisadero & Scott Sts.), (415) 776-1506, *Authentic Mexican*
 Don't expect to find the usual run-of-the-mill Tex-Mex or Cal-Mex food. This place is for the purist, Mexico City–style. Start with a sampler of three varying salsas made daily, then go for one of the Oaxacan mole dishes chased with a fantastic margarita or two. . . . Grab your coworkers for a post "close the deal" celebration. It's a lively hot spot that welcomes happy people with open arms and endless tequila-laden margaritas.

Doidge's, 2217 Union St. (bet. Fillmore & Steiner Sts.), (415) 921-2149, *Breakfast/Brunch*

This is hands down the best breakfast or brunch in the entire city. Sit at the counter alone and indulge with cinnamon French toast, house-baked scones or baked poppy seed toast. The small dining room in the back is great to sit and linger after a Saturday night of cocktails and dancing. The hangover cure is the famous breakfast casserole with Italian sausage, new potatoes, green onions, and tomato. Now, grab a blanket and take a nap in Washington Square Park (see Tripping, North Beach). You might wake up good as new. . . . Opens at 8 A.M. and serves until 12:30 P.M., 2:30 P.M. on weekends.

Dragon Well, 2142 Chestnut St. (bet. Pierce & Steiner Sts.), (415) 474-6888, *www.dragonwell.com, Tea for Two*

It may not be the Year of the Dragon, but your good fortune is knowing about this place. In the mood for cheap Chinese without the "cheese" factor associated with your average noodles-to-go joint? Then dine in or take out at this sunny location known for its innovative cuisine chinoise. We suggest the Tea-Smoked Duck ($7.95) as an entrée and pot stickers filled with Napa cabbage to start ($5.50). Grab a fortune cookie on your way in . . . and out. One may not be enough! The most expensive item on the menu is $10.95. *Psst . . . make plans to meet for tea instead of coffee. It's a nice Asian alternative to the American java jolt.*

Fuzio, 2175 Chestnut St. (@ Pierce St.), (415) 673-8804, *Casual Fusion*

Never be lonely for lunch. Join in the fun at this lovely, casual place where you will be treated like a Queen Bee (okay, you still qualify for princess with a little help from Retin A). Sit along the bar and watch the kitchen dole out consistently tasty food. Don't be scared away by the fact that this is a "chain-aurant" . . . the other locations are equally good. See other locations in Castro/Noe Valley and Downtown/Soma.

Greens, Building A, Fort Mason (bet. Marina & Buchanan Sts.) (415) 771-6222, *Vegetarian View*

Original location for sprouty Bay "Janes." For 20 years or more this has been *the* favorite San Francisco vegetarian restaurant. Its reputation extends 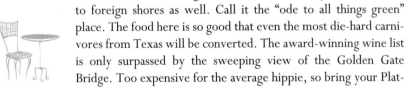 to foreign shores as well. Call it the "ode to all things green" place. The food here is so good that even the most die-hard carnivores from Texas will be converted. The award-winning wine list is only surpassed by the sweeping view of the Golden Gate Bridge. Too expensive for the average hippie, so bring your Platinum Visa and book ahead—it can take up to two weeks to get a reservation. *Psst . . . be sure to pick up one of their cookbooks so you can recreate the sumptuous dishes at home when you are feeling domestic!*

The Grove, 2250 Chestnut St. (bet. Scott & Pierce Sts.), (415) 474-4843, *Solo Dining*

Two communal tables set the ideal stage for a lunch or dinner, or just a coffee break if you're on the go! Order the apple chicken salad, vegetarian chili, or "mom's meatloaf." Those with tot-in-tow will appreciate the peanut butter, banana and honey sandwich . . . actually, it's still our favorite! Or the chicken potpie is the absolute cure for colds and homesickness. *Psst . . . save room for the house specialty: "organic pie." Wow!*

Irrawaddy, 1769 Lombard St. (bet. Laguna & Octavia Sts.), (415) 931-2830, *Alternative Cuisine*

Can't bear one more night on the town with Pan-Asian fusion food? Opt for this sexy, sultry wild card where you'll dine on exotic Burmese fare. The excellent blending of Indian and Chinese cooking techniques makes for a wonderful meal. Kick off your shoes, slink down to one of the sunken tables, and relax. Great to go to with the girls for an alternative evening, or kick off a romantic weekend with your new crush! The possibilities are limitless. Pretend he is Yul Brynner and you are Deborah Kerr. . . . It could happen!

La Canasta, 3006 Buchanan St. (@ Union St.), (415) 474-2627, *Mexican To Go*

Get in line for the best homemade, authentic, Mexican-food take-out joint in the city. Convertible Porsches pull up and double-park to get this fabulous grub . . . and you just never know what cutie might be in the driver's seat! Caramba! Prepare to wait, but use your time wisely to choose between the taquitos rancheros and the empanadas de queso for appetizers. The tacos are outrageously delicious, all served in corn tortillas. The burritos with rice, beans, and salsa are to die for and the tamales, still in their husks, are a must! No unhealthy ingredients are used, and the tamales are low in fat and lightly salted. Delivery available in the area from 4 to 9 P.M. daily.

La Nouvelle Patisserie, 2184 Union St. (bet. Fillmore & Webster Sts.), (415) 931-7655, *www.lanouvellapasterie.com, Lunch With Mom*

This true French pastry shop is a charming place to rest aching toes on a Union Square shopping quest. Serving breakfast and lunch, but we go for the fabulous authentic desserts—a great midday sugar rush! Brides-to-be should take note of the "wedding cake appointment" consultation with Nelly, the wedding cake goddess, from Sat. at 11 A.M. to 5 P.M., by appointment only. It's heavy-duty stress deciding between traditional butter cream frosting and raspberry ganache, especially with your mother "helping." Be transported by the beauty of the shop and fulfilled by the sweets. No Amex.

Pane e' Vino, 3011 Steiner St. (@ Union St.), (415) 346-2111, *Italian Trattoria*

You will be transported to the heart of Italy by entering the doors of this special eatery. The white stucco walls and dark wood windows with lace curtains are true to the Italian look. Speaking of looks, if you ever considered helping a guy get a green card, look no further! Just try not to break into hives when he takes your order. . . . Limited but sumptuous menu features exotic pastas, including the inventive risotto del giorno. Chef/Owner Bruno Quercini serves fresh fish from the grill as well as heartier dishes like grilled rack of lamb with a red wine sauce ($19.95). Leave room for the dolci, like a tiramisu that incites seizures, or try the white chocolate ice cream topped with espresso and whipped cream. *Psst . . . take a peek at the lovely herb garden in the rear of the restaurant. It's so pretty. Don't miss their more modern distant cousin on Beverly Boulevard in Los Angeles.*

Peet's Coffee and Tea, 2156 Chestnut St. (bet. Steiner & Pierce Sts.), (415) 931-8302, *Afternoon Pick-Up*

See details in The Heights.

Plumpjack Café, 3127 Fillmore St. (bet. Filbert & Greenwich Sts.), (415) 563-4755, *Neighborhood Favorite*

After a short closing for kitchen renovations, Plumpjack Café is back with a vengeance. Chef Keith Luce is at the helm after stints with the White House (yes, *the* White House) and the world-famous Little Nell in Aspen. Request to sit on one of the three leather banquettes for the best view of the

whole room. Jennifer Lopez would, why not you? The place feels like a private club and the room itself is beautiful and intimate, perfect for conversation, be it business or personal. We love the luxurious white tablecloths, a necessity for any civilized meal. One of the most reasonably priced wine lists in San Francisco.

Uniquely American fare, with menu changes daily. Entrees from $7 to $30.

Pluto's, 3258 Scott St. (@ Chestnut St.), (415) 775-8867, *Homesick*

On the road and the thought of one more pretentious meal and snotty waiter make you crazy? Here lies the answer. Home-style cooking served cafeteria style in a cool setting. Oversized salads and sandwiches as well as hot dishes and vegetables served at unbeatable prices. Just like mom would serve . . . if she ever cooked at all! Now don't forget to brush your teeth before bed, dear. Open from 11:30 A.M. to 10 P.M.

Rose's Café, 2298 Union St. (@ Steiner St.), (415) 775-2200, *Neighborhood Favorite*

Situated on a sunny corner, this is the sister restaurant to Rose Pistoli (see Eats, Nob Hill). Not as flashy, more homey feeling, but every bit as delicious. The menu rocks! We can think of a dozen or more reasons to eat here for breakfast, lunch and dinner. The tables outside are perfect for alfresco snacking while taking a break from the Union Street hustle and bustle. The goat cheese salad and mussels accompanied by a half carafe of white wine will have you back on the beat in no time at all. Open daily from 7 A.M. to 10 P.M.

SF Pizza, 1602 Lombard St. (bet. Gough & Octavia Sts.), (415) 567-8646, *www.bestsfpizza.com, Exotic Pizza*

Pizza for the more discerning palate. This pizza is the brainchild of a five-star chef who masterfully created a crunchy crust that is creatively topped with nontraditional ingredients. Popular choice? Chicken pesto with garlic and tomatoes. Beer and wine are on hand for a snack postmovie at the Metro Theater on nearby Union St. Cash and local checks only. Pizzas range from $7.95 to $19.95 (the lobster version). Open from 2 to 11 P.M. daily, later on weekends if it's crowded. Don't blame us if you become an addict.

Three Seasons, 3317 Steiner St. (bet. Lombard & Chestnut Sts.), (415) 441-1298, *Neighborhood Newcomer*

This cute Vietnamese restaurant serves contemporary food. It's casual and fun to eat at the sake bar. Just don't get too carried away on the rice wine if you're driving! Dinner only, daily from 5 to 10 P.M.

Working Girls' Café, 3101 Fillmore St. (@ Filbert St.), (415) 775-5228, *On The Run*

The convenient corner location makes it easy to grab an interesting sandwich on your way back to the office, or a reliable breakfast as you head in! Lunch includes selections like mixed deli sandwiches, unique fresh salads, soup du jour served with French bread, and hot entrées like vegetarian lasagna. Breakfast ranges from the simple bagel to scrambled eggs with herbs, cheese, and tomatoes. Grab an espresso while you wait for your meal, and be proud that you will make your meeting on time with something delicious to eat! *Psst . . . boys welcome too! Need to cater a lunch at the office? Offering sandwich trays, Greek platters, and desserts for any occasion, big or small. Other locations, Downtown, 239 Kearney St. (bet. Sutter & Bush Sts.), (415) 398-1390, and 100 Spear St. (@ Mission), (415) 495-8995.*

Yoshida-Ya, 2909 Webster St. (@ Union St.), (415) 346-3431, *Local Yuppie Japanese*

Yakitori, skewered meats, are the piéce de résistance at this longtime favorite Cow Hollow eatery. Excellent sushi and good hibachi keep the yuppies with booster seats in tow alongside Japanese nationals coming back time and time again. We love to sit upstairs on the floor in true traditional style and pretend to relive *Memoirs of a Geisha! Psst . . . nearby Ace Wasabi, 3339 Steiner St. (bet. Chestnut & Lombard Sts.), (415) 567-4903, is an alternative with the same quality food, but the crowd is hipper and the wait is longer. Call about Bingo night, when the stage is set with pretty people and loads of rowdy fun.*

Zinzino, 2355 Chestnut St. (bet. Divisadero & Scott Sts.), (415) 346-6623, *Modern Italian*

Brought to you by the guys who created The Grove in the same neighborhood. Wood-fired Neapolitan pizzas and gelato sundaes have us helplessly hooked. Try the extra-crispy roast chicken and sample the mouthwatering thin pizza crust. This is a must in the neighborhood. Always at the top of one of SF's "Best Of" lists.

♦ Good to Know:

The Chocolate Bear, 2250 Union St. (bet. Fillmore & Steiner Sts.), (415) 922-5711, (888) 505-BEAR, *www.chocolatebear.com*

Need chocolates made in the shape of your company's logo? No problem. Stop by for a taste of fudge or truffle at this fun shop with all things cocoa. Eighty percent of their business caters to corporate clients, but feel free to buy at this Union Street location. "A day without chocolate is unbearable!"—Jane, circa 2001.

Not to Miss:
Perry's, 1944 Union St. (bet. Buchanan & Laguna Sts.), (415) 922-9022, *Burgers & Boys*

"The Heights" (Pacific, Presidio, Laurel) ....

Café Kati, 1963 Sutter St. (bet. Webster & Fillmore Sts.), (415) 775-7313, *Class Act*
Utter elegance and gustatory perfection in Pacific Heights. The fabulous food turned out here nightly should be considered a culinary masterpiece. Drool over the looks but delight in the taste of their succulent blackthorn cider-marinated pork. It's a visual feast as well as a taste bud bonanza. Chef Kirk Webster is a real San Francisco treasure. Bon appetit, girlfriend! Open nightly.

Chez Nous, 1911 Fillmore St. (bet. Bush & Pine Sts.), (415) 441-8044, *Neighborhood Newcomer*
Let your shopper shoulder take a break at this perfect afternoon spot for a lunch break while on a Fillmore shopping spree. The breezy and delightful atmosphere will refresh even the weariest of die-hard shopaholics. Stop by and put your party on the list before serious hunger pangs kick in, because there is always a slight wait. No Amex.

Crepe N'Coffee, 2821 California St., (@ Divisadero St.), (415) 776-8866, *Cheap Eats*
Girls on the go, take note! This is a friendly corner spot with bright yellow walls, for a sunny breakfast or quick lunch. Solo girls will find it easy to dine here on Greek salads and delicious light dessert crepes. The breakfast menu includes eggs, omelets, and crunchy bagels. *Psst . . . experts agree that people who eat breakfast live longer and burn more calories throughout the day, so make haste!*

Curbside Café, 2417 California St. (@ Fillmore St.), (415) 929-9030, *Late Sunday*

As the name says, this is a great place to park curbside . . . well, at least your Vespa! The spinach salad with pine nuts, feta cheese and vinaigrette is worth the crush of the crowd. Bring the Sunday newspaper for the heavy wait . . . it's small and always packed with educated city dwellers who obviously know a good thing when they park it!

Dot, Miyako Hotel, 611 Post St. (bet. Laguna & Post Sts.), (415) 922-7788, *Sleek Newcomer*

Formerly Yo Yo Bistro, Dot has come on the scene in the nick of time! It's too new to know if this place will stand the test of time, but judging by the big hype and the big-name creator, Nick Graham, it has the deck stacked in its favor. The two-story dining room features the Nouvelle American concoctions of chef Noel Pavia.

Food, Inc., 2800 California St. (@ Divisadero St.), (415) 928-3728, *www.FoodIncUSA.com, Lunch / Brunch*

Great place for breakfast (from 9 to 10:30 A.M.), brunch or lunch in a casual setting with incredible food. This menu is chock-full of salads, sandwiches, individual pizzas, soups, quiches and "house specialties." Whatever you fancy, it's all delicious. Just don't be in a rush to get back to the office because service can be slooow. *Psst . . . go for the heart-shaped waffles with maple syrup on Saturday morning with your Latin lover or yuppie boyfriend. Molto romantica! Custom catering for social or business occasions too.*

Jackson Fillmore Trattoria, 2506 Fillmore St. (@ Jackson St.), (415) 346-5288, *Authentic Italian*

Southern Italian food is served at this tiny Upper Fillmore trattoria. The décor leaves a lot to the imagination, but the marvelous complimentary bruschetta and hearty grilled meats more than make up for the lackluster interior. This place would make your Sicilian mother green with envy! Reservations for three or more only. Open seven nights a week for dinner only, 5:30–11 P.M.

The Meetinghouse, 1701 Octavia St. (@ Bush St.), (415) 922-6733, *Neighborhood Favorite*

Barbie would dine here. This place is adorable! It rates so high in our "Jane" book that we have booked a widely standing reservation. This darling place provides wonderful innovative food to 14 tables of devotees daily. Don't selfishly devour the entire bread basket before your outstanding meal arrives in the hands of the friendly waitstaff. Go early if you can't bear to wait! Open daily for dinner, but they stop serving at 9:30 P.M. They assume Barbie needs her beauty sleep—little do they know! Reservations highly recommended.

Mifune, Japan Center, 1737 Post St. (bet. Buchanan & Webster Sts.), (415) 922-0337, *Quickie Noodles*

There's nothing like these delicious noodles on the go in the heart of Japantown. Steamed soba and udon are just the ticket if you are rushing to a movie at the nearby Kabuki 8! The atmosphere is nothing to write home about, but who cares when you are in and out with a low-calorie meal for under $15. Parking available at the Japantown Center.

Morpho, 1980 Union St. (@ Buchanan St.), (415) 447-8275, *www.morpho-sushi.com, Hip Sushi*

Take the tiny flight of stairs into sushi heaven. This neighborhood newcomer has the feeling of being in the heart of Japan with your favorite crowd of *Wallpaper* magazine-toting hipsters. The owners, Channel and Roylni, are an ultracool couple and hands-on restaurateurs. She designed the place and he oversees the kitchen. The small bar is ideal for a quick cold sake and spicy tuna hand-roll on the go. The sushi bar winds through the restaurant to the back, where a small square-shaped room has a retractable roof for sunny days. It's so girly, with butterfly-shaped seat backs in baby blue and pastel yellow tones. A must!

Patisserie Delanghe, 1890 Fillmore St. (@ Bush), (415) 923-0711, *Fergie Backlash*

Get ready to taste some of the best French-style pastries that money can buy Stateside. In the neighborhood for 17 years, owners Dominique & Marie-Jeanne serve up petit fours, raspberry crunch and other out-of-this world sumptuous sweets. The space itself is conveniently situated on a large corner—double-park, dash in, and catch a glimpse of the pro bakers in the exposed kitchen at the back while grabbing a self-serve coffee and pondering which dessert to impress your guests with tonight!

Peet's Coffee and Tea, 2197 Fillmore St. (@ Sacramento St.), (415) 563-9930, *Coffee Break*

Running to an appointment in the neighborhood or needing some "shopping fuel?" Hit this famous coffee emporium—one of many branches in the Bay Area—that is just right for a break in the afternoon. *Psst . . . this is one of the best shopping areas on the West Coast, so a little java jolt could be in order.*

Pizza Inferno, 1800 Fillmore St. (@ Sutter St.), (415) 775-1800, *Junk Food Binge*

A reliable place for lunch or dinner if you need something quick, cheap and oil-soaked to sop up last night's white-wine binge, you devil girl! Individual pizzas with "lowfat" Mozzarella cheese are the way to go. *Psst . . . happy hour is from 4–6:30 P.M. and again from 10 P.M. to closing every night for beer and wine. We love the Pear Cider, but if you're a wine snob, then bring your own "Beaujolais" for a two-dollar corkage fee.*

Vivande Porta Via, 2125 Fillmore St. (bet. Columbus Ave. & Sacramento St.), (415) 346-4430, *Italian Trattoria*

Can't take one more pretentious waiter or, worse yet, the thought of cooking after a day at the office? Here lies the answer. This is a true insiders' tip to one of the city's most treasured eateries. Sample authentic pastas (the risotto is to die for) rival any Tuscan grandmother's kitchen. The place is packed—and they don't take reservations—so plan to sit cheek to cheek and wait. Save room for dessert, which is always fresh and exciting. *Psst . . . re-create the whole meal at home with fancy food items on hand and for sale "à la carte." Olive oils, homemade pastas, prosciutto, cheeses and all the finishings.*

✒ *Not to Miss:*
Benihana, Japan Center, 1737 Post St. (bet. Laguna & Webster Sts.), (415) 563-4844, *Great For Kids*

Hayes Valley/Civic Center ·····························

Brother-In-Laws Bar-B-Que, 705 Divisadero St., (@ Grove St.), (415) 931-7427, *Southern Alternative*

Let's face it, when you think of San Francisco, you don't really think of great barbeque . . . but you should! These folks have brought the South to your doorstep. You'll catch the delicious odor of pigs on the spit from blocks away and make a beeline to pick up a "to go" order of the best-tasting ribs, chicken and brisket west of the Mississippi. We think it's their secret sauce that makes everything so succulent, good to the last lick. You can occasionally find a place to perch inside at one of the scattered tables strewn with paper napkins, but we think it's more fun to make a pig out of yourself in the confines of your own apartment watching a rerun of *Babe*. The usual sides: baked beans, cole slaw, greens and potato salad.

Frjtz, 579 Hayes St. (@ Laguna St.), (415) 864-7654, *www.frjtzfries.com, Local Hang*

Belgian fries are a must as well as savory crepes (try the Matisse: smoked salmon, sour cream and chives, $6.50) or a sandwich called Basquait (grilled chicken, pesto mayo, red onions and melted Swiss on focaccia, $6.95). Ultramod music is spun by DJs on Saturday from 8 P.M. to midnight. Beer, wine, and champagne only. Just pray that the music puts you in a trance so that you don't notice your expanding thighs. *Psst . . . sexy potty that is worth a visit, with glow-in-the-dark toilet ring and black light.*

Hayes Street Grill, 320 Hayes St. (bet. Franklin & Gough Sts.), (415) 863-5545, *Pre/Post Theater*

"Just get me to the show on time!" American seafood, specifically the highest-quality fish served in the neighborhood, if not the whole city. The setting is conservative but exciting, considering you never know when an opera star from the nearby Opera House might dine here late after a night of Boheme-ing. Specials are set daily according to what's fresh. The calamari is a must for starters. Nice small bar for a drink if you are a stranger looking to have a quiet drink while gazing upon walls adorned with black-and-white head shots of famous patrons.

Jardinerie, 300 Grove St. (@ Franklin St.), (415) 861-5555, *Be Seen*

Ultrasexy, dramatic restaurant and bar designed by the famed Pat Kuleto. We love the round bar, small yet ultra-"Jane." Book the Balcony table—although reservations are scarce for *any* table, overlooking the bar is the best seat in the house for people watching or better yet, getting engaged! Live jazz keeps the pace going as you dine on lobster strudel and foie gras. The Cosmos are the drink of choice. Be sure to wear your prettiest La

Perla lingerie and Alberta Feretti little black dress; this place deserves your best from the inside out.

Millennium, @ Abigail Hotel, 246 McAllister St. (bet. Hyde & Larkin Sts.), (415) 487-9800, *Candlelit Eggplant*

Is your cutie screaming for root vegetables at the top of his lungs? Put your carnivorous drive aside because the best way to lure this boy's heart is with piles of vegan cuisine in this romantic atmosphere. Squash never felt this sexy. If your instincts are right you could wind up in the "Love Suite" at the Abigail Hotel, upstairs!

Powell's Place, 511 Hayes St. (bet. Laguna & Octavia Sts.), (415) 863-1404, *Soul Food*

Blink twice and you just might see Huck and Jim floating by the window. You're not going insane; it's just the dementia from this incredible "down-river," home-style food. Fried chicken, smothered steak, charred ribs, roast beef, greens, black-eyed peas, and the best corn muffin this side of K-Paul's in New Orleans. Got the picture? Cots not provided for after-lunch naps. Open 9–11 daily. *Psst . . . great post-happy hour destination after early cocktails at the W Hotel lobby (see Tripping, Downtown).*

Suppenkuche, 601 Hayes St. (@ Laguna St.), (415) 252-9289, *Deutschland*

Solo girls will feel welcome at this stark modern home of German beer and authentic fare. The communal tables are perfect for noshing on Bratwurst and sipping one of the 28 exotic German brewskis in an unthreatening yet fun environment. Hurry, the last seating is at 10:30 P.M.

Tartine Café Francais, 244 Gough St. (@ Fell St.), (415) 553-4595, *Light Lunch*

Soups, salads and cookies are served in this tiny, closet-sized French café. It's all so lovely and great for us girly girls. Open from 10 A.M. to 4 P.M.

Zuni Café, 1658 Market St. (bet. Franklin & Gough Sts.), (415) 552-2522, *Citywide Favorite*

Zuni has been a 20-year treasure that has stood the test of time for unique design, diverse clientele and an innovative menu. See and be seen sipping a Cosmo or pink champagne while nibbling on the corn polenta or something simple like a cheeseburger. Extremely popular with locals and tourists alike. The copper bar is a stand-out, as well as the stellar service and desirable location.

Haight-Ashbury

Bean There, 201 Steiner St. (@ Waller St.), (415) 255-8855, *Custom Coffee*
Massive windows allow you to look out onto the adorable tree-lined street at passersby as you sip lattes all day . . . well, at least until 9 P.M. The pastries are the best of the best from bakeries around town. Good to know that you won't have to spend all day traipsing around stalking your favorite muffins! Their French-press coffee is delightful as an alternative to cappuccinos. Cash only.

Crepes on Cole, 100 Carl St. (@ Cole St.), (415) 664-1800, *Light Lunch*
On a beautiful day there's nothing better than to sit outside at one of the six patio tables and dine on tasty chicken pesto crepes while pouring over Sunday's *Chronicle*. Forget about your big presentation tomorrow morning and savor the sunlight, the food and a good book! Locals socialize and mingle in this friendly neighborhood haunt. Cash-poor girls will be delighted to pay $3.95 to $6.95 for a variety of crepes. Open daily from 7 A.M. to 11 P.M., midnight on weekends.

EOS Restaurant & Wine Bar, 901 Cole St. (@ Carl St.), (415) 566-3063, *Neighborhood Favorite*
This is one of the city's finest casual, chic destinations for out-of-this-world cuisine from renowned chef Arnold Eric Wong. Exquisite Asian-Fusion dishes appear at your table as culinary works of art—as you know, presentation is everything! Enjoy the industrial sleek setting as you savor an excellent wine from their comprehensive list, obviously heavy on California vineyards. Save room for the Bananamisu, a combination of tiramisu with bananas. We're beginning to glow just thinking about it! All desserts are worth starving six days to justify the splurge. Parking and reservations are scarce, but worth the struggle.

Indian Oven, 233 Fillmore St. (bet. Haight & Waller Sts.), (415) 626-1628, *Ethnic/Indian*

Indian food central! Bay Area girls and the boys who love them flock to this Lower Haight tandoori haven. The recent expansion helps to lessen the exhausting wait for a table—although we'd wait the length of time it took to build the Taj Mahal for the bowls of legume-based stew and sizzling clay-pot tandoori with hot nan. Excellent value too, for worker babes on a budget!

Kate's Kitchen, 471 Haight St. (@ Fillmore St.), (415) 626-3984, *Hangover Cure*

Young hipsters come here to hang, nosh and pontificate on the state of the New Economy. Hearty breakfasts are the answer when you have been out all night with friends or if you have a day of errands ahead and want a big carbohydrate jolt. It's a bit out of the way if you're not local, but it's worth the trek. If you would walk on fire for hot biscuits and gravy, and fabo pancakes, then this is your ticket to Nirvana!

Thep Phanom, 400 Waller St. (@ Fillmore St.), (415) 431-2526, *Thai Glory*

Looking to impress a client with your international taste savvy? Get off to a good start by suggesting this impressive authentic Thai restaurant. The service alone makes you feel like a princess worthy of such spoils. Prepare to wait, and wait and wait some more. Not to worry . . . food this delicious deserves a strong appetite, not to mention a strong will! Open nightly from 5:30 to 10:30 P.M. *Psst . . . thank goodness for Botox—it'll iron out the furrow in your brow when you see the wait list.*

✦ *Not to Miss:*

All You Knead, 1466 Haight St. (bet. Clayton & Masonic Sts.), (415) 552-4550, *All-Day Breakfast*

The Castro/Noe Valley ⋯⋯⋯⋯⋯⋯⋯⋯⋯⋯⋯⋯⋯⋯⋯⋯

Anchor Oyster Bar, 579 Castro St. (bet. 18th & 19th Sts.), (415) 431-3990, *Seafood Standard*

Intimate room with stainless-steel tables packed with people back to back, side by side, shucking oysters, peeling shrimp, and eating buckets of mussels, tossing it all back with white wine. Locals galore.

Barney's Gourmet Hamburger, 4138 24th St. (@ Castro St.), (415) 282-7770, *Prime Beef*

Go the first time for the best burgers in town, but return for the curly fries and oversized onion rings. Talk about something to fix your PMS symptoms! There's something on the menu for everyone, even non-meat eating babes. Sit in the patio in the rear and contemplate the pros and cons of swearing off carbs, meat, and bad boys, once again, starting tomorrow. See other location in Marina/Cow Hollow.

Café Luna Piena, 568 Castro St. (bet. 18th & 19th Sts.), (415) 621-2566, *Outdoor Garden*

Best-kept secret in the Castro area. This place is the cat's meow! Contemporary Italian/American fare with an engaging menu that changes quarterly. Local joint for those looking to blend into the neighborhood—no tourists allowed! (Just kidding.) Breakfast/brunch includes favorites like corned-beef hash and eggs, spicy homemade fennel sausage and the house specialty, Eggs Luna Piena, poached eggs topped with smoked salmon, served with creamy polenta and dressed with shrimp bisque. For lunch, try the portobello burger with goat cheese and arugala, and for dinner, fried calamari (incredible) served with fresh fennel and a spicy aioli. Or, go easy with the eggless Caesar salad. Be seated outside on one of the two tiers of the wooden deck that seats about 70. Serving breakfast/brunch 11:30 A.M.–3 P.M., weekdays. Brunch, 9 A.M.–3 P.M. Reservations accepted.

Firefly, 4228 24th St. (@ Douglas St.), (415) 821-7652, *Exotic Home Cooking*

Tucked away between two apartments, this is a fine place for foodies or those who love great fusion food. It's a romantic little jewel that consistently turns out innovative comfort food like shrimp-and-scallop pot stickers. Here butter is not just butter, it's something a bit more tasty, with different infusions of flavor. The menu changes every couple of weeks, but you are sure to find something to please your finicky "Jane"-girl palate. Open 5:30–10 P.M. daily. *Psst . . . the end of 24th St. is always a bit foggy, adding to the charm of your dining experience. Reservations are a must.*

Fuzio, 469 Castro St. (bet. 18th & Market Sts.), (415) 863-1400, *Casual Fusion*

See details in Marina/Cow Hollow, other location in Downtown/Soma.

Mecca, 2029 Market St. (bet. 14th & Dolores Sts.), (415) 621-7000, *www.sfmecca.com, Party Central*

If the weekend came and went too fast, spend your Sunday nights at this bang-up fun place serving seafood specialties like iced shellfish and shrimp dumplings. Drag performances are intermittent, with delish tidbits to nibble on before reality strikes and your pumpkin arrives to take you home early—it is a "school night," you know.

No Name Sushi, 314 Church St. (bet. 15th & 16th Sts.), no phone, *Treasure Hunt*

This place really has no name and no phone number. But, one thing is for sure: this insiders' hideaway destination is a well-kept secret on the must-do list for all sushi/sashimi junkies. We have been known to drive all the way from Marin County if we are having a real hankering. Highest quality raw fish this Bay city has to offer. No drama, just the goods. Good luck finding the place. . . .

Sweet Inspiration, 2239 Market St. (bet. 16th & Sanchez Sts.), (415) 621-8664, *Dessert & Coffee*

If you've beeen a good girl and eaten well at Alice's in the neighborhood (grease-free, California-style Chinese food), reward yourself for such good behavior with dessert and coffee from this gem. (Suggest it casually at the table and then demand it if your party does not see eye to eye.) Serving scrumptious cakes, tarts and pastries until 11:30 P.M. on weekdays, 12:30 A.M. on weekends. Cash only. *Psst . . . Alice's is located at 1599 Sanchez St. (@ 29th St.), (415) 282-8999.*

Zodiac Club, 718 14th St. (@ Market St.), (415) 626-7827, *Horoscope-Themed*

What's your sign, baby? This wacky place serves astonishingly good Mediterranean food, and the menu changes monthly according to the stars. The atmosphere is equally strange; it's nearly totally dark inside except for votive candles and the various Zodiac signs backlit to add glow to your meal. Maybe it will be in the "stars" for you to get the raise you have been vying for? It's enter-taining and a culinary delight. Would we leave you in the dark? Never.

✦ Not to Miss:

Miss Mellie's, 4123 24th St. (@ Castro St.), (415) 285-5598, *Noe Brunch*
Hot 'n' Hunky, 4039 18th St. (@ Castro St.), (415) 621-6365, *Late-Nite Burgers*
Café Flore, 2298 Market St. (@ Noe St.), (415) 621-8579, *People Watching*

Mission

Atlas Café, 3049 20th St. (bet. 20th & Alabama Sts.), (415) 648-1047, *Local Hang*

This grungy neighborhood coffee shop is without a doubt the anti-Starbucks! The java chain gangs around this joint. Most patrons are card-carrying members of Greenpeace, PETA, and the Phish fan club, drawn together by the basic desire to sip their caffeinated beverage of choice in a funky relaxed space with other high-minded individuals bent on world re-form. Looking for an activist cutie? Just order that double macchiato and keep your eyes open!

Blowfish, 2170 Bryant St. (bet. 19th & 20th Sts.), (415) 285-3848, *Rock 'n' Roll Raw Fish*

If not the best sushi in the city, this is definitely the most entertaining place to eat it and pick up a gorgeous chef in the process! The crowd spills out onto the street during peak hours as the hip and hopeful vie for entry into this sushi multimedia funfest. Art on the walls, techno on the turntable and multiple TV screens displaying God knows what all lend a chaotic and enticing quality to the surroundings. The artistic and architectural presenta-tion of the food makes up for any slips in the quality department. This "Create Your Own Leaning Tower Of Pisa" philosophy applies to the dessert menu as well; the green tea cheesecake is as visually mesmerizing as delicious! And did we say the chefs were hot? Order with a wink. . . .

The Blue Plate, 3218 Mission St. (@ Valencia St.), (415) 282-6777, *Uptown Down Home*

Not your average "blue plate special" . . . in fact there is really nothing blue about the plates at all, just exceptional postmeal satisfaction with little batter-induced bloating. Prepare for a more experimental approach to "down-home" cuisine! Chef/Owners Ian Wolff and Cory Obenour have attracted a loyal posse by taking the staples of home cooking and adding gourmet flair. Try the simple, incredible Niman-Schell pork chop if you're a purist, or deviate a bit with crusty polenta with bacon and arugula, a salad with grilled peaches and mizuma, huckleberry potatoes and granola-crusted cobbler as the piéce de résistance!

Circadia, 2727 Mariposa St. (@ Bryant St.), (415) 552-2649, *Coffee Shop*

Looking for "Chandler" (A.K.A. Matthew Perry) types? You just might find them here . . . or at least some cutie clones worth flirting with and saving from themselves! Stop by for a casual cappuccino—all the dot-commers do. Cell-phone-toting patrons linger and talk about their latest IPOs on the comfy vintage sofas (okay, garage-sale sofas). Owned by Starbucks (now they're trying to invade the comfy couch locales) so don't look for anything too outrageous, just a great place to park and java.

Delfina, 3621 18th St. (@ Dolores St.), (415) 552-4055, *Media Darling*

First of all, for those that remember The Bistro in L.A., you know to order the chocolate soufflé the minute you are seated. It's out of this world, but takes time to fluff while you munch through your main courses! This much-talked-about eatery was recently expanded to meet the overwhelming demand fueled by its new "in" status. Happily, we report that it still remains true to the hype. Casual yet sophisticated. The menu runs the gamut from basic comfort food (think roast chicken with mashed potatoes) to the slightly more exotic Chilean sea bass served with brussel sprouts for a unique twist. Small bar is great for the solo diner. Eat, drink and be merry. *Psst . . . don't try to buy the original art . . . contrary to popular belief, it's not for sale! Prices range from $7 to $22.*

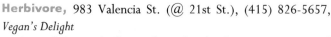

Herbivore, 983 Valencia St. (@ 21st St.), (415) 826-5657, *Vegan's Delight*

One of the city's finest places for the "veggies anonymous" crowd. Seat yourself; you may wait a bit during busy hours, but it's worth it if dairy and meat are dirty words in your vocabulary.

While you wait there is plenty of artistic visual temptation . . . the walls are lined with photos of succulent berries that whet your appetite in the dimly lit, pretty room. The young, trendy, tattoo-friendly crowd has picked the mushroom lasagna as a fave. Otherwise, the wraps, soups, salads, and sandwiches are also healthy and delish!

La Rondalla, 901 Valencia St. (@ 20th St.), (415) 647-7474, *Meat Lovers*

Yes, it is fun to say "best abondigas." But really, these are the best meatballs, as in meatball soup, in town. Their girth is somewhere between that of a golf ball and a baseball; the meat is still pink on the inside and the huge pieces of zucchini, potato and carrot give new meaning to the phrase "La sopa that eats like a meal." Throw in a squeeze of lemon—and perhaps a strawberry margarita on the side—and you'll realize that no matter how many swank new restaurants open in the Mission, La Rondalla will always stand head and shoulders above them all.

La Villa Poppi, 3324 22nd St. (bet. Mission & Valencia Sts.), (415) 642-5044, *Intimate Italian*

Authentic Italian food brought to you by a husband-and-wife team who is on hand to serve delicious Tuscan food. Greg Sweeting does it all, prepping, cooking and cleaning. Roselynn does everything else to make this place the charming, intimate dining wonder that it is. The menu changes monthly, so don't expect to get bored with the spaghetti and meatballs around here. It's cheaper than a ticket to Florence and just as satisfying. Closed on Sunday & Monday.

Panchita's Café, 3115 22nd St. (@ Valencia St.), (415) 431-4232, *Tiny Mexican*

Viva Mexico! Original menu for lovers of authentic Mexican fare. Not your average Tex-Mex: placate your palate with plantains and cream and warm roasted-chili salsa with chips before a meal that will make you a repeat offender. The owner attended the Culinary Institute of America to perfect his "chops" a couple of years ago and never looked back . . . the food is muy fantastico! Ole!

Slanted Door, 584 Valencia St. (@ 17th St.), (415) 861-8032, *Neighborhood Favorite*

Enter the wonderful culinary world created by Charlie Phan, chef and owner of this San Francisco culinary haunt. (If you must know the genius, he will come to the table to meet and greet!) The authentic Vietnamese cuisine is really out of this world. It's always packed with two floors of "foodies" in pursuit of innovative perfection on a plate. Order the Shakin' Beef, the chicken clay pot, or the crispy Imperial rolls. The inviting, yet spartan, décor matches the creative menu. Reservations a must at this perennial hot spot . . . lunch is easier to "walk-in." Two tables downstairs are "first come, first serve" at all times. Valet parking is available. Our friend Eddie suggested that his tombstone read: "Died happily upstairs at the Slanted Door." Prices range from $5.75 to $24.50.

Taqueria El Toro, 598 Valencia St. (@ 17th St.), (415) 431-3351, *Mexican On The Go*

Authentic, healthy Mexican served cafeteria-style. Be prepared to stand on line during peak hours. It's worth the wait for the freshest of fresh tacos, burritos, seafood dishes and especiales. We love the 100 percent commitment to "no MSG, no preservatives and no bull." Speaking of no bull, it's delicious! Open 10 A.M.–10 P.M. daily. *Psst . . . same owners have a second outpost in the neighborhood, Taqueria Pancho Villa, 3071 16th St. (bet. Valencia & Mission Sts.), (415) 864-8840. Open until midnight.*

We Be Sushi, 538 Valencia St. (@ 16th St.), (415) 565-0749, *Solo Dining*

If you're hankering for your weekly sushi fix and the new budget won't permit anything too outrageous, this is the place for you. You will feel right at home dining alone on delicious rolls and cold sake. Excellent quality.

Watergate, 1152 Valencia St. (bet. 22nd & 23rd Sts.), (415) 648-6000, *Very Elegant Victuals*

Unlike its ultratrendy neighbors, this place is *molto elegante!* The cuisine is French-Asian, with interesting sauces that compete with any edible delectable on the Left Bank. The dark wood sets the tone and makes for the perfect cozy place to bring Mr. Right. Maybe he will be inspired to call you Mrs. Right! Closed Sunday & Monday, dinner only. Costs $14–20.

Woodward's Garden, 1700 Mission St. (@ Duboce St.), (415) 621-7122, *Secret Hideaway*

Be the girl with the inside scoop: situated in a somewhat-out-of-the-way spot, under the freeway and in the Mission district, this little (and we mean little, less than 25 seats) hideaway is a genuine find. It's cozy and welcoming even though the neighborhood can be less than desirable at times. Bring your appetite and relax over a yummy duck breast while feeling the heat of the kitchen! Vegetarians will find options too. Very romantic, so take advantage of this fine food, low costs, and low lighting, if he asks where you would like to go for dinner tonight! Closed on Monday & Tuesday. Dinner only. Prices run from $10 to $25.

Other Neighborhoods/Counties

Ton Kiang, 5821 Geary Blvd. (@ 22nd & 23rd Aves.), (415) 386-8530, *Dim Sum And Then Some*

Seen one too many Jackie Chan movies lately? The best of the best in fresh dim sum for babes with the Asian nibbles. Pick and choose from an inventive assortment of variations on the dim sum theme: itsy bitsy crunchy ribs, giant lightly fried prawns, out-of-this-world shrimp dumplings accented with chive, crispy roasted duck that melts at your fingertips not to mention your tongue. . . . It's a whole new world of miniature food for the neophyte, and a great find for the dim sum fan club. Now if only you could eat just one!

Treats

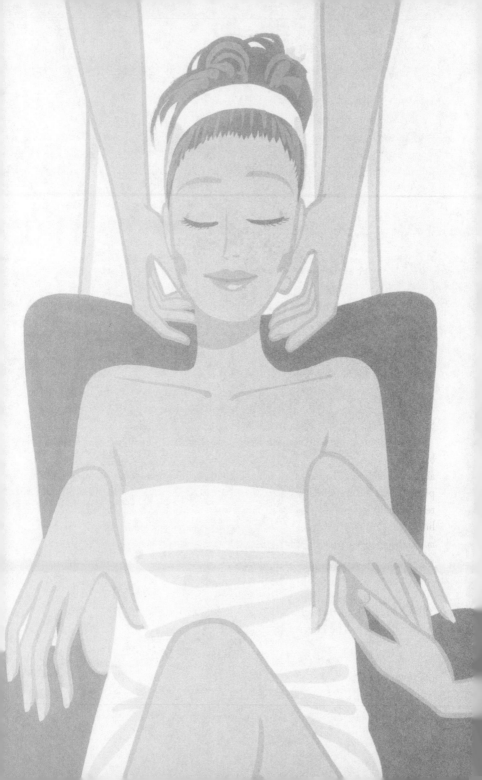

77 Maiden Lane, 77 Maiden Lane, 2nd fl. (bet. Grant & Kearny Sts.), (415) 391-7777, *Socialite Headquarters*
Wondering where all the ladies-who-lunch go after their two-hour gab-and-crab fest at Balboa Café (see Twilight, Marina/Cow Hollow)? They are beelining for the ultimate pampering salon to get waxed, rubbed, polished, dipped and coifed before they head off to a fundraiser for the SF Opera. The extensive menu of services is designed to pamper and beautify in one fell swoop! Spa packages are the perfect gift, but the prices range from $250 up. Men are welcome too . . . if they promise to behave! *Psst . . . if nuptials are in your future, wedding parties are their specialty.*

Angela's Nails, 225 Front St., 2nd fl. (bet. California & Sacramento Sts.), (415) 677-8660, *Reliable Nails*
O great mystery of life! Upstairs holds the answer: a good manicure and wax. Just as you would expect, it's clean and it's fast. No pretense and no appointment necessary. Dash in, dash out. . . . Now, if only the rest of your day wasn't so hairy! Other location, 743 Pine St., (bet. California & Sacramento Sts.), (415) 986-2027.

Acme Head & Body, 266 Sutter St., 2nd fl. (bet. Grant Ave. & Kearny St.), (415) 989-2263, *Hip Hair*
This place is fun, with a retro 1950s-style setting. Scott has been in the business of making women beautiful for some 20 years. Frank Sinatra tunes and a delicious neck massage prepare you for an experience that is sure to please even the most discerning downtown power girl! All stylists are internationally trained to give you a cut that is sure to turn heads as you bee-bop into XYZ (see Twilight, Downtown) tonight for cocktails. *Psst . . . for a midweek Shiatsu rubdown, let these pros help you to chill out, and take on the rest of your hectic week in de-stressed style.*

Architects & Heroes, 580 Bush St. (bet. Stockton & Grant Sts.), (415) 391-8833, *www.architectsandheros.com, Neighborhood Favorite*
See details in The Heights.

Beate Comment, 450 Sutter St., 23rd fl. (bet. Paul & Stockholm Sts.), (415) 393-1490, *Room With A View*

In need of a vacation, but you blew your budget on a vintage Vespa you couldn't live without? Take a minijourney without ever packing a bag! Beate wants you to feel transported. We love the manicures that last forever and the individualized facials that cater to your particular needs and the facials are otherworldly. Ask for Jill if Beate is booked. It's a pretty place, complete with ship-style portholes and personalized attention. Blink, blink, you are back to reality and booking your next visit without the cost of an airline ticket or seasickness! Open Tues.–Sat. 9–6 P.M.

Cinta Salon, 23 Grant Ave., 2nd fl. (bet. O'Farrell and Geary Sts.), (415) 989-1000, *The Works*

This full-service salon is the ideal place for city girls looking for superb repair under one roof with no headache. Cinta, the chic owner, knows "what a girl wants." Grab a sleek blow-dry, a painless bikini wax and a stick of Dentyne Ice, and you are good to go! Costs: blow-dry with a senior stylist $40, highlights $130, relaxer $100, facials $75, body bronzer application $85, full-face threading $50, French manicure $20.

Carlton Hair International, @ The SF Shopping Center, 865 Market St., #C28A (@ Powell St.), (415) 495-8300, *Cut/Color To Go*

Scared silly by the thought of going to a "chain" for a trim or manicure? This "un-chain" started in South Africa and subsequently began popping up all over Southern California. The philosophy: a convenient location combined with high-quality service (think opposite of Super Cuts). This is their first foray into the Bay Area, and they are a welcome addition for the downtown girl in a hurry! Get a sleek blow-dry ($40–50) or a quickie manicure ($15) on your way to an important meeting. The cable cars stop nearby, and they are open until 8 P.M. *Psst . . . don't miss the chance to pick up some "Fear of Flying" herbs at the front of the salon before your next overseas jaunt! No, they are not Erica Jong–endorsed aphrodisiacs!*

Cowboys and Angels, 207 Powell St. (@ O'Farrell St.), (415) 362-8516, *Trendy Hair*

Set in an industrial loftlike space, this is an optimum place to get a hip cut that's not so far out you will frighten or be frightened . . . but you may possibly delight your friends and colleagues with your fashion savvy! Louise Bamowski and her cool and groovy pack of stylists are able to listen to your wildest hair dreams and translate them into reality. You won't look like Gwen Stefani unless you ask to. All trendiness aside, enjoy a delicious cappucino or latte while you browse through the latest edition of *Vogue,* clipping glamorous dos to consider. Your nerve is intact, and your hair is in great hands . . . so go for it! Haircuts $55–85, full highlights $150.

Elevation Salon & Café, 451 Bush St. (bet. Grant Ave. & Kearny St.), (415) 392-2969, *Mod Squad*

We love being different with time! Offering great hair care while you dine in the chic, inviting museum-style café, munching on sandwiches, salads, or a garden burger. Be adventurous and opt for an inviting new twist to your old look under the color wand of Van. Finish it all off with a gloss/toner, a double espresso and your daily vitamin. Picasso would approve! Closed on Sundays.

Equilibrium, @The Hotel Monaco, 501 Geary St. (@ Taylor St.), (415) 346-7337, *www.SPAEQ.com, De-Stress*

It's a little known fact that this full-service spa for facials, massages, fitness, meditation, manicures, pedicures, waxing and body wraps is open to the public even though they are located in the hip Hotel Monaco (see Tripping, Downtown). We "Jane" girls are reluctant to let the word out because this is our favorite secret hideaway to rejuvenate our bodies, souls, and minds. All of the services are innovative and seemingly tailored to your individual problems: the Jet-Lag Facial (masks with active ingredients to tighten the skin's appearance, 90 min. for $135), Spa Equilibrium Pedicure (sea salt scrub and peel with a mint foot mask, $55), Anti-Stress Aromatherapy Body Wrap (body scrub followed by essential oils and milk lotions, 90 min. for $170), Personal Visualization (to access your inner wisdom and balance your emotions, 60 min. for $85), plus many more. Arrive early or stay afterwards and use the glamorous eucalyptus steam room, sauna and whirlpool. *Psst . . . it is coed, so bring your swimsuit. Also, they offer their services on demand to nearby hotels that do not have facilities.*

Erma McLaughlin, @ Joseph Cozza Salon, 30 Maiden Lane, 5th fl. (bet. Grant Ave. & Kearny St.), (415) 433-3030, *www.josephcozzasalon.com, Lasting Nails*

When another quickie file-and-paint job just won't tide you over, book a session with Erma for a pedicure and manicure that soothe the soul and last a long time! The salon itself is comely and in the heart of Union Square. The friendly assistants go out of their way to make sure you are comfortable through your entire visit. After changing into a plush robe and having your feet soaked and bathed in hot water, be prepared to let the luxury begin. Sip tea to the gentle tunes that serve as a perfect backdrop to your "stress-less" treatment. Erma exfoliates the whole leg and foot, applies heated creams, massages, files and polishes until you pass out from the luxury! The whole experience is a perfect way to unwind after a hectic week at the office and before kicking off a romantic weekend with your honey. It's worth the extra cash as it will save you time, money and your sanity! Costs: manicure, $20; pedicure, $40 plus.

It's Yoga, 348 Folsom St. (@ Market St.), (415) 543-1970, *www.itsyoga. net, Neighborhood Favorite*
This is the South of Market shrine to stretching. The busiest hours are mornings and evenings when gaggles of local girls (and boys!) flock to the one of four levels of classes. Sign up ahead of time and prepare to downward dog, mat to mat! Midday classes are filled with local artist types. Showers are available to cool down and perk up for your hot postyoga date! *Psst . . . we suggest the midday classes for between-meeting breaks, but parking is costly in the nearby lot and parking in front is scarcer than truffles in August!*

Maiden Lane Salon, 111 Maiden Lane, Suite 303 (bet. Grant Ave. & Stockton St.), (415) 981-2426, *www.maidenlanesalon.com, Wedding-Day Bliss*
"Your beauty is in good hands: ours." That motto sets the tone for this haven dedicated to making you look, and therefore feel, beautiful. This full-service salon offers special services like paraffin treatment for your toes ($15), lactic acid treatment (alternative glycolic peel for sensitive skin) $40, or an eyelash tint ($20). Adding to their special touch, they use and sell some of the best products to take home: Peter Thomas Roth, Pevonia, Phytologie, De Lorenzo and more. *Psst . . . they are the best when it comes to bridal beauty packages!*

Mary Thé Skin Care, 153 Maiden Lane (bet. Grant Ave. & Stockton St.), (415) 788-8431, *No-Fuss Facials*
In a neighborhood that is not lacking in places to beautify, this simple salon is dedicated to "face!" It's a great option for those looking for an extraordinary facial performed by one of the lovely team of aestheticians, who cares more about your skin and your personal needs than hawking products. It's a simple white-on-white space with multiple facial rooms. $85 for a 75-minute session.

Nails For You, 17 Drumm St. (bet. Sacramento & California Sts.), (415) 788-5081, *Manicure Must*

This reliable nail salon is a convenient pit stop in the Financial District. Unlike the typical file, rub and polish crew, they have a secret touch that makes their manicures last and last. It's quick, friendly and convenient . . . $26 for manicure and pedicure. *Psst . . . with hands that look that good afterwards, you may want to book an appointment with the palm reader in the same building!*

Skin Rejuvenation Clinic, 251 Post St., Suite 310 (@ Stockton St.), (415) 788-SKIN, *Facial Specialist*

This is the ideal place for the "not-ready-for-the-knife" crowd. Eva Patel is the nondoctor for those who want more than a facial but less hassle than a dermatologist's office. She spent years as a surgical assistant but is trained as an aesthetician. With that understanding, she gracefully delivers her treatments with the precision of a surgeon and the ease of a relaxing facial. Start with the glycolic/lactic acid peels for a quick lift ($60), and work into her more advanced procedures. The space itself is as enchanting as the treatments! *Psst . . . her custom line, Skin Rx, has one of the best sunscreens that money can buy. Nongreasy and sheer!*

Spa Nordstrom, @ Nordstrom, 855 Market St. (@ 5th St.), (415) 243-8500, *www.nordstrom.com/spanordstrom, Grand Dame*

In a city with a lot to offer, this spa is the quintessential destination for the girl who needs to be pampered and "chill." Enter the generic elevators in the Market Center and punch the button. . . . Start to feel the calm before you arrive! Who doesn't want their feet cleaned in a wooden bowl and rubbed with lemon, while sipping on herbal tea in a plush robe? And that's all before you even start! Every service is transforming, leaving you with a feeling that you don't care what it costs. You will be renewed slowly as the pressures of life melt away. There is a remarkable level of privacy in the way the spa is laid out. *Psst . . . looking for something new? Book the European Hydro Tub treatment ($50); the magic waters will make you feel your Euro best! Or try a French pedicure ($50) before you set sail for the weekend.*

Sheirling, 525 Second St. (bet. Brannon & Bryant Sts.), (415) 974-6940, *Environment Friendly*

Be still and be beautiful! Unveil the enchantress within you at this environmentally friendly salon and day spa. They are all about helping you relax, renew, restore, and achieve your own personal balance. Set in a sleek yet retro loftlike space with groovy vintage-style barbershop chairs, this place can handle any "issue": polish change ($15), Aveda Express Facial ($50, 45 minutes), brow consultation and design ($30), Cyber Relief Massage ($45) and our "Jane" favorite, the Himalayan Rejuvenation Body Treatment. This full-body regimen balances your individual dosha (five-element diagnosis) through exfoliation, warm oil massage, and steam, promising to bring about mental clarity and total rejuvenation. Hey, it's cheaper than a shrink and much more psychically satisfying, to boot. Closed Sun. & Mon.

Yelena Spa for Women & Men, 166 Geary St., Suite 1107 (@ Stockton St.), (415) 397-2484, *www.yelana-spa.com, Neighborhood Favorite*
Shhh . . . sharing this "secret Russian technique" of facials at the skilled hands of Yelena is tough for us to do. Forget what you know about traditional facials: after an extended hour of cleaning, exfoliating, extracting (yes, it hurts, but none of the usual redness accompanies her unique approach) and finishing with a delicious hand, foot, and shoulder massage, you'll be just waiting to exhale! Our bet is that you'll come out looking like a Bond girl. Now sashay into Foreign Cinema (see Twilight, Mission) and order a martini cocktail; shaken, not stirred. Costs: start at $78 for a European Facial, and Body Treatments start at $65.

Yosh for Hair/Gina Khan, 173 Maiden Lane (bet. Stockton St. & Grant Ave.), (415) 989-7704, *www.yoshforhairsf-ginakhan.com, Best Dye*
Yosh has been a San Fran innovator in hair care for over 17 years, and let's not forget Gina, who has worked with Yosh for over 25 years! She is recognized as one of the world's foremost hair coloring authorities; she teaches and is a three-time recipient of the Haircolor USA Creative Artist Award. The modern yet warm salon is welcoming, with soft, indirect lighting and gorgeous orchids on the counter. The whole staff is educated in the latest techniques and hottest styles from around the world, and they recommend individual cuts and unique color to suit your lifestyle as well as your body and face shape. Cuts by Yosh are $125 with blow-dry; master and senior designers are $86 and $69 respectively. Custom highlights are up to $135, plus an added surcharge for "color virgins."

Zendo, 256 Sutter St. (@ Grant Ave.), (415) 788-3404, *www. salonzendo.com, Queen For A Day*

Urban girl alert! This is a fabulous place to take the edge off. Step into an uninteresting office building and step off the elevator into this slice of paradise in the midst of the hustle and bustle of Union Square. Go with the easy vibe that reeks of aromatherapy oils. Prepare to be pampered by some of the city's finest treatments. Their haircuts, waxing (less painful than most!), and facials are of particular note. Try the Rejuvenation Facial ($120 for 90 minutes) using techniques like initial skin analysis, massage, exfoliation and mask application followed by a luscious moisturizer. Haircuts $55, purifying $85 for 50 minutes, Seated Express Massage $2 a minute.

Vidal Sassoon, 359 Sutter St. (bet. Grant Ave. & Stockton St.), (415) 397-5105, *www.vidalsassoon.com, Precise Cuts*

When trying a new salon seems too daunting, never fear, this is the most reliable destination for cuts and color. As Carly Simon once sang, nobody does it better, year after year, and city by city, continent by continent, than this chain to beat all chains, when it comes to precise hair cuts for the masses. Don't be put off by that idea because all of the stylists are highly trained in the Sassoon way of cutting which has been touted throughout the years by stylish women around the world. Dare to try a new over-the-top look or just shape-up your mane that has been growing-out since you chopped it all off after the big break-up. *Psst . . . did you know that Vidal Sassoon created the classic "bob" haircut in 1963?*

⚘ Not to Miss:

Elizabeth Arden Red Door, 126 Post St. (bet. Grant Ave. & Kearny St.), (415) 989-4888, *Neighborhood Favorite*
De Kroon Salon, 303 Sutter St. (@ Grant Ave.), (415) 398-6474, *Natural Style*

Nob Hill/Russian Hill/North Beach/Chinatown ....

Crunch, 1000 Van Ness Ave. (@ O'Farrell St.), (415) 931-1100, *www.crunchfitness.com, Get In Shape*

High-tech fitness in a high-tech setting. This is a megawatt place to get in shape and practice your flirting skills on the cute trainers, who have fitness down to a science! A huge selection of classes daily such as Femme Fatal, Booty Kickin' Step, and Wash Board Abs will keep it interesting, along with the usual Stairmasters, EFX, and Lifecycles. Grab a cool smoothie on the go and save calories for your sumptuous dinner at Tommie Toy with your new "boy toy!" Costs: $23 a day or $150 a month. Other locations in major cities such as New York, Miami, Chicago, Los Angeles, and Atlanta. *Psst . . . exhibitionist's dream: the bathrooms are of special note because they put you on display! Frosted glass protects private parts, but a spotlight illuminates uh . . . certain things. You sexy show-off!*

Jackson Place Salon, (in The Courtyard), 633 Battery St., Suite 117 (bet. Pacific Ave. & Jackson St.), (415) 399-1044, *Hidden Gem*

This full-service salon and spa is a great destination when you are in the mood to be pampered in a no-nonsense environment. Expect modern up-to-the-minute looks by one of the five stylists. Owners Alla Kaplun and Lori Mitcheli bring fabulous products to you, such as the Italian line Terrax (great for really dry hair), and Bumble & Bumble (gotta have the "dry shampoo" powder). Offering haircuts ($50), color ($50 and up), and "gel" nails ($40). Let facialist Susana pick a facial to fit your needs for that moment. We love the Vitamin C Treatment ($60). Grab a 15-minute "On-the-Go" special by Debra Rubin for a mere $20. Now don't you look good—knock 'em dead today.

Mister Lee, 834 Jones St., 3rd fl. (bet. Sutter & Bush Sts.), (415) 474-6002 or (800) 693-2977, *www.misterlee.com, Beauty Central*

Sound body, sound mind. Enter the world of Mister Lee. (Leave this page of the book open for your paramour to see!) Let the world music set the tone as you enter this hideaway on the third floor, where Egyptian murals and filmy curtains greet you before a delicious massage. We love the hydrotherapy bath massage that uses whirlpool-esque jets of water, strategically placed on body pressure points such as fingertips, lower back, and pectorals. It's guaranteed relaxation that Cleopatra would envy! Other salon treats are: Glycolic Peels ($80), Algae Wrap Pedicures ($35 and up), Cellulite Treatments ($140), and fantastic haircuts that were given rave reviews by *Vogue* ($45 and up). "One Perfect Day," $375. *Psst . . . early birds want to take advantage of the 7:30 A.M. appointments, and night owls can prowl in until 8 P.M. on Thursdays. Sunday is open for groups, or book ahead if you know you need a fix!*

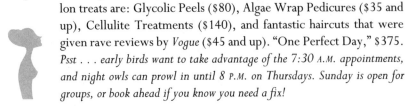

Nob Hill Spa, @ The Huntington Hotel, 1075 California St. (@ Taylor St.), (415) 345-2888, *www.nobhillspa.com, Neighborhood Newcomer*

The tony location is just the initial tip to the Nirvana that awaits you. Attached to the historic Huntington Hotel (see Tripping, Nob Hill), this oasis is dedicated to peace and wellness. Designed by SF Feng Shui guru Seann Xenja, with one-of-a-kind cultural antiques and accents. The best part is that you can partake of it all for a daily fee of $25, waived with the purchase of a 50-minute treatment. Check into the "sanctuary," complete with lockers, robes, and slippers, and choose your playtime "poison." Linger around the pool overlooking the magnificent city skyline before heading off to enjoy a Champagne Facial (champagne combined with exotic Chinese herbs, $185). Okay, Posh Spice, don't expect to find Jack Kerouac here! It's ritzy, baby! *Psst . . . book the exclusive private massage room with fireplace or opt for the couples' massage room.*

Salon Andres, 55 Grant Ave., 4th fl. (bet. Geary Blvd. & O'Farrell St.), (415) 397-9767, *Queen For A Day*

A beautiful salon that combines a 30s-style deco elegance with modern high ceilings fit for the Millenium. The lounge-style sitting room downstairs is a cool place to wait with your complimentary glass of wine. Relax and sip before one of the friendly staff escorts you for a fab cut by one of San Francisco's best shear-lings (starting at $35). Or, if a mild case of adult acne takes over your face, book a blissful facial from the magical hands of Rayleen. Other services include yummy spa manicures, pedicures, and hair color. Now, don't you feel better?

Marina/Cow Hollow

2001 Nails, 2213 Union St. (@ Fillmore St.), (415) 775-5838, *Magic Manicure*

We dare you to find a quicker, more thorough manicure in this fair city! Even the most well-dressed "it" girls and socialites drive all the way from Marin County for a French manicure from these pros. A bit generic from the outside, it's clean and snappy on the inside. The proof is in the pedicure!

Acabello, 2423 California St. (bet. Fillmore & Steiner Sts.), (415) 922-7577, *Blow-Dry*

In a city that changes its loyalties to salons as fast as the stock market's loyalty to the high-tech business, this place has been around for over five years, so they must be doing something right! We love the custom artwork on the walls, for mindless gazing as we have our hair made over. In a rush but need a little je ne sais quoi? Book a sleek blow-dry. Closed on Sunday & Monday.

BeneFit Cosmetics, 2219 Chestnut St. (bet. Scott & Pierce Sts.), (415) 567-1173, *www.benefitcosmetics.com, Makeup Application*

See details in The Heights.

Gorilla Sports, 2324 Chestnut St. (@ Scott St.), (415) 292-8470, *www.gorillasports.com, Sweat It Out*

The name is the tip-off: a gym for those who take exercise very seriously, not for those looking to lift a few weights and call it a day. A fun atmosphere; it's more conducive to those already in shape, as well as "January girls" who sign up in full-blown resolution mode. Expect plenty of encouragement from staff and patrons along with a wide array of options to fit anyone's schedule and level of fitness. Some of the cutting-edge group classes include: Boxing, Tae Kwon Do, Pilates, Spinning. The cardio equipment is state-of-the-art, and they offer a nice selection of free weights for traditionalists. The first visit is free, so go for it! Membership only for future visits. See other location in The Heights. *Psst . . . for your A.D.D.-prone child, there are kids' karate classes offered.*

Heaven Day Spa, 2209 Chestnut St. (@ Pierce St.), (415) 749-6414, *www.heavendayspa.com, Full Service*

This multilevel spa/salon has much to offer to the girl on the move! Grab a massage, or a body wrap, from one of their talented aestheticians. Other unique services on hand include private yoga from Veera Sanjana ($125), lunchtime peels (30 min.), quick Aroma Steam (15 min. for $10), healing acupuncture ($90), or perhaps you will need a blow-dry after your treatment, for $25 and up. This is a one-stop shop for beauty and wellness. Open seven days a week, until 8 P.M. including Monday.

High-tech, 2007 Divisadero St. (bet. Sacramento & California Sts.), (415) 928-0324, *Afternoon Delight*

This is a trustworthy place to get a quick nail or wax job. It's clean, efficient and just what you need to get ready for an important presentation or date. Offering manicures ($8) and pedicures ($16), $20 for both. Waxing available too. Open 9 A.M.–7 P.M. daily, 10 A.M.–6 P.M. Sunday.

Michaela, @ Ringolevio Salon, 2660 Gough St. (@ Union St.), (415) 272-2593, *Healing Hands*

Massage is known to improve circulation along with your general state of well-being! Michaela Boehm originally studied massage in Thailand, and then became certified in acupressure at the Institute in Berkley. Her touch is deep, powerful, and not for those looking for a fluffy rubdown. After a long flight, we recommend Acu Oil, which combines the Swedish technique with stress-relieving acupressure. The salon is clean and mellow and will help you forget the 17 new messages on your cell phone. $30 for 30 minutes. By appointment only, closed on Mondays. *Psst . . . need a birthday gift for the hard-to-please client? Gift certificates available.*

Novella Salon and Spa, 2238 Union St. (bet. Fillmore & Steiner Sts.), (415) 673-1929, *www.novellasalonandspa.com, Peaceful Treatments*

Enter the peaceful world of Novella, complete with incense and mood music. The services are all designed to pamper and beautify your hair, hands, feet and skin. Spa packages are the perfect indulgence for that special someone's birthday. We loved our deep-conditioning hair treatment ($45) and de-stress Eye Treatment ($25). Try the cutting-edge treatment ampoules as an addition to your regular facial. A nice selection of products "to go" will enable you to recreate your spa experience at home: Pevonia products from Switzerland, lavender-filled eye pillows and Aveda cosmetics. No Amex accepted, but debit cards are welcome.

Ringolevio Salon, 2660 Gough St. (@ Union St.), (415) 272-2593, *Skin Care Pro*

What else is going on at Ringolevio? Nona Harrison and Elaine Unterreiner are two in-house, highly talked-about aestheticians who approach skin care from a holistic angle. Facials, peels, waxing, tenting, and various body treatments complete the list of personalized services.

San Francisco Yoga Studio, 2159 Filbert St. (bet. Fillmore & Calhollow Sts.), (415) 931-YOGA, *www.usyoga.org, Hot Movements*

Does a time crunch keep you from your crunches? Relax and get to it! Tony Sanchez, a Bikram student and practitioner, holds yoga court in his adorable studio. His sessions are swift, down to 60 minutes from the standard 90-minute Bikram way. You'll be back at the office before anyone notices you're gone! The studio itself is pared down to free your mind from all of the craziness of the Cow Hollow streets.

Solar Planet, 3151 Fillmore St. (@ Greenwich St.), (415) 922-7200, *Pigmentation Dilemma*

It is certainly not fashionable to be tan these days, but a little color is in order before you don that strappy number for the ballet tonight. Solar Planet is equipped with several Dr. Muller tanning beds, most particularly the Omega and the high-powered Orbit; in other words, the Rolls-Royce in tanning circles. The trustworthy staff is knowledgeable about the business of sunning and will help determine which treatments are best based on your skin's texture and color. Perhaps the best treatment for you oh-so-fair-skinned girls is a tan from a bottle. Yep, they offer application too, complete with a relaxing deep-tissue massage. Either way, they make sure you leave with a glow that rivals "blushing" after your first kiss!

Spa Radiance, 3061 Fillmore St., 2nd fl. (@ Filbert St.), (415) 346-6281, *www.sparadiance.com, Neighborhood Favorite*

If sudden amnesia overtakes your brain, or you happen to misplace this book, do not forget this one name in SF beauty. Since its inception in 1975, Spa Radiance has been touted as one of the city's most treasured spots. Angela Umansky, a third-generation Russian aesthetician, combines modern technologies like dermabrasion with old-world remedies from the south of France to make magic. Set in a comfy two-story Victorian home, enjoy some preservice tea in a darling china cup! Some of the packages are aptly named: "So You've Got A Problem" facial, the "Jet Lag Facial" ($95), or Sharon Stone's favorite, the much coveted "Bed Of Roses" massage by Jerry ($210 for 120 minutes). Using actual rose petals to exfoliate and steam, Jerry then kneads you like dough—the Pillsbury boy will have nothing on you. Follow it up with a makeup application, a manicure or a Brazilian bikini wax with Anastasia, who is the queen of waxing at this most-treasured cozy place of beauty.

Union Square Apothecary, 2185A Union St. (bet. Fillmore & Webster Sts.), (415) 771-1207, *Day Spa*

The hot dot-commer who still has a job and has moved in next door hasn't noticed you? We've got the answer! Step down the stairs into the wonderful world of Shiad, a cosmetic chemist, and let him work his magic. Utilizing a huge selection of custom oils and fresh serums, Shiad carefully blends the perfect fragrance to match your natural scent. Or one of the fabulous facials, cellulite treatments, a body polish or self-tanning application should do the trick! Ask for custom-made Lip Smoother balm and the aromatherapy starter kit on your way out the door. Now you know why *Self* named them one of the 10 best in the U.S.! *Psst . . . ask about the "pheromones" if you dare. He houses 1,400 of them, and custom tailors combinations of your choice. One is bound to match your mysterious prey!*

Vanishing Point, 3218 Fillmore St. (@ Lombard St.), (415) 292-4955, *Hair Be Gone*

Fuzzy Wuzzy was a bear, Fuzzy Wuzzy needs a wax . . . now! Or does she? East Coast Gotham girls are leading the way in permanent hair removal and now it's traveled west. This astonishing technique uses light to damage the hair shaft, inhibiting growth permanently. (There is a small amount of pain involved that is supposedly equal to the snapping of a rubber band against your skin. Right . . .) It's timely and costly, but what's more enticing than the thought of never having ingrown hairs on your bikini line again? Priceless at $125 per 15 minutes. See other location in Castro. *Psst . . . the recent addition of Botox injections (all by dermatologists), collagen and microdermabrasion make this the one-stop shopping for beauty enhancements (at this location only).*

Yoga Haven, 3303 Buchanan St. (@ Lombard St.), (415) 775-9642, *Sweating Required*

If you need to sweat out your frustrations, or stretch out the kinks in your back from biking through Napa with your buff beau, look no further! These classic Bikram classes are literally hot, hot, hot, as you plow through 26 different poses (84 poses for the advanced masochist). Run by a husband-and-wife team, along with help from their siblings and both mothers, it's a family affair guaranteeing 90 minutes of massive sweating. Kudos for the superb ventilation in the hot room, encouraging breathing in the most uncomfortable of situations. You'll be as relaxed as a jellyfish after a quick shower and cool as a cucumber for the big presentation this afternoon!

Not to Miss:

Berenice Salon, 2115 Union Sq., 2nd fl. (bet. Fillmore & Webster Sts.), (415) 345-8898, *Facials & More*

"The Heights" (Pacific/Presidio/Laurel) ....

A Body Of Work, 2797 Union St. (@ Baker St.), (415) 351-2797, *www.abodyofwork.com, Rehabilitation Workout*

Forget the old concept of "no pain, no gain." If you are suffering from weak abs or a true injury, this is a brightly lit place to stretch your way to health and a hot body! Jean will help you maneuver through the web of machines (think Pilates) that incorporate the concepts of rotational mobility and the rehabilitation of your body. The studio itself is huge, but don't be scared away—it still feels private and personal. Seventy dollars per session, with discounts for packages. Beginners may opt for the Fundamental Series: $195 includes five private sessions, evaluation of health, posture analysis, and a workout program. *Psst . . . try their other location in Sonoma, 17311 Arnold Dr., (707) 938-5593*

Addison, 2321 Pine St. (@ Fillmore St.), (415) 931-9513, *Hip Hair Cutter*

Formerly of Architects & Heroes, Addison books up at least one week in advance, so plan ahead for his full attention . . . it's worth the wait ($75). A sleek and modern place for master cuts, this tiny salon has only six stations on two floors. The "of the moment" looks are carefully churned out by some of the city's best talent. This is the ultimate "Jane" place. Products for sale include the all-natural MOP and the ever-so-necessary Phyto products. *Psst . . . use the Phyto #9 leave-in conditioner: the best if your color is "enhanced." We would travel to France to stock up if necessary.*

Architects & Heroes, 2239 Fillmore St. (bet. Clay & Sacramento Sts.), (415) 921-8383, *www.architectsandheroes.com, Neighborhood Favorite*

Under new ownership, this oh-so-cool (and oh-so-pricey!) SF salon is still one of the best places in the city to get an incredible haircut. All of the stylists specialize in the Sassoon method, which means precise yet fashionable cutting. The salon itself is sleek, chic, the perfect backdrop to hair designs that will last. In fact, your cut will look just as good when you attempt to recreate the look yourself the next day. Really! Don't forget to pick up some Kiehl's Silk Groom, sold at the front, on your way out. Ask for Jody if you are thinking of color. Open seven days a week, until 9 P.M. Wednesday–Friday. See other location in Downtown. *Psst . . . allot extra time for parking (a nightmare), so you won't miss your appointment!*

BeneFit Cosmetics, 2117 Fillmore St. (bet. California & Sacramento Sts.), (415) 567-0242, *www.benefitcosmetics.com, Makeup Application*
These San Francisco twin sisters, Jean & Jane, have made quite a name for themselves in the Bay Area and beyond. Their cosmetic line is famous for the lip pump, a topical wand of magic that makes lips full and sexy. Or try BeneTint, a burgundy stain, to give cheeks a natural "glow." But our personal favorite: go glam to your office Christmas party with false eyelashes! Application on the spot for $15–20. If you are jonesing for something a little more permanent, they tint lashes, wax and offer a short but sweet menu of facials ($35–$65). Walk-ins welcome, but book ahead if you know your big dates ahead of time. Open seven days a week. See other location in Marina/Cow Hollow.

Body Gallery, 1527 Baker St. (@ Bush St.), (415) 776-6641, *www.thebody-gallery.com, One-On-One Training*
Can't bear another boring run on the treadmill? Diversify your options. Based on a Pilates-style workout, this team of professionals is trained to help you achieve immediate results by strengthening your muscles while protecting your back. These workouts seem so effortless, it's tempting to drift off into never-never land while staring at the lovely art-lined walls owner Susan Copich has amassed for your viewing pleasure. The workout starts at $60 per session, but the price goes down when you buy in bulk. Try the $35 semiprivate session if you are on a budget. By appointment only. *Psst . . . if you are an artist, or know one, she is always looking for emerging artists to feature in the studio.*

Chase Manning Studio, 3628 Sacramento St. (bet. Locust & Spruce Sts.), (415) 567-1911, *Casual Cuts*
Tucked into an adorable white alleyway, this elegant shop is as inviting as the street that leads to it! This is a great traditional salon that welcomes locals as well as the "informed" traveler. Any place that offers the par excellence Rene Fueture products and a glass of white wine during your blow-

dry is all right by us ($40)! Although this charming place will lure you in, the street outside is lined with great boutiques for postcoif shopping.

David Oliver, 3366 Sacramento St. (bet. Presidio Ave. & Walnut St.), (415) 563-2044, *Famous Haircutter*

Touted by the local and national press as *the* man to go to if you want to look younger and . . . more beautiful! Situated on one of the best streets in the city to window shop, this sun-filled salon is delicious. David, a dashing Englishman, trained under the tutelage of his father and the Vidal Sassoon Salons in London, then came to the States to manage Sassoon salons in Chicago and SF. He opened his own SF outpost in 1982. The ladies-who-lunch brigade recommended him to fix Barbara Bush's hair when she was in town! He also sells some of our favorite products like Terax (Italian), Tend Skin (the answer to in-grown hair), and Bumble & Bumble (NYC). Manicures, waxing, and makeup application also available! Cut & blow-dry by David, $70. Hmm . . . wonder if he could introduce us to a fellow Brit . . . perhaps a Guy Ritchie clone?

Defy Gravity, 3611 Sacramento St. (@ Locust St.), (415) 921-8313, *Stretching Plus*

If staying flexible is the key to staying youthful, then this sunny Presidio Heights studio is a great find. Offering an alternative to spinning and stepping your life away at a traditional gym, machines that were invented by Joseph Pilates allow you to relax while you push, pull, and roll your way to ultimate fitness without any risk of injury. Private and "duet" sessions. The name itself gives you a good idea of the many different ways your body will contort if you know what you are doing. Trust them, they know! Be sure to wear something that allows you to move easily.

Global Yoga, 2425 Chestnut St. (@ Divisadero St.), (415) 346-9493, *Stretch And Sweat*

Who couldn't use a little tune-up now and then? Formerly Yoga Zone, this place is the hottest yoga studio in town—literally. If you can't stand the heat, get out of the studio! This unassuming second-story location is home to throngs of devotees. Dedicated to the Hatha Yoga and the Bikram Method, classes are taught exactly as Bikram teaches. Mary J. Jarvis, the fearless leader, swears that her studio is about healing chronic ailments (old snow-ski injuries), correcting poor posture (too many hours on the Internet!), all the while slowly changing the shape of your body. Mats can be rented for a dollar. First class is $10, and the second one is free for new students. Twelve dollars for drop-ins. Or pay $95 for a one-month unlimited pass. *Psst . . . enroll the kiddies in the Yoga for Children. Also, mommies-to-be can be accommodated with slightly altered postures.*

Gorilla Sports, 2450 Sutter St. (@ Divisadero St.), (415) 474-2699, *www.gorillasports.com, Sweat It Out*
See details in Marina/Cow Hollow.

JT Nails, 1848 Fillmore St. (bet. Sutter & Bush Sts.), (415) 563-4373, *Reliable Nails*
You have a million things to do this Saturday. Check one more thing off the list! Neighborhood girls flock to this clean, quick and cheap nail salon. Book ahead, or arrive early. Otherwise prepare to wait a bit. Costs: $8 plus tip.

Kabuki Springs and Spa, 1750 Geary St. (@ Fillmore St.), (415) 922-6000, *www.kabukisprings.com, Ultimate Relaxation*
For you "Jane" girls who are skeptical about the notion of communal bathing, put your doubts aside and make this spa your destination. There is not enough room in this book to rave about the experience at this Japanese-style spa. The space itself is designed to encourage harmony and relaxation, down to the subtle music. Just go, and we bet you will be adding this phone number to your Palm V before you reenter the harsh reality of life outside these walls. Women-only baths on Wednesday, Friday, and Sunday, where nudity is encouraged. Tuesdays are coed, so bathing suits are required, thank gawd! For $15 you can enjoy the full facility (hot pool, cool plunge, sauna and steam room). Or book a fabulous massage ahead of time, and then relax in the baths for the price of the massage! Open from 10 A.M.–10 P.M. seven days a week. *Psst . . . parking is available at the Japan Center garage next door.*

Marilyn Jaeger Skincare Studios, 415 Spruce St. (bet. Sacramento & California Sts.), (414) 751-0647, *Waxing Headquarters*
Marilyn Jaeger's Brazilian bikini wax has made her the most-talked-about gal by those in the know. Ever since Gwyneth Paltrow beamed about her newfound "freedom" in all of the fashion magazines, it's all the rage Stateside. Not for those who are shy about exposing their private parts to a

virtual stranger but, if you are dying to be the "bare-o-ness" on the beach or in the bedroom, she will make it seem like no big deal. Don't forget: she trained under Anastasia Soare (J. Lo's brow master) and shapes the best arches this side of St. Louis. Forty-five dollars on initial visit and $35 after. *Psst . . . book ahead if you know your schedule over the next three months because she books up for months on end, although she has been known to work until the wee hours to accommodate the faithful!*

The Mindful Body, 2876 California St. (@ Divisadero St.), (415) 931-2639, *www.themindfulbody.com, Buy Happiness*

Voted the best yoga studio in the Bay Area in *SF Chronicle* (2000). The space itself is in an old brick laundry, and the classes are offered in two large rooms with steel beams and leaded skylights. An extensive variety of traditional yoga classes and private training is available. You used to see all women with a few men hiding in the corner, but now they are "cross-gendered" for the New Millennium. How mod! Think Hatha, Ashtanga, Pre/postnatal, and Power Flow classes. Michael Cooper is supposedly the crème de la crème instructor. A few of our favorite perks: Introduction to Meditation on Saturday afternoons, the bubbling hot tub for relaxation after class, Organizational Stress Management for "terminal rage," in-house acupuncturist and facials too! No Amex accepted. Twelve dollars per class, $11 if you pay the 75-dollar membership fee.

Nail Pretty, 3315 Sacramento St. (bet. Presidio & Walnut Sts.), (415) 673-9818, *Maintenance Madness*

Need a sure thing? Go for a quickie pedicure and ask for Naly. It is the best $15 we have invested in a long time! Open 9:30 A.M.–7:30 P.M. daily.

Naja Cosmetics, 1850 Fillmore St. (bet. Sutter & Bush Sts.), (415) 345-8301, *www.najacosmetics.com, Makeup Application*

This one-of-a-kind cosmetic store offers complete makeup application for that special party or better yet, that special day. Naja is a former makeup artist who perfected her craft in the advertising world. Enjoy the fruits of her experience and expertise: perfect application and a clean line of modern colors from which to choose, including components such as custom-blended powders for even the most difficult skin tones. We bet that she could give any famous line a run for their money! After the relaxing application, pick up some of the great-priced custom skin-care and body products that are so in demand that other SF stores rep them as well! *Psst . . . in case you have a hot date in the near future, ask for a consultation to help recreate your look at home.*

Parsnips, 2915 Sacramento St. (bet. Divisadero & Broderick Sts.), (415) 409-0004, *Ideal Cuts*

Looking for a charming place in the neighborhood for a trim or blow-dry? This is an ultrafeminine place with terracotta-colored walls and an intimate three chairs for a snip and dry. Melisa, one of the owners, "moonlights" as an interior designer. By the looks of this place we would trust her with our home as well as our head. Plenty of locals agree. Closed on Monday.

Presidio Heights Salon, 3470 Sacramento St. (bet. Laurel & Walnut Sts.), (415) 346-2086, *No Hair*

Locals flock to this neighborhood place where Alice, Vivian and Cecilia treat their patrons to the best low-cost nail treatments, facials and waxing. No appointment necessary, but it gets crazy busy in peak times, so book ahead if you have a favorite aesthetician. Open 9:30 A.M.–7:30 P.M. daily, 10 A.M.–6 P.M. Sunday. Manicure & pedicure together for $18 plus tip.

Snippety Crickets, 3562 Sacramento St. (bet. Locust & Laurel Sts.), (415) 441-9363, *Children's Cuts*

This cute shop specializes in "cuts 4 kids" ($15). The walls are lined with photos of first-haircut success stories, and there are tons of toys to keep the little ones entertained before and after the big event! Just in case Junior falls in love with one of the toys, most are priced for "tantrum intervention" sale. Imagine that, ha! If you are on the run, they cut moms and dads too.

Strong Heart Strong Body, 3366 Sacramento St. (bet. Presidio Ave. & Walnut St.), (415) 755-8550, *Individual Attention*

"We help you invest in yourself" is the mission statement of this state-of-the-art facility. Looking to commit to a personal exercise regime (again!)? Let the effervescent E. A. facilitate your dreams. Dedicated to keeping your program interesting enough to keep you on track and boredom-free, E.A. shoots for long-term mental and physical benefits. Here you go: develop a plan, establish realistic goals, avoid injuries, vary the workout and make the most of your time. What time? Too good to be true? With a little luck and a lot of devotion, great things can happen. *Psst . . . expecting mothers are welcomed as part of his highly popular pre and postnatal programs.*

✐ Not to Miss:

High-tech, 2007 Divisadero St. (bet. Sacramento & California Sts.), (415) 928-0324, *Cheap Nails*

Simply Balanced, 2410 California St. (@ Fillmore St.), (415) 567-4349, *Stretch & Tone*

Hayes Valley/Civic Center

Creative Nails, 191 Franklin St. (bet. Oak & Fell Sts.), (415) 861-8100, *Reliable Pedicure*

Yes, it is another of those "quickie" places that seem to be spreading faster than Nail Envy, but this place offers pedicures that seem to last forever! They also offer a quick touch-up if you've broken a nail. Try a more elaborate set of acrylic nails or silk wraps if you are going to the opera and want to feel like a diva! One of the few salons in the 'hood, so take note and grab a quick wax as well if you are in a real pinch.

Finger Tip, 1309 Sutter St. (bet. Van Ness Ave. & Franklin St.), (415) 567-2092, *Fake Nails*

Go to this simple place for a reasonable, *fast,* fashionable set of acrylic nails. A new set costs around $30, a fill around $15. Jenni is the girl with the magic touch who makes sure that you are massaged, coiffed and out the door in no time at all, with plenty of cash left over to spend at American Rag across the street.

Louie, 4 Brady St. (bet. Gough & Franklin Sts.), (415) 864-3012, *Hair Guru*

This is a great destination for a fab cut, color and overall new look. Situated on an adorable little street, this not-so-hidden treasure is a perfect place to linger over coffee while you mentally prepare for the new you. The owner, Joel, is the man to oversee your color and make sure that your cut is exactly like that torn-out picture of Hillary Swank from *InStyle.* His carefully selected team is equally talented. You will be genuinely "swanky" as you slink down the street to meet your friends at nearby Zuni Café (see Eats, Hayes Valley). Haircuts are $55–75, color starts at $60 and goes up to $145 for double process.

Mes Amis, 193 Franklin St. (@ Fell St.), (415) 558-7118, *Custom Cuts / Blow-Dry*

Going to the ballet with your beau? Meet him at "will call" and come here to get a remarkable trim and blow-dry before curtain call. This is a seemingly out-of-the-way place to go for just a haircut and blow-dry, but we know of one "Jane" girl who gets more attention for her haircut by Jean than when Sharon Stone shows up across the street at Hayes and Vine Wine Bar (see Twilight, Hayes Valley). This small, friendly salon is dedicated to making you look beautiful for less cash than a cocktail at Bix (see Twilight, Nob Hill). Okay, maybe that's a wee bit of an exaggeration, but it is assuredly affordable without compromising style. *Psst . . . if Jean is booked, his staff is equally attentive and talented.*

Oxenrose, 500 Hayes St. (@ Octavia St.), (415) 252-9723, *www.oxenrose.com, Neighborhood Favorite*

Calling all cool girls: take note of Oxenrose, a fashionable place dedicated to hair and hair alone! It is a spacious place for cuts, color, perms, relaxers and special up-dos. The staff is feisty, knowledgeable and ready to help any girl navigate a new look or just get a touch-up between looks. Prices range from $35 to $95, depending on the service. Serving yummy espressos and other Italian favorites by Illy from the coffee bar in front to give you that morning jolt. Who said beauty is painful? This place is an ode to beauty the easy way.

Haight-Ashbury

Edo Salon, 601 Haight St. (@ Steiner St.), (415) 861-0131, *Blow-Dry*

What a delightful place to beautify! Situated on a sunny corner in the Haight, book an exceptional blow-dry here from John. We can't rave enough about how relaxing, yet committed to excellence, this place is. Look marvelous before heading into a week of hectic meetings or social occasions.

Marie Rua, 791 Haight St. (@ Scott St.), (415) 626-6674, *Chic Hair & Spa*

Named one of the "Top 200" salons in the country by *Salon Today* magazine in 1999. Originally started in the late '90s by Maria Malone as a hair salon across the street, she gained notoriety for her edgy looks and funky stylists. Needing a place to recuperate from all their good press, they walked across the street and opened a serene spa that is so peaceful you can hear your pores getting cleaner! The simple treatments are as individual as the space in which they are performed, complete with classical music and fragrant candles. "No cell phones" policy. An upscale place with downtown sensibilities and prices: Glycolic Acid Treatment ($35), Refresher Facial (30 min. for $35), Underarm Wax (Ouch! $17), Makeup Application ($50 and up), Foot Reflexology & Salt Scrub (30 min. for $35), and more. Hair salon, 798 Haight St. (@ Scott St.), (415) 626-6674. Open 11 A.M.–7 P.M., until 8 P.M. on Thurs., 10 A.M.–6 P.M. on Sat.

Skin City, 323 Divisadero St. (bet. Oak & Page Sts.), (415) 255-4777, *Neighborhood Favorite*

This is one of the best places in all of San Fran to get customized, cutting-edge skin care with specialists committed to bringing you the best services and products. Girls of all shapes and sizes from the Bay Area come here to seek relaxation, solve a skin condition, or just reduce the signs of aging. The Clinical facial is 60 minutes of massage, exfoliation, extraction and moisturizing to correct acne-prone skin. The Intensive Hydrating facial is perfect after one too many Cosmopolitans at Shanghai 1930 (see Twilight, Downtown), or try our personal favorite, which includes a healing paraffin mask and the unique Beard Treatment that addresses the problem of those little witch hairs under your chin. Unbeatable off-the-beaten-path lines of skin-care products are on hand to help you with home upkeep between facials. Also, waxing, electrolysis, lash tinting, eye treatments, chemical peels and microdermabrasion available. Open Mon.–Fri., 11 A.M.–7 P.M.; Sat. & Sun., 10 A.M.–5 P.M.

Spaghetti & Ravioli, 210 Fillmore St. (bet. Waller & Haight Sts.), (415) 863-7843, *www.spaghettiravioli.com, Full Service*

Upon entering this spacious salon, you will be entralled by all the varieties of high-end skin-care products, whose displays cleverly divide the space. Owners Mark and Devin make sure that clients have any and every beauty regime required under one roof: extensions, cuts ($50–85), makeup application, color (cost depends on need, "correction or beauty enhancement"), and the best of all, the Diamond Peel Experience™, the equivalent to microdermabrasion. Introduction for $125, and a series of six stays the same price.

Yoga Tree, 780 Stanyan St. (@ Waller St.), (415) 387-4707, *Intimate Style*

A great place for virgins . . . yoga virgins, that is! If you are looking to relax into the California pace, enter here. The classes themselves are set in a lovely two-room space, separated by grand orange curtains and cloud murals, that gives the feeling of being outdoors. They also offer advanced classes for the seasoned pro. Both levels are treated with equal care. *Psst . . . Michael Cooper, who is listed as one of the best teachers by the* SF Chronicle, *teaches here occasionally. Call ahead for his schedule.*

The Castro/Noe Valley

The Art of Aesthetics, 211 Church St., Suite C (@ Market St.), (415) 487-9217, *www.artofaesthetics.com, Fab Facials*

Need a spa treat on a Snickers budget? Here's the best facial that lasts 90 minutes and only costs $45. Situated in the Debuce Park area, this lovely spot offers hardwood floors and lots of windows with light pouring in, and peaceful orchids add a nice touch to the whole experience as you sip tea before your treatment. Waxing, microdermabrasion and back treatment round out the list of services designed to spoil as much as heal. *Psst . . . repeat clients rave over Monika, one of the gorgeous aestheticians, whose beauty could intimidate or inspire.*

Bold & Beautiful Skin Care by Bella, 4081 24th St. (@ Castro St.), (415) 550-8700, *Personal Service*

Problem skin is no problem with Bella in the neighborhood! Her commitment to European-style skin care is unparalleled. Nothing like a flawless complexion to put sparkle in your step and your love life! Other services include the "Facials for Aging" (scary thought!), the Bio-Electric Face Lift and a fantastic glycolic acid peel. All cost between $70 and $90. Let her give you back your youthful glow, or help you get it the first time around. Open Wednesday through Saturday. *Psst . . . if you are allergic to cosmetics, consider the option of permanent cosmetics . . . a Bella specialty!*

The Castro Day Spa, 4105 19th St. (@ Castro St.), (415) 487-9666, *www.castrodayspa.com, Simple Pleasures*

Reliable neighborhood day spa that provides some great packages for your body and spirit! Opt for the "Hold My Calls" (75 min. minipackage @ $75), "Stop The World" (2½ hrs. for $150), or perhaps ("Capture The Moment" (2 hrs. for $150) is more your speed. Surprise your best friend on her birthday with "The Ooh-Ah!" (3¾ hrs. for $250). This second-story low-key environment is the perfect locale for your afternoon getaway! Open Tues.–Sat. until 6:00 P.M. *Psst . . . they now offer the pain-free Dermaglow—the particle skin exfoliation device for those who don't want to undergo laser or chemical treatments.*

Elisa's Beauty & Health Spa, 4028A 2nd St. (bet. Noe & Castro Sts.), (415) 821-6727, *Bath House*

Need some spontaneous spa-ing? Walk-ins are welcome seven days a week! Don't count on swanky decor or a stellar score in the white-glove inspection at chez Elisa, but do count on reliable spa services. The broad range of treatments offered include waxing ($30 for bikini), lash tint ($25), glycolic acid peels ($60), deep-tissue massage ($55 for 55 minutes), and steam/sauna/hot tub ($12 an hour). Frequent users of the "wet" services should inquire about the discount cards at the front desk. *Psst . . . the lovely aquarium entertains while you wait.*

Hairplay, 1599 Dolores St. (@ 29th St.), (415) 550-1656, *www.hairplay.com, Hip Hair Care*

Oversleep on your already bad bedhead? Don't let the cheesy name scare you away. This neighborhood favorite will give you a fabulous blow-dry on the run. If you're in the mood for more than a "Band-Aid," schedule ahead for a precise cut and color. The diversity of the hip clientele ensures that whatever look you are looking for is available at the hands of their stylists. San Francisco native Fritz Clay is the handsome innovator who specializes in his own unique techniques. His client roster is as diverse as his attitude. Fun environment to start your transformation! Open on Sundays too, from 10:30 A.M.–5:30 P.M.

Integral Yoga Institute, 770 Dolores St. (@ 21st St.), (415) 824-9600, *Stretch Out*

Expand your mind, if not your spine, while you get in touch with your inner voice in a grand Victorian mansion. The pretty and spacious rooms are almost outdone by the gorgeous views of the city! Practicing traditional Hatha style of yoga ($8 per class). Not in the mood to move, but just need a midday stress break? Try the lunchtime meditation session that includes no sweating and lots of veggies.

Jungle Red, 4233 18th St. (bet. Collingwood & Diamond Sts.), (415) 934-9755, *Hip Hair*
Quiz: what was the name of the nail polish used in the 1940s classic film, *The Jungle?* Hint, hint, hence the name of this fashionable industrial salon. The stylists are talented as well as calm and kind. Ask for Scott if a cut is in order. He will work to help create any look your heart desires. Closed on Sun. & Mon.

Vanishing Point, 4092 18th St. (@ Castro St.), (415) 552-0600, *Hair Be Gone*
See details in Marina.

Mission

Lori Anderson, call for location, (415) 863-1884, *Peaceful Facial*
Trust your skin to the loving hand of Lori in the Potrero Hills neighborhood. Everything about this facial appointment will lead to two results: total relaxation and beautiful skin. She has extensive training, and will ask a series of questions before your facial to decide what to focus on for your particular skin condition. After she performs her magic, which includes a series of exfoliations, gentle extractions, masques and moisturizers, she gives a tender massage while you drift off to Nirvana. Products from Pevona are on hand as well. Back to reality, you will be a better-looking and feeling person for knowing her!

Ellie Herman Pilates Studio, 3435 Cesar Chavez St. (@ Valencia St.), (415) 285-5808, *East Meets West*
Tucked away in San Francisco's latest hot nightlife district, Ellie's is a true treasure; well worth a trek all the way from Pacific Heights! Owner/Instructor extraordinaire, Ellie offers several different ways to enjoy her studio: try the "drop-in" yoga-style mat classes ($12), grab your best friend or coworker for a duet training session ($30 ea.), or walk on the wild side with a "threesome" ($20 per person)—not that kind, you naughty girl! Go

full-tilt and have her train you one-on-one ($50 per session). Ellie also offers two holistic studios featuring acupuncture, massage and other Eastern therapies. Get tucked, get pricked and get squished all under one roof! Open seven days a week.

Glama-Rama, 417 S. Van Ness Ave. (@ 15th St.), (415) 861-GLAM, *Neighborhood Favorite*

What a fun place to go for a cut in this neighborhood that is not exactly "glamour girl" turf! What is a girl to do? Adventurous "Janes" will trust us and book an appointment at this truly wacky, kitschy, downright hilarious palace. The space itself is a loftlike square room painted Pepto-Bismol pink, with various odd, vintage barber chairs, and antique vanities at each station. Swarms of hipster glamour girls congregate for highlights, haircuts and marvelous up-dos for special nights on the town. There is a casual sitting area in the front for reading and relaxing. Better yet, peek at the funny collection of wigs ranging from the ridiculous to the sublime—naturally we could not leave without one (or two) of the reasonably priced treasures ($30–40). Good for a costume party or "his" seven-year itch, you be the judge. Raquel Welch wears one, why not you? Costs: $30–50 for cuts, $55–100 for color/highlights. *Psst . . . no time to fuss? Buy some of the Bumble & Bumble "dry shampoo" for sale in the front. It is a powder shampoo that will hold you over without compromising style and cleanliness. If hair extensions are your obsession, they do an awesome job at creating that Penelope Cruz look for $500–750.*

Jonathan Russell, Master of Tai Chi, 2101 Mariposa St. (@ Vermont St.), (415) 671-0120, *www.taichiSF.com, Self-Defense*

Planning to live until the next millennium in this stress-filled universe? This is a good place to start. Meet Jonathan Russell, who studied under world-renowned Master T.T. Liang. His Potrero customer base boasts a large demographic of young women who now want to explore the mind-body connection. Who said your body couldn't contort into 150 postures? Beginners are welcome. Be brave and go for it ($15 per session). *Psst . . . he teaches at Slovenian Hall on Wednesday nights from 6:30–8:30 P.M. Voted the best Tai Chi instructor in the city by the highly respected SF Weekly in '99. He also teaches at various health clubs such as 24 Hour Fitness, Gold's, Golden Gateway, and more.*

Other Neighborhoods

Iyengar Yoga Institute, 2404 27th Ave. (@ Taraval St.), Sunset, (415) 753-0909, *www.iyisf.org, Preventative Measures*

With 25 years' experience in teaching people how to "calm their minds, relieve stress and keep your self healthy," the IYI is a top-notch facility. Not to mention the oldest yoga center in the U.S.! Beginners should just show up with bare feet, an empty stomach and fitted clothes that can stretch. Offering five levels of classes for those looking for more than a quick fix. You can actually realign your posture after years of wearing high heels on those hills! Their monthly schedule of seminars, like "Yoga for People With Careers," coordinates nicely with your new regime. Kids, pregnant women and seniors are welcome. Drop-ins too, $15 a session or $60 for five classes. *Psst . . . there is plenty of street parking.*

Tea Garden Springs, 38 Miller Ave. (@ Sunnyside St.), Marin, (415) 389-7123, *Asian Delight*

If you are venturing outside the city and are enticed by the idea of an Asian Tea Garden with facials and treatments . . . look no further! Book ahead, and get ready for a little slice of Eastern heaven! Step into paradise, starting with a tiptoe across a babbling little spring garden and finishing with an antiaging facial (never too young to start!), or share a Saturday afternoon with your significant other with the aromatherapy bath and massage in a suite built for two!

Citywide:

Alison Siegal, (415) 608-8985, *Massage On Location*

Just landed after a week of boring meetings, delayed flights and strange hotel pillows? No need to panic, just keep the phone number of this talented SF masseuse close at hand . . . or better yet, call from the plane! Whether you need her to come to your house, your hotel or your office, she is equipped to travel and bring her healing treatment to your doorstep. She is trained in acupuncture, reflexology and other deep-tissue massages. No need to name drop about her client list, just know that she is prepared to make any girl-in-need better in the time it takes you to say ouch! Ahhh! *Psst . . . she only massages women clients.*

Andrew Castellanos, (415) 440-4494, *Personal Masseur*

Have crick, will travel. If you have lifted one too many heavy computer bags in and out of the rental car, let this dashing therapist use his therapeutic hands on your knotted shoulders and beyond. No, not that far beyond, you trollop! He uses the shiatsu method as a base, and then tailors the method to your body, using other techniques such as reflexology and deep-tissue massage. We are religious about our appointments with Andrew. He knows how to work out the kinks and discover ones we didn't know we had!

Le Sanctuaire, call for address, (415) 401-6930, *Personalized Facials*

Those who know, know: Rebecca Whitworth's skin-care services are out of this world. She delivers one of the best skin-care packages that the Bay Area has to offer. We die for her special packages ($140): a sumptuous facial, a lip and eyebrow wax, a special enzyme mask followed by a gratifying hand, foot and head massage. The icing on the cake? You can buy her luxurious line of organic skin care after you are reeling from the results of her treatment! Trust us, Rebecca is one of "us," with a heart as gentle as her touch. By appointment only. Closed on Sun. & Mon. except for "emergency" only. *Psst . . . products can be ordered by e-mail: lesanctuaire@earthlink.net.*

⌀ *Good to Know:*

Need to get a quick workout before you head off to Sonoma for the weekend? **24 Hour Fitness** is just that! With locations throughout the city (and the West Coast) that are open 24 hours a day. Check for locations at *www.24hourfitness.com.* Take advantage of the 10-day free pass if you join or pay $15 per day. Fitness update: Netpulse exercise bikes on the premises!

Traumas

Downtown/Soma/Union Square

Adolph Gasser, 181 2nd St. (@ Howard St.), (415) 495-3852,
Lens Crazy
 Your Kodak disposable just won't hack it on your African safari. Come
here for the best camera for the best photos and the best memories imaginable. They have the best camera equipment selection in the city, and a
rental division too!

At Your Service Inc., 247–249 3rd St., (@ Howard St.), (415) 543-
7444, *Laptop Catastrophe*
 Your laptop crashed yet again, before "the week from hell" has even begun. Take a deep breath and rent a computer for the week from these folks.
Both Mac and IBM available. *Psst . . . they also have a notary public on staff for
any last-minute witnessing.*

Beaver Bros. Antiques, 1637 Market St. (bet. 12th & Brady Sts.),
(415) 863-8391, *Rent-A-Life*
 If you're planning a theme party, or decorating a set, this place is a two-
storied haven for has-been memorabilia and furnishings. A prop master's
delight, you will find everything you need to "set the scene." The selection
is large enough to allow you ample opportunity to examine all the options
from bygone eras.

Britex Fabrics, 146 Geary St. (bet. Stockton & Grant Sts.), (415) 392-
2910, *Suzy Homemaker*
 Bolts and bolts (four floors!) of every material, texture and pattern fabric your little heart desires. After three generations, these guys have cor-
nered the market on trims, laces, and ribbons for the entire Bay Area. The
one-stop destination for anyone short on cash and long on time to whip up
a new "something" before a Friday-night date, or just change the lining in an
old favorite skirt and replace the trim on a beloved tablecloth . . . all before
the stroke of midnight! Open 9:30 A.M.–6 P.M. Monday through Saturday,
till 7 P.M. on Thurs. & Fri.

Brooks Cameras, 125 Kearny St. (bet. Post & Sutter Sts.), (415) 362-
4708, *Snap Shot*
 An oldie but a goodie—catering to lens maniacs since 1945, this is still

the best bet for new and used camera gear, along with a repair department and video transfer service. Say cheese!

Citicomm Wireless, 1116 Folsom St. (@ 7th Street), (415) 861-6888, *www.citicomm.net, Time Saver*

Reach out and touch someone. . . . Whatever your cellular needs are, they can be fulfilled here; yet another cellular provider looking for an honest girl's business. Let them dazzle you with charm and cellular accessories. Who said diamonds were a girl's best friend? In the New Millennium it's her cell phone, honey!

Copy Write, 191 Battery St. (bet. California & Pine Sts.), (415) 433-4488, *www.copywriteprinting.com, Internet Interruptus*

In the heart of the financial district and your e-mail is down? You are in luck: scurry to this convenient outpost for all things PC and Mac, where they can hook you up with Internet access until 8 P.M., seven days a week. Since when have you worked on a Sunday? You just never know when duty will call, or at least inspiration!

DiPietro Todd Salon, 177 Post St. (bet. Grant Ave. & Kearny St.), (415) 397-0177, *Rainbow Connection*

A little tight on cash this month and you tried to "touch up" your color at home, and now someone with violet hair is looking back at you in the mirror. Don't cry—this sleek and swanky hair joint is known for corrective color and cleaning up disastrous attempts to "home improve." But full recovery doesn't come cheap, so next time you'll remember it's cheaper to get it done right the first time! Best benefit? Open for services on Monday, traditionally a day we all have to suffer through with no beauty care!

Focus Gallery, 2423 Polk St. (bet. Union & Filbert Sts.), (415) 567-9067, *Incriminating Evidence*

Need to develop last night's pictures from the "den of sin" before someone else does? Call John at Focus Gallery and rent a private darkroom. You never know what or who might come into focus! Didn't we warn you about wanton acts of senseless abandon? Open Tues.–Sun. Noon–10 P.M., until 6 P.M. Wed. and Sat.

Going in Style, 865 Market St. (bet. 6th & 7th Sts.), (415) 512-9477, *www.goinginstyle.com, Have Fanny Pack . . .*

Your new beau invited you on a weekend whirl to Mexico, and your luggage has seen better days? Hop into this comprehensive travel accessory store, where the motto is: "If it fits in a bag, we have it." They carry many one-of-a-kind travel items along with full selections from top luggage companies such as Le Sport Sac, Swiss Army, Timbuk 2, and Eagle Creek. We love the silk "maps" that double as chic scarves! Pick up a teleconverter for your cell phone, a weather radio, a collapsible umbrella, and a world clock in one fell swoop. Don't forget those groovy Aquis towels that dry in half the time of a normal towel, and if you are planning on roughing it in questionable pensions or hostels, take along a luxurious Dream Sack silk sleeping sack! Daniela, the store manager, is ready to help you off to a great trip whatever your destination.

Grand Central Sauna and Hot Tub, 15 Fell St. (@ Market), (415) 431-1370, *Heated Measures*

It's Friday morning . . . your secret crush just called and asked you out, so you need to lose twenty pounds by sundown. Whom do you call? Wrap yourself in Saran Wrap and head to the sauna—here. You can rent sauna space or a hot tub by the hour as you watch your fingers shrivel into little nubs of wrinkled flesh. Bleach your hair à la Ursula Andress and get in that Swedish Babe mode. The cozy private rooms are made for relaxing and . . . well, let's just leave it at that.

Great Entertainer, 975 Bryant St. (bet. 7th & 8th Sts.), (415) 861-8833, *Fats Domino Obsession*

Your boyfriend bet you a trip to the Islands if you beat him at pool on Thursday night. Need to brush up on your "four ball in the side pocket" routine? This is a girl-friendly yet appropriately "divey" place to practice, shoot a few frames and hang out with friends! 11 A.M.–2 A.M., seven days a week.

Green Door, 441 Stockton St. (@ Sutter St.), (415) 397-4181, *Knock And Knead*

Open until 4 A.M. for night owls with painful necks. Your shoulders have migrated above your ears after a nerve-wracking week of wheeling and dealing, so head to this no-frills massage parlor for high-quality service and reasonable rates. Your basic hour massage is $60. They have a great reputation and have been in business for over 14 years. No Amex.

Harrison & Bonini, 1122 Harrison St. (bet. 7th & 8th Sts.), (415) 861-8300, *Hammer Helpers*

You are moving to the 'burbs, and as a lifetime city dweller feel like a fish out of water there. The least you can do is equip yourself with the latest in home tools, from fly swatters to brooms to garden hoses to rakes to God knows what all. . . . You will find your "moving to the 'burbs survival kit" within these walls, or at least the FOR SALE BY OWNER sign when you decide to move back to Nob Hill where you belong! They close at 4 P.M. daily.

Headlines, 838 Market St. (bet. Stockton & Powell Sts.), (415) 956-4872, *Boutique Meets Ticket Outlet*

See details in Castro/Noe Valley, other location in Marina/Cow Hollow.

Dr. Jones & Associates, 120 Battery St. (bet. Pine & California Sts.), (415) 391-4466, *Demonic Dentures*

"Ouch, my aching tooth" is not a great way to start a date, a vacation or a huge presentation to your biggest client. Not to fear: Dr. Jones to the rescue. From cavities to caps to broken crowns, he and his team have your smile and your sanity covered. Take two aspirin and give him a call.

Ken's Wheel Service, 737 Harrison St. (bet. 3rd & 4th Sts.), (415) 543-1815, *Vehicular Boo Boos*

Car bomb . . . or your car *is* a bomb—however you want to look at the equation, Ken is there to help align those tires or fix those squealing brakes, a common phenomena in the Hilly City.

Dr. Seth Matarasso, 490 Post St. (bet. Mason & Powell Sts.), (415) 362-2238, *Professor Pimple*

Mount Vesuvius relocated to your chin yesterday and is about to erupt. . . . Maybe it's time to cut down on the French fries, stress and late-night debauchery, and get an appointment with a skin professional. Dr. Matarasso is one of the best and most sought after in town, so expect to have to wait to get an appointment. However, all things come to those who wait—he has been known to work miracles on problem skin, and he has great bedside manner to boot!

Passport Agency, 95 Hawthorn St., 5th fl. (bet. Folsom & Howard Sts.), (415) 538-2700, *International Departures*

If you suddenly feel an unexplainable urge to spend the weekend in New Zealand, we can't make any promises about severe jet lag, but this would be a good place to start planning. By appointment only, and you must be set to travel within 14 days to use this service. Use this automated phone line to set an appointment. For an additional $35, you can get an "expedited" passport in about two weeks, otherwise you will get it back in less than six weeks. Open from 9 A.M.–4 P.M. weekdays.

Photo Exchange, 351 3rd St. (@ Harrison St.), (415) 512-7950, *Memory Retrieval*

No glitz, no glamour and no frills, but you will get your pictures back in an hour . . . and isn't that all you really wanted? Closed on Sunday. *Psst . . . if it's time to renew that passport, get some photos taken while you wait!*

Post Office, @ Macy's, 180 O'Farrell St. (@ Stockton St.), (415) 397-3333, *Shop & Ship*

Shop till you drop and still have time for timely correspondence. After you're ready to drop dead from dressing room hyperventilation, drop that credit card payment in the mail on your way out! It's the only post office in the city open on Sun., 11 A.M.–5 P.M. Or Mon.–Sat., 10 A.M.–5 P.M.

Quetzal, 1234 Polk St. (bet. Bush & Sutter Sts.), (415) 673-4181, *E-Mail Crisis*

Unlike some Internet cafés, where computers seem like an afterthought, at Quetzal they are the centerpiece: 10 new iMacs in a rainbow of colors with high-speed DSL access at only 16 cents per minute, $9.95 per hour. But the café has much more to offer: coffee drinks in supersized cups; a serious menu of sandwiches, bagels, breakfast items, salads, soups, pizzas, and beverages; and big-screen TV. And the three most important café qualities: good lighting, comfortable seats and lively background music. Named after the iridescent bird that is Guatemala's national symbol, Quetzal's tall ceilings, huge windows and rotating display of artwork make it an airy, uplifting place. When asked if the place ever features live entertainment, the counterman responded, "Just the characters from the neighborhood."

Rand McNally, 595 Market St. (@ 2nd St.), (415) 777-3131, *Lost Highway*

The last time you took a trip, you missed your plane, lost your luggage and got taken for a ride by your "economy" hotel. Now you have full-blown travel anxiety. But stop! Check out one of these nifty (and free) travel lectures! Great info, helpful hints and other travel enthusiasts make this a festive learning experience. Past lectures have included: "Road Trip USA" and "Cheap Airfare Strategies"—and who couldn't use some cheap airfare these days? Lectures are ongoing, call for details. Generally held 5:30–6:30 weeknights.

The Rawhide, 280 7th St. (bet. Folsom & Shipley Sts.), (415) 621-1197, *Hoe-Down Fetish*

You've just met the man of your dreams on an airplane, and he has asked you out for dinner and dancing on Friday . . . line dancing. What's a girl to do? Show up at this joint for a crash course in Two-Step and Line Dancing. . . . You'll be ready to sweep your newfound cowboy off his feet in no time. (Tony Lamas not included.) Monday–Friday at 7:30 P.M.; $2 admission includes classes! *Psst . . . this is definitely a gay club but it's very "straight-friendly."*

San Francisco Cleaners, 2123 Polk St. (bet. Broadway & Vallejo St.), (415) 776-7890, *Stripped Clean*

Dribbled Diet Coke down the front of your new Armani at lunch? Don't panic, just swing the suit by this reputable cleaners on your way home from work. They stay open later than most on weeknights. How you get home now that you're naked is your problem, baby! Open Mon.–Fri. 7 A.M.–8 P.M., Sat. 8 A.M.–6 P.M., Sun. 12 P.M.–6 P.M.

San Francisco Democratic Party, 100 Van Ness Ave., 25th Floor (@ Fell St.), (415)-626-1161, *Right-Wing Phobia*

You fear that a right-wing conspiracy is responsible for the no-smoking policy in your new office building and feel the stare of Charlton Heston every time you watch *Ben Hur.* . . . It's time to take action! Join the party and volunteer to help get your candidates elected. You'll sleep better knowing you have made the effort . . .

San Francisco Republican Party, World Trade Center, 1 Maritime Plaza, Suite 336 (@ Battery St.), (415) 989-1259, *Left-Wing Phobia*

You have begun to fantasize about Howard Stern and legalization of pornography . . . it's time to get a grip! Sign on the dotted line and actively help keep America from the infiltration of deviant and immoral behavior. Of course, you'll have to cool it a bit yourself, missy!

San Francisco Sports Medicine Clinic, 120 Battery St. (bet. California & Pine Sts.), (415) 931-9255, *Inflamed Vanity Syndrome*

That little stubbed toe is refusing to heal after you tripped over your surfboard . . . and to add insult to injury, it's so swollen you can't squeeze into your favorite Jimmy Choos. Head for this orthopedic clinic specializing in feet and ankles, and be back on the road to health and high heels in no time. Just don't tell them about your motivation for recovery.

Shell Pharmacy, 77 Battery St. (bet. Pine & Bush Sts.), (415) 981-5373, *Junkies And Junk*

You need drugs and you need them now! Okay, probably an Advil will do. This is your hometown pharmacy—whether San Fran is your true hometown or not. Pharmacist Don Dezordo is helpful and ready to attend to all your pharmaceutical needs, big and small.

Site for Sore Eyes, 140 Battery St. (bet. California & Pine Sts.), (415) 412-2020, *Braille Avoidance*

Have you been struggling to read *InStyle* late at night before bedtime? Do your eyes feel tired all the time? Maybe it's time for a checkup. This is a great place to get a thorough yet low-key eye exam, and to order any corrective lenses they prescribe while you are there. Great selection of frames too.

Soma Cleaners, 201 Spear St. (@ Howard St.), (415) 777-9995, *Ring Around The Collar*

Yet another spiffy dry-cleaning service for the overworked and underpaid white-collar worker bees. Good prices, quick service.

Speedway Copy Systems, 227 Front St. (bet. California & Sacramento Sts.), (415) 434-4959, *Duplication Complication*

When you've forgotten to make copies for your 8:30 A.M. meeting, and it happens to be 8:15, you've got a need for speed, baby! Run into this efficient copy center for quick copies and no headache getting to your meeting on time.

Laura Stropes, 862 Folsom St. (bet. 4th & 5th Sts.), (415)587-3559, *"The Needle-izer"*

Come in for a little chi balancing by "Dr. Laura" . . . bringing Eastern healing arts to out-of-whack Westerners. Whether it's a specific injury, general back pain, flu, or allergies, she's got you covered. As the Chinese say, "where there is pain, there is no flow, where there is flow there is no pain." So flow, baby, flow; just don't look when they are inserting the hundreds of teeny-tiny needles. By appointment only.

Travelers Medical Clinic, 490 Post St. (@ Mason St.), (415) 981-1102, *Sick Celebs*

If Ashley Judd caught the flu while filming in the Bay Area, she would have sought out this health haven. Where the stars go when they get sick . . . do stars even get sick? We'll have to take their word for it!

Tuxedo Shop, 109 Geary St. (bet. Stockton & Grant Sts.), (415) 391-5325, *Black & White Clothing*

You swore you would never date a guy who didn't own a tux . . . but promises are made to be broken, especially when Mr. No Tux is so adorable. However, you have a black-tie event this weekend that you want him to attend. This store offers wide selection and fast alteration on rentals so that Mr. No Tux will be transformed into Mr. Monkey Suit in no time. . . . Whether he likes it or not is another question altogether. Basic rental package, $50.

Verizon Wireless, 199 Pine St. (@ Battery St.), (415) 543-9797, *Disappearing Cellular*

No ringing in your purse, no vibrating in your briefcase, no blinking light . . . Did you accidentally leave your cell phone "somewhere" on the planet over the last three hours? The ladies' room at the restaurant, the taxi, the airport lounge, the salon—it's a needle in an urban haystack! Cut your losses, because time is money, and let this helpful staff get you started again with the same number. Then again, you could lose Mr. Wrong forever with a new cell identity . . . it's cheaper than plastic surgery!

Wireless Depot, 865 Market St. (@ 5th St.), (415) 348-8661, *www.ewirelessdepot.com, Ground Control*

You are supposed to meet that cute guy you met on the street for a drink at 7 P.M., but you can't remember where and you don't have a cell! Every urban gal needs her Bat Phone, and this is a great place to start your hunt for cellular freedom. User-friendly sales staff and extensive selection make this a sure bet, Batgirl! And now you can track down Batboy without looking for a pay phone.

Dr. Joanne Yee, 101 Spear St. (@ Mission St.), (415) 495-8600, *See and Be Seen*

Eye strain is becoming the fastest growing complaint of the computer age. . . . If you are feeling it too, opt for this friendly optician, who can give you the best comprehensive vision analysis, perform refractive surgery or fit you for corrective lenses. Then you'll have plenty of time to swing by the market for that bag of carrots you should have been eating all along.

⊘ Good to Know:

Dazzle your man with the shoe scoop: the best shine for his Pradas is from the dapper Famous Wayne, on the corner of California and Market St. He won't be hard to find . . . just look for the guy with the big smile, brushes in hand and jazz music playing in the background.

In the high-priced overnight world of FedEx, nothing beats the U.S. Postal Service for economical reliability. Love letters via FedEx just don't have the same panache as the ones that arrive with the 34-cent "Love" stamp. . . . Try the main Post Office downtown, 180 Steuart St. (@ Howard St.), (800) 275-8777. Open Mon.–Fri. 7 A.M.–6 P.M., Sat. 9 A.M.–2 P.M.

Nob Hill/Russian Hill/North Beach/Chinatown ⋯⋯⋯

Broadway Cigar & Liquor, 55 Broadway (@ Columbus Ave.), (415) 397-1310, *All-Night Party*

You and your friends are pulling an all-nighter . . . an all-night fest, that is, and have run out of libations? Not to worry . . . This is one of the few late, late, night liquor stores in the city. Make a pit stop at midnight, and you'll be partying till the crack of dawn. *Psst . . . we don't advise drinking alone while watching Bette Davis flicks on DVD all night.*

Cost Plus, 2552 Taylor St. (@ Bay St.), (415) 928-6200, *Wacky World Fare*

It's your father's 80th birthday . . . and let's face it, he has literally everything? What do you do? Head here to this quirky store filled with even quirkier imports. Imported paraphernalia and memorabilia from all over the world including, but not limited to: Tijuana taxi horns, Moroccan goat bells and the more subdued teak coffee tables. If they don't have it, then it isn't to be had.

Joni Max, 909 Hyde St. (bet. Bush & Pine Sts.), (415) 929-4630, *Hoover Thighs*

If the thought of the knife is too terrifying, check out the Euro-brilliance of Dr. Zingaro's (see next entry) sidekick, Joni Max. She practices Endemologie, a nonsurgical European body-contouring technique that is all the rave. The process itself feels like a semismooth suctioning rubdown and is supposed to make cellulite disappear after upwards of ten visits. She is also a massage therapist, so what could be better than ten massages and the possibility of dimple-free thighs? We must warn you that Joni is also a personal trainer and just may put you on a program to work those dimples out the old-fashioned way.

Dr. Edmond Zingaro, 909 Hyde St. (bet. Bush & Pine Sts.), (415) 929-4630, *Silicone Valley*

You aged forty years overnight. . . . Must have been that fourth Cosmo that sent you over the edge! Seek out Mr. Fix-It for the upper-crust crowd of Nob Hill for a little fountain of youth tasting. While this is his private office, Dr. Zingaro is chief of plastic surgery at San Mateo Hospital. Your crow's feet couldn't be in better hands . . . and better in his hands than on your face!

Marina/Cow Hollow

Back in Balance, 1952 Union St. (bet. Buchanan & Laguna Sts.), (415) 561-9575, *Spinal Tapping*

Meet Dr. Michael Schauer. This killer lady is one of San Francisco's crunch masters. Also a chiropractor, she'll have you back in balance in no time! She also offers massage and nutritional counseling at this center for integrative health. Call ahead for an appointment or to "drop by" because hours can vary from day to day.

Burton's Pharmacy, 2016 Chestnut St. (bet. Fillmore St. & Mallorca Way), (415) 567-1166, *Pills, Potions And Purses*
   Pick up your prescription and your purple toe polish in one fell swoop! A full-service pharmacy. Beauty products include Elizabeth Arden and Clarins, along with fantastic Vera Bradley bags and great travel cosmetic bags.

Joellen Donahue Ermes, 2087 Union St. (@ Webster St.), (415) 731-4328, *Eastern Healing*
   Your doctor thinks you are a hypochondriac, your husband thinks you're nuts and you just think you're dying. If you have unidentifiable aches, pains or malaise, it could be a job for this fantastic acupuncturist and herbalist. When all else fails, or before anything fails, it's great to explore Eastern medicine and holistic health.

Francoise, 1952 Union St. (bet. Laguna & Buchanan Sts.), (415) 563-2199, *Waxing Psychic*
   Why did Joe run off to Tibet with all of my La Perla thongs? Why am I not married, with a cook and social secretary, and 2.7 babies? When will my boss die the slow and painful death she deserves, evil cow that she is? If the pain involved in pruning your privates makes you question the meaning of life and destiny, then this salon is for you. Their "tarot reader-in-residence" will make sense of it all and then some.

Headlines, 2301 Chestnut St. (@ Scott St.), (415) 441-5550, *Boutique Meets Ticket Outlet*
   See details in Castro/Noe Valley, other location in Downtown/Soma.

Horseshoe Tavern, 2024 Chestnut St. (bet. Minorcka & Fillmore Sts.), (415) 346-1430, *Testosterone Alert*
   Girls just want to have fun with boys who know how to have fun. If you are looking for "action" you are sure to get lucky. You have tried all the proper ways to meet a nice young boy, like the Racquet Club, mixers for young opera enthusiasts, even purposefully wiping out on your roller blades in Golden Gate Park, with no success. Here at the Horseshoe, where there are plenty of boisterous boys on the loose looking to have a good time, you might get your chance.

The Postal Chase, 3053 Fillmore St. (bet. Filbert & Union Sts.), (415) 567-SHIP, *Mystery Address*

You've decided to place a personal but need a mailbox for all your prospective suitors' love letters. . . . This is a great address to have! You'll have 24-hour access to your box and can receive UPS, FedEx, and faxes. You can also call and check on your mail, or have them hold it for you while you are on an extended vacation with your new beau. . . .

Sun Days, 2286 Union St. (@ Steiner St.), (415) 292-4490, *Casper Crisis*

Going to Hawaii to celebrate your promotion? One of the best ways to assure that you're not going to "burn, baby, burn" is to get some color before you hit the beach. We know tanning isn't fashionable, but sometimes a girl's gotta do what a girl's gotta do! Their high-speed tanning machines promise safer and quicker results than the older models—no more claustrophobic "coffin-style" beds. It's clean, quick, and the music and in-room telephone will put you at ease. See other location, Castro/Noe Valley.

"The Heights" (Pacific/Presidio/Laurel)

Access Chiropractic, 2410 California St. (@ Fillmore St.), (415) 921-2325, *Manipulative Lumbar Lady*

The weekend trip to Bali seemed like a good idea after seven martinis, but after 20 hours on the plane in the middle seat in the back row, it feels more like a bad dream where you are hit by a car and paralyzed from the neck down. Enter Victoria Moore, D.C., who will guide you back to health with one crunch to the left and one crunch to the right. Stand up, sit down, fight, fight, fight!

Automotive Clinic, 2035 Divisadero St. (bet. Sacramento & California Sts.), (415) 563-2915, *Car Hospital*

AAA to the rescue yet again. . . . The friendly staff at this garage will assist you with all your automobile needs. You just can't beat this grease pit in a neighborhood lacking in car repair garages.

The Brown Bag, 2000 Fillmore St. (@ Pine St.), (415) 922-0390, *Paper Drought*

Refill your Filofax, buy that pound of lime green paper you crave, pick up thank-you notes for last night's birthday dinner party, buy those water colors for your nephew and throw in some playing cards for the plane trip to Timbuktu . . . it's all here. Paper addicts will delight in this fantasyland for just about anything to write on. What a fun place to browse.

The California Pacific Medical Center, 2333 Buchanan St. (bet. Sacramento & Clay Sts.), (415) 563-4321, (800) 225-5637, *www.cpmc.org, White Coat Roulette*

If you left your heart somewhere other than San Francisco and need a "transplant," look no further. This is a good place to start if you're new to the area and want to make sure your medical bases are covered. Helpful staff and even more helpful personalized referrals make this a comfort zone for the newly relocated. Physician referral at its finest. They have a 24-hour emergency service.

City Cycle, 3001 Steiner St. (@ Union St.), (415) 346-2242, *www.city-cycle.com, Two-Wheel Addiction*

Your boyfriend has become a cycling freak, and in order to spend more time together you have decided to take the plunge into this mysterious world of padded-fanny bike shorts and shoes with clips. These people do not rent bikes, but they will custom build one for you for a mere $5,000 or so! They also do great repairs and stock all the biking paraphernalia and clothing you could ever want or need. Turn into a biker babe before someone else takes your seat! *Psst . . . their motto is "service is king."*

Cobbler's Bench Shoe Repair, 3308 Sacramento St. (bet. Walnut & Presidio Sts.), (415) 567-3555, *Shoe & Shrink*

You managed to snag your croc Manolo heel in the grate and are hobbling around in a state of shock. . . . Visit the endearing Zavo Ishac, who will treat your shoes—and you!—with care! Open Mon.–Fri. 8 A.M.–6 P.M.

The Desk Set, 3252 Sacramento St. (@ Presidio St.), (415) 921-9575, *Madame Printer*

He popped The Question and wants to get married next month! Hurry to this efficient outfit and get those invites printed in-house ASAP. Owned by a woman, only she would understand your impossible predicament. Just be sure to order your thank-you notes from her when you get back from Bermuda!

Duxana, 1803 Fillmore St. (@ Sutter St.), (415) 673-7134, *www.duxbed. com, Back Relief*

"The bed your back has been aching for." All about bedding, this is a supreme selection of custom headboards, featherbeds, down comforters, duvet covers, pillows, shams, sheets, blah, blah, blah. In the Scandinavian tradition, it's simple and sleek. This is the real deal for all of the "bird 'n tree" girls. It's the best of the best for the minimalists who demand to be pampered, for at least eight hours a day.

Fillmore Hardware Co., 1930 Fillmore St. (bet. Bush & Pine Sts.), (415) 346-5240, *Gidget Goes Hardware*

Your life is incomplete without a floral doormat? Help is on the way if you venture into this girly hardware haven for all things feminine and functional. Since 1941 they have been helping us change lightbulbs and outfit our San Francisco kitchens. FYI: no pastel-colored nails. Open Mon.–Sat., 9 A.M.–6 P.M., Sun 11 A.M.–5 P.M.

Fotek, 3499 Sacramento St. (@ Laurel St.), (415) 563-3896, *Photo Lust*

You've gotta have 'em and you want 'em now! Well, you might have to wait an hour or so but the quality is good and the service friendly! This one-hour photo finishing store also takes passport pictures and sells disposable cameras and film. You're out of luck if you're looking for professional camera equipment.

Grove Center for Health and Creativity, 1739 O'Farrell St. (@ Fillmore St.), (415) 775-6145, *www.grovecentr@aol.com, www.grovecenter.com, Lung Aerobics*

Do you hyperventilate into your child's brown paper lunch bag because life has gotten too overwhelming? Take Faith Hill's advice and just "Breathe"—literally. The "Breatherapy" technique taught here can change your life. Taught by registered "breatherapist" Surupa, this transformational technique will teach you how to handle all sorts of stressful situations through the manipulation of your own breath. Pretty nifty, and cheaper than traditional psychotherapy at about $25 per class. *Psst . . . they also offer other kinds of personal-growth classes and lectures.*

Hardware Unlimited, 3326 Sacramento St. (@ Presidio St.), (415) 931-9133, *Hints From Heloise*

You can't remember what you came to buy? Don't worry, you'll find whatever you are looking for here, from Weber Grills for summer barbecue to cut roller shades for your new boudoir. If you can't take your kitchen because it is so cluttered, then organize it with their brilliant kitchen organizer. Since men can't resist a babe with a drill, power tools are also available for your little "home improvement!" *Psst . . . they make keys as well.*

Jet Mail, 2130 Fillmore St. (bet. California & Sacramento Sts.), (415) 922-1265, *Post Office Blues*

When there is not a stamp in sight, these friendly "jet setters" offer UPS and FedEx along with all the hardware you need to ship your goodies near and far. Boxes, money orders, Notary Public, and gift cards are just a few examples from the hodgepodge of products and services offered. FedEx drop off and pick up until 4 P.M. When "rain, snow or dark of night" just isn't enough. . . .

The Junior League of San Francisco, 2226A Fillmore St. (bet. Clay & Sacramento Sts.), (415) 775-4100, *Oedipal Complex*

You woke up this morning and had turned into your mother overnight . . . You didn't know where to go or what to do . . . until now! This philanthropic civic organization of women has a strong history of community service geared toward family, children, the needy and all aspects of socio-cultural improvement! Stereotype: social worker-bee Stepford wives; reality: women of all ages from all walks of life mobilizing to make a difference. Wouldn't mom be proud? Membership is recruited on an annual basis; active members are required to commit to fulfilling a certain number of hours of service on annual projects that include fund-raising and community service.

Kerner Chiropractic, 3106 Fillmore St. (@ Filbert St.), (415) 563-2452, *Captain Crunch*

You've bent over, you can't get up *and* you wore a miniskirt with high heels today. Enter Dr. Brian Kerner, D.C., who can help you with this, plus anything from carpal tunnel thanks to your laptop to headache thanks to your visiting in-laws. Walk-ins welcome.

Kimmel's Stationery, 2144 Chestnut St. (@ Pierce St.), (415) 921-8828, *www.kimmels.citysearch.com, Paper Roses*

You woke up the day after your honeymoon and had a panic attack about all those thank-you's. . . . A year seems like a blink of an eye? Not to worry. This comprehensive yet sleek store is lined wall-to-wall with note cards, stationery, office supplies, and fine gifts. It can get a bit crowded so prepare mentally for the challenge! *Psst . . . pick up an inkwell while you're at it, because you'll need it for all those notes. Fountain pens are much more sophisticated than ballpoint, my dear.*

Kimono Shige Nishi Guchi, 1581 Webster St. (@ Post St.), (415) 346-5567, *Turning Japanese*

Your boyfriend developed a geisha fetish? Now that you have the concept even in the realm of consideration, this is a great place to browse, and possibly buy a gorgeous kimono and salvage your relationship. The subservience role-playing is up to you, naughty one.

Kuk Sool Won, 1641 Fillmore St. (bet. Post & Geary Sts.), (415) 567-5425, *Samurai Wanna-Be*

You haven't been the same since you saw *Crouching Tiger.* Master Kwan Jang Nim can show you a thing or two at this traditional Korean Martial Arts studio. Now, where to find one of those darling white pantsuit things? Classes available for all ages.

Martin Dollard, 3429 Sacramento St. (bet. Fillmore & Webster Sts.), (415) 673-7708, *Bow Wow Wow*

This gourmet Pet-o-Rama for the funky Felix translates into all things dog in Presidio Heights. Does your pooch suffer from a little Seasonal Affective Disorder? Nothing like a custom birthday cake to brighten his day! Well, that and one of those expensive lamps that . . . never mind! Just grab a matching collar and case to fulfill his canine fashion craving!

Mark M. Morris, O.D., 2149 Chestnut St. (bet. Pierce & Steiner Sts.), (415) 922-0616, *Temporary Blindness*

When carrots (not the diamond kind, silly girl, they always work) just aren't cutting it, have your eyes checked and possibly corrected by one of the Bay Area's best. Then, of course, your next move will be to find the trendiest glasses in town. Four eyes can be sexier than two! True emergencies are okay as well. Open Mon.–Sat., 9:00 A.M.–3:00 P.M.

Murata Pearls, 1737 Post St. (bet. Laguna & Webster Sts.), (415) 922-0666, *Pearl Salvage*

Your mother's pearls didn't manage the limbo at last night's company luau as well as you did. . . . After spending the latter part of the evening picking them out of the sand on the faux "beach," you'd like to return them to their original state of grandeur. This is the place—they do restringing and carry a large selection of pearl jewelry. Might be nice to find a matching pair of earrings for your newly restrung heirloom.

PO Plus, 3450 Sacramento (bet. Walnut & Laurel Sts.), (415) 921-6644, *Happy Wrap*

When you're running your own show, you need to be prepared for little emergencies, like having to send your wedding dress to Japan for your crazy friend who has eloped and needs it fast, so you can get back to business. This place is great for the home-office "Jane" girl: boxing, taping, packing, shipping, faxing, Notary Public, and key copy. Domestic and international shipping available.

Psychic Reading by Velisha, 2120A Fillmore St. (bet. Sacramento & California Sts.), (415) 776-7989, *Spooky Shrink*

Your therapist doesn't know the answer, your friends are no help, even your mother has no advice to give. . . . Maybe you just need a metaphysical tune-up from Velisha. Then again, sometimes what you don't know can't hurt you . . . but isn't it fun to find out? Open 10 A.M.–9 P.M.

School of French and Translation Service, 500 Sutter St. (@ Powell St.), (415) 362-3666, *Voulez-vous coucher avec moi?*

When your new Parisian lover leaves a note on your pillow in his native tongue and you don't speak French . . . *Le voila!* The answer lies within these walls—in more ways than one. You can learn the language and give some semblance of longevity to the relationship, or just have the note translated and go buy that sexy teddy you've been eyeing at Neiman Marcus in Union Square. Life is grand, *ma chere! Psst . . . this staff does heavy-duty business translation service as well.*

Silver Tux Cleaners, 3001 Sacramento St. (@ Broderick St.), (415) 567-0703, *Exotic 409*

In a fit of passion, your new husband spilled red wine on your wedding dress at the reception. Before you head to divorce court, drag the big pile of white organza to these wedding gown specialists and let them give it a whirl. They do great dry-cleaning in general, and also offer alterations, and drapery and leather cleaning as well. Let's face it, you're not going to wear that gown again anyway, with or without the stain!

Soko Hardware, 1698 Post St. (@ Buchanan Mall), (415) 931-5510, *Random Needs*

Your Japanese gardener is holding your begonias hostage until you bring him lunch and a new trowel. Kill two birds with one stone at this strange little joint that sells everything from gardening tools to rice cookers and chopsticks . . . and just about anything else that you can imagine that falls somewhere between those two extremes.

Toyoko's, 2418 Chestnut St. (@ Divisadero St.), (415) 921-2131, *Nip And Tuck*

The vintage dress that you just bought needs altering before Friday night. Start by praying, and then wait on line at this busy shop and hope. This place is jumping with people waiting to get fitted or to pick up their stuff, though, so don't get your hopes up too high. She is the best in town. Open Tues.–Fri. 10 A.M.–1 P.M., 2 P.M.–6 P.M., Sat. 10 A.M.–3 P.M. Closed Sunday, Monday and every fourth Saturday.

Vino, 2425A California St. (@ Fillmore St.), (415) 674-8466, *White Wine Crisis*

Chilled wines at a discount! Bodda bing bodda boom! Okay, you party girl on a budget who somehow planned a spontaneous Valentine's Day party for all of your singleton friends, stock up here without going to the poorhouse. The eclectic mix of French, Italian, Portuguese, and Chilean wines will guarantee a good time.

◈ *Good to Know:*

Baker Beach, off Lincoln Blvd. in the Presidio, *Disrobe And Dive*

You are channeling the spirit of Lady Godiva . . . Try a little skinny-dipping in the federally owned park that allows bathing in the buff in certain areas. It's very legal and very "Lady"-like to go for it, my friend.

Hayes Valley/Civic Center

California Culinary Academy, 625 Polk St. (@ Eddy St.), (415) 771-3536, *Marriage Crisis*

The honeymoon is over and your mother-in-law is coming for dinner next week. Don't run away from home—run here for a crash course in cooking that just might save your new marriage. Offering continuing education for beginners as well as experienced cooks, plus a variety of weekend classes. At the end of the class day, you'll feast on the "ever-changing buffet that you helped prepare" as you mix and mingle with the members of other classes and the chefs who instruct them. $125 per class. *Psst . . . don't miss their fantastic Sunday lecture series. Now you can give your fancy-chef-wanna-be girlfriend a run for her money.*

Lava 9, 542 Hayes St. (bet. Octavia & Laguna Sts.), (415) 552-6468, *Mad Cow Repair*

While the extra five pounds you put on over the holidays is barely noticeable to you, has it left your leather pants in a state of "stretched-out" stress? Venture to Lava, where you might be enticed to buy one of their groovy new designs while you drop off your "bloated" pants for repair. They do great leather cleaning as well.

Marriage License, One Dr. Carlton B. Goodlet Pl. (bet. McAllister & Grove Sts.), (415) 554-4176, *Hopeless Love*

"White Lace and Paperwork, A Stamp For Luck and You're On Your Way. . . ." Yes, you've only just begun. I Love Him, I Love Him Not, *but I really love that cushion-shaped diamond.* Whatever the reason, be prepared for the altar like the good Girl Scout you were. We shouldn't have to tell you that these days an MRS is harder to come by than an MBA. Open weekdays, 11 A.M.–4 P.M.

San Francisco Public Library Literacy Program, 100 Larkin St. (@ Market St.), (415) 557-4388, *I Before E*

You've been reading *Cosmo* for so long, tackling a novel seems like climbing Mount Everest in your Manolo Blahniks. To get back in the land of the literate, how about volunteering to help someone else learn to read? Sharpen your own skills at Project Read while you help another adult achieve their dream! You must be 20 and have a high school degree or the equivalent to qualify as a tutor.

Volunteer Center of San Francisco, 1675 California St., Suite 70 (bet. Polk St. & Van Ness Ave.), (415) 982-8999, *Guilt Trip*
 Longing for a purpose beyond your own self-promotion? *Voilà!* This center operates as a kind of melting pot for nonprofit and civic organizations and the volunteers that fuel them. If you're longing to participate in a worthwhile cause, they can steer you in the right direction. All true "Jane" girls have a heart for the needy, so join in and make a difference.

Zeitgeist, 437B Hayes St. (@ Gough St.), (415) 864-0185, *Antique Watches / Repair*
 So your rich uncle didn't leave you the vintage Hamilton like he promised? Never fear, this is the best place to purchase an investment timepiece. Do Gruen and Bulova ring a bell? Zeitgeist's master watch and clockmaker restores antique watches to their original grandeur. He will also repair modern-day watches and jewelry, all the while handling your precious gems with loving care. No American Express.

Haight-Ashbury

Cookin', 339 Divisadero St. (bet. Page & Oak Sts.), (415) 861-1854, *Cut-Rate Cuisinarts*
 Told your new beau you were a gourmet chef and the only thing in your kitchen is a plastic fork? While we don't condone bald-faced lying, at least you can fake it until you make it thanks to this emporium for recycled kitchen equipment and sundries. They have it all, from pots, pans, and blenders to cookie cutters, and everything in between! Outfit your kitchen and then hit the cookbooks by Martha Stewart or our favorite, *The Splendid Table.*

Gamescape, 333 Divisadero St. (bet. Page & Oak Sts.), (415) 621-4263, *Personality Disorder*
 Your boss told you to "lighten up," and you aim to please. Check this place out for all sorts of fun and games. Every board game your heart desires and more: Parcheesi, Clue, Life, Twister, Travel Scrab-

ble, books on scoring card games, and a healthy selection of video games. Just remember, bringing a Play Station to the office might be taking his advice a bit too far.

Martini Cleaners, 401 Divisadero St. (@ Oak St.), (415) 863-7717, *Spoiled Chanel*

Highly recommended by our friends in the Haight as *the* place to take your one-of-a-kind vintage and designer items for dry-cleaning.

Mendel's Art Supplies and Stationery/Far Out Fabrics, 1556 Haight St. (bet. Ashbury & Clayton Sts.), (415) 621-1287, *Paper Chase*

Late to work . . . and out of ink for your printer? Pop into this crazy place and pick up those office supplies along with a sketchpad for lunch break doodling, while at the same time checking out their eclectic selection of fabrics, feathers, and buttons. Feathers and fax paper and pastels . . . Makes sense to us, unless, of course, you are looking for traditional office supplies.

Roberts Hardware, 1629 Haight St. (bet. Clayton & Belvedere Sts.), (415) 431-3392, *Self-Defense Tools*

Why is it every time you need a screwdriver or a hammer, you can't seem to find it in the closet where you last saw it? Head over to this hard-core hardware establishment that has been hammering away at home improvement since 1931. They'll get your tool chest well stocked with the basics in no time flat!

San Francisco Stained Glass Works, 345 Divisadero St. (bet. Page & Oak Sts.), (415) 626-3592, *Glass Houses*

House-sitting for your friends last weekend, your "little" pool party got out of hand when you threw a Manolo sandal through their stained-glass window. These folks can repair the damage, or teach you to do it yourself—if you've got enough time before your friends return from Paris.

SFO Snowboarding, 618 Shrader St. (bet. Haight & Waller Sts.), (415) 386-1666, *Outdoor Ware*

Going to Lake Tahoe for the weekend with your new crush, and he insists on snowboarding instead of skiing? Let the pros of SFO fit you with boots and bindings, $45 for the weekend. Impress him by being prepared with some excellent equipment. Peruse and purchase some cool snowboarding clothes, not as sexy as ski-bunny tight pants, but a heck of a lot more comfy and grunge-chic.

Tools of Magick, 1915 Page St. (bet. Shrader & Stanyan Sts.), (415) 668-3132, *Spells And Smells*

You just got dumped by Mr. Right Gone Wrong and want to put a hex on him? Enter here: all sorts of paraphernalia for the professional and the amateur magician, witch, warlock and run-of-the-mill soothsayer. Grab a little oil, some incense, a candle or two, and some bat wings, and you're ready to rock! Uma, the owner, will be happy to help you cook up a hell of a spell . . . or just pick some delicious incense to pull you out of your fickle-friend funk.

Zen Center, 300 Page St. (@ Laguna St.), (415) 863-3136, *Stress Less*

Feel a full-on nervous breakdown in your future? You need to seriously chill out and learn the art of relaxation. This serene retreat, geared toward encouraging awareness, and "all things Zen," offers numerous classes, lectures, workshops, and meditation sittings. Call for a calendar of upcoming events and ask for Vicki Austin if you have specific questions.

The Castro/Noe Valley

Ames, Locksmith & Security Co., 3977 24th St. (bet. Noe & Sanchez Sts.), (415) 282-7919, *Locked Out*

You've locked your keys in your car . . . again. These folks will come to your rescue without even rolling an eyeball. Waste no more time trying to wiggle your way into the car with a coat hanger, just give them a ring 24 hours a day and help is on the way. Friendly and fast are the operative words.

Baghdad Café, 2295 Market St. (@ 16th St.), (415) 621-4434, *Late-Night Craving*

Serving breakfast into the wee hours of the morning: until 4 A.M., which, for this somewhat sleepy town, is late. Eggs for the famished or pancakes for the "over-served," plus an extra cup of coffee, especially if you plan to drive home to Marin County. *Psst . . . the crowd is*

predominately lesbian, but after a night of lecherous men at Charlie's (see Twilight, Marina/Cow Hollow), a room full of girls seems like a respite.

The Bead Store, 417 Castro St. (@ Market St.), (415) 861-7332, *Cheaper Than Diamonds*

You're a nervous wreck and need some monotonous task to take your mind off the office. Or, out of cash to buy something chic to update last year's black dress? Make cool jewelry with that Stevie Nicks flair that is so "in." Browse among a million beads, pick your favorite specimens and start stringing, or let them string your "design" for you if you find that threading makes you more nervous than you were before! Who knows . . . you could start a cottage industry if your artistic sensibility lends itself to crystal pebbles.

Headlines, 557 Castro St. (bet. 18th & 19th Sts.), (415) 626-8061, *Boutique Meets Ticket Outlet*

You have thirty minutes to plan and get ready for your Friday-night blind date . . . help! Come here for a cute outfit and tickets to a concert, play or sports event. You just never know how much talking you're going to want to do with Mystery Date. What if you get Poindexter? At least you'll look good.

Isa's Salon & Day Spa, 3836 24th St. (@ Church St.), (415) 641-8948, *Hair Crisis*

This full-service day spa boasts some of the best "beauty supplies" and emergency hair care in the area and, better yet, they are open seven days a week to treat conditions such as extreme dry hair, color disasters, hair loss and French-fried tresses. Even "hat head" can be remedied in a pouf. Planning a rendezvous in the wilds? A quick vegetable eyelash tint ($15) will help preserve your "natural beauty" while you commune with nature and your honey. Spa packages are available for those in search of total transformation. Open T–F, 10 A.M.–8 P.M., Sat. 9:30 A.M.–6:30 P.M., Sun. 11 A.M.–6 P.M., Mon. 10 A.M.–7 P.M.

Leer's German Specialties, 1581 Church St. (@ 28th St.), (415) 282-6803, *Helga In The City*

Trapped in your *Sound of Music* fantasy and can't get out? Go here . . . everything German from makeup, magazines and records to gourmet food and beer. Grab a wiener and some lip gloss and you're good to go, fraulein. "The Noe is alive with the sound of traffic . . ."

Sun Days, 3985 17th St. (@ Castro St.), (415) 626-8222, *Casper Crisis*
See details in Marina/Cow Hollow.

Tuggey's, 3885 24th St. (bet. Church & Sanchez Sts.), (415) 282-5081, *Hardcore Hardware*
Open since the early 1900s, these folks don't mess around with hammers and hoses. If you can't find it here, then it is not to be found . . . and if they can't help you, nobody can. Aren't you relieved, my little Homer Formby? Open seven days a week, 8:30 A.M.–6 P.M., later on Sat.; Sun., 11 A.M.–3 P.M.

✦ *Good to Know:*

Cruisin' the Castro? Call (415) 550-8110 to get another historical perspective of the city via walking tour—by far the best way to see the neighborhood.

✦ *Not to Miss:*

Europhoto, 4077 24th St. (@ Castro St.), (415) 824-7318, *Instant Pleasure*

Mission

Body Manipulations, 3234 16th St. (bet. Guerrero & Dolores Sts.), (415) 621-0408, *Body Art*
You have been stricken with Daredevil Disease, so go for it, girlfriend. A little tattooing and a stud in your tongue might go a long way toward your recovery! They'll paint you and pierce you to your heart's content. (FYI, we know a few plastic surgeons that can help you tomorrow morning when you return to your senses.)

Good Vibrations, 1210 Valencia St. (bet. 23rd & 24th Sts.), (415) 974-8980, *www.goodvibes.com, Lubes And Tubes*
A sexy supermarket. For the sexually curious or the passionately

playful, this hip and groovy emporium offers everything a feisty gal needs when she's down on her luck or just looking for battery-operated action. Got it? *Psst . . . user-friendly for the shy and quiet types. They even have instruction manuals for the more studious! Credit card purchases are billed discreetly as Open Enterprises.*

Harrington Bros., Inc., 599 Valencia St. (@ 17th St.), (415) 861-7300, *Interim Landlord*

Help! Your landlord has given you a month's notice, but that was a month ago. . . . You need to be out by Friday and you're not quite sure where you are going next! This moving and storage company is the best for "crisis intervention." Reliable—they even have their own line of home furnishings when you do decide on your new pad! After watching them steamroll through your stuff, you'll have built up quite an appetite for dinner at the Slanted Door (see Eats, Mission). Moving never tasted so good . . .

Lost Pets, 1200 15th St. (@ Harrison St.), (415) 567-8738, *AWOL Afghans*

While taking in the sights on your visit to dog-friendly San Francisco, Fido decided to branch out on his own and was led astray by a promiscuous poodle! These folks will do their best to help relocate your pet before you turn into a stressed-out pumpkin. They do charge a nominal finders fee, payable by check or credit card. . . . We love the continually updated recording with the descriptions of recently located "escapees." Rest assured that your "best friend" will be back with you with the help of these folks. Open 12 noon–5:30 P.M., Wed. until 7 P.M.

Lost Weekend Video, 1034 Valencia St. (@ 21st St.), (415) 643-3373, *Terminal Boredom*

You've got every cable channel, book and magazine imaginable, and still your brain is set to implode from boredom. Check out the groovy selection at this eclectic film rental shop. They have new releases, short films, cult flicks, and indies shot in San Francisco itself. Variety is the spice of life; the spice of life is chocolate; chocolate makes you fat; being fat makes you cry . . . time for a tearjerker and another Reese's! Open Sun–Thurs. 12 P.M.–10 P.M., Fri.–Sat. 12 P.M.–11 P.M.

Oxygen Bar, 795 Valencia St. (@ 19th St.), (415) 244-2102, *Breathe Easy*

Have you spent one too many nights on the town polluting yourself with loud music, tequila, and wild boys? Prepare to detox: Welcome to the wacky world of Oxygen. H_2O is meant to cleanse and reenergize, and this part bar (no booze) part spa (all Zen ode to a *Star Wars* hot spot) is ready and waiting for your weak little self to arrive. The space is cool with tubes protruding from the lime colored walls. Hook-up and enjoy flavors such as "Euphoric," a blend of lemon, chamomile, and marjoram, or "Relax." Feeling sexy? Try the "Aphrodisiac." Chill to the groovy, if not eerie, tunes that put you in the mood for the menu of aromas. And we are not just blowing hot air! Ten dollars for 10 minutes, $15 for 20 minutes, $25 for 40 minutes. *Psst . . . throwing a surprise party for your best friend? They will deliver to your door or you can book the whole place and puff the night away with all of your buddies!*

Paxton Gate, 824 Valencia St. (@ 19th St.), (415) 824-1872, *Seriously Bugged*

Taking taxidermy to a whole new level. The inventors of the new stuffed-bat therapy will welcome their new world of dead beasts and a few dead bugs. We were transfixed by the butterfly nets, only to look upon large glass cases of dearly departed creatures tacked to boards. Then again, whatever floats your boat. Seriously, if you are an insect enthusiast, check it out.

Psychic Horizons, 972 Valencia St. (bet. 21st & Liberty Sts.), (415) 643-8800, *www.psychichorizons.com, Bliss Deficient*

Stressed to the max? Need a little perspective on your job, your relationship, your inner child? Then come hang out and meditate with these folks on Tuesdays at 7:30 P.M. Wear loose-fitting or comfortable clothes and prepare to sit, meditate and discuss the night away. . . . You'll wake up the next day better for it! Free.

San Francisco Motorcycle Club, 2194 Folsom St. (@ 18th St.), (415) 863-1930, *Leather Babes*

Is your *Easy Rider* obsession interfering with your performance at work? Go from Charlie's Angel to Hell's Angel in one night. This is the second-oldest motorcycle club in the country (established in 1904) and welcomes visitors and first-timers at 8 P.M. on Thursdays. Members ride all different kinds of bikes and are generally a fun group! You never know—you might run into Lauren Hutton. *Psst . . . never leave home without your baby blue helmet and silk Hermes scarf for pro-tection!*

The San Francisco School of Art, 667 Mission St. (bet. 2nd & 3rd Sts.), (415) 543-9300, *Van Gogh Wannabe*

You have become a person without a life or a hobby. Your left brain has shut down completely. Nothing like a little submersion into the arts to stimulate your creative side and uplift your spirits! Choose from a variety of art classes that will set you back on track to join the land of the living and culturally fulfilled. Open registration.

Scarlet Sage Herb Co., 1173 Valencia St. (bet. 22nd & 23rd Sts.), (415) 821-0997, *www.scarletsageherb.com, Relaxation Fix*

Calling all nature babes to the herbalist next door! Soothe your mind and body, not to mention your spirit, at this comprehensive haven for ho-listic health. Find yourself entranced by the wide array of herbal alternatives to detox your life. We love the bugleweed and the marshmallow root.

Star Wash, 392 Dolores St. (@ 17th St.), (415) 431-2443, *Maytag And Movies*

If local San Franciscan Sharon Stone did her own laundry, she would do it here. It's Sunday night and you can't find a pair of clean anything in sight! Chic and clean, with classic flicks thrown in to entertain you while you "slave" away on those whites and colors. Just don't get distracted by the cutie at Dryer Three and mix your Fuchsia La Perla set with your new Lorenzini white shirt; pink is out for Fall. *Psst . . . the staff is excellent, with ex-tremely helpful attitudes.*

X-21 Modern, 890 Valencia St. (@ 20th St.), (415) 647-4211, *Prop Rental*

Amazing stuff for sale and rent! This huge warehouse stocks props, fur-niture and a wide array of other accessories for the mid-century-minded gal. The inventory is astonishing and includes the best of art deco, vintage office furnishings, paintings and sculpture, ceramics, glassware and more. This place is fabulous . . . we want to live here! We picked up a brand-new '50s red rotary-dial "Bat Phone" for our bedroom, that only takes calls from suitable suitors, and a six-piece white porcelain butterfly tea set from Ger-many. Otherwise, it is a blast to while away a few hours poring over the eclectic collection of stuff. *Psst . . . there is a huge basement holding as much stuff as the main floor. Don't miss it.*

Other Neighborhoods

B & B Pet Store, 4820 Geary St. (@ 12th Ave.), Richmond, (415) 221-7711, *Bone Gallery*

Buffy the Labrador has gone into a depression . . . something must be done! Perhaps a little gift. . . . Considered the best pet store in town, although slightly off the beaten path, they offer extensive product selection and individualized attention from an informed staff . . . and the price is right! Everything under the sun for your pooch, plus a whole lot more for the pet lovers of the Bay Area. . . . Worth the extra trek.

California Martial Arts Academy, 2901 Clement St. (@ 30th Ave.), Sea Cliff, (415) 752-5555, *Self-Defense*

"Everybody was Kung Fu fighting . . ." If you can sing the tune to this song, then your rear end probably needs a lift by now. Get in gear and in shape while building stamina, confidence and the skills to protect yourself from would-be attackers. They focus on the oldest form of the martial arts, Kung Fu, and will start off at the introductory level, which teaches the basic techniques and philosophy of the discipline, as well as some self-defense skills. Costs: $10 for the intro class.

Call of the Wild, 2519 Cedar St. (@ Euclid St.), Berkeley, (510) 849-9292, *www.callwild.com, Claustrophobics Anonymous*

Feeling like a caged animal? Howling at the moon from the windows of your Nob Hill apartment? Break out of your city shell with a wild adventure care of Carole Latimer and her fabulous company, catering to ballsy and outdoorsy gals worldwide! Land on Mount McKinley's Ruth Glacier via bush plane, explore Alaska or just participate in a groovy Bay Area day-hike. They've got you covered with experienced guides, pretrip instruction, group equipment including tents and great food, all adding up to a Grade-A adventure. Over 20 years in the biz of "babes in bizarre places." Won't your neighbors be relieved when the howling subsides?

Italian-American Social Club of San Francisco, 25 Russia Ave. (bet. London & Mission Sts.), Ingleside, (415) 585-8059, *Noodle Withdrawal*

You just spent the summer in Tuscany researching . . . well, researching *la dolce vita!* Now you are in total withdrawal, complete with anxiety attacks and the need to wear heavy black eyeliner. Snap out of your funk here with a fabulous dinner and dancing to live music among authentic Italian-Americans and others who love Italy! Reservations required but you need not be Italian-American to attend. Every fourth Friday of the month (except December) at 7:30; $19 for nonmembers.

Krispy Kreme Doughnuts, 32450 Dyer St. (@ Alvarado-Niles St.), Union City, (510) 471-6121, *www.krispykreme.com, Sugar Attack*

Finally. The hot glazed arrived in the Bay Area in early 2001, and not a moment too soon—for years, we've been yearning for this special treat to make its way across the country from the Southeast. There is no doughnut like the Krispy Kreme. Period. By now, you should know the drill: when the round neon sign—Hot Doughnuts Now—lights up, it's go time. The warm, freshly baked balls of dough are just heading out from their shower of sweet glaze. You can get them plain, filled with a delightful berry goo, decorated with sprinkles, or even covered in chocolate. And for just a few precious moments, the world disappears but for the quiet explosion of taste as a stream of sweet cream pours from inside the floury paste, cooling the hot glaze. It's no wonder the place sells its own line of hats, T-shirts, and mugs. Krispy Kreme fans have created a cultlike following, which has been mighty good for business. *Psst . . . the Winston-Salem, N.C.–based company went public shortly after opening in Union City and its stock sold like, well, hot doughnuts.*

Punahele Island Grill, 2650 Judah St. (@ 32nd Ave.), Sunset, (415) 759-8276, *Hawaii Five-O*

Sick of all of the dot-commers and want to fulfill your desire to "drop out" and head for the Islands? This relatively atmosphere-free room is authentic Hawaiian luau; in fact, you almost feel you're at, say, a wedding reception as you sit next to strangers at long folding tables. But no one remains a stranger and, not surprisingly, Punahele Island attracts a large number of native Hawaiians. A live luau band plays the real stuff—not old Don Ho hits—moving more than one middle-aged woman to get up and hula dance in the aisles, remembering the steps she learned as a child. Everyone in the joint hoots and hollers, egging on the next dancer. Even though it's in Outer Sunset, the place is packed to the rafters every Friday and Saturday night. As for the food, it's so authentic that a big pile of macaroni salad comes with every order—only true Hawaiians know that macaroni salad is the unifying food of their modern culture. Mounds of shredded pork on every plate are so succulent they dissolve before you can begin to chew. Reservations are a must for groups larger than two; expect to bump elbows with the diners next to you.

The Sewing Workshop, 2010 Balboa St. (@ 21st Ave.), Richmond, (415) 221-7397, *Fashion Emergency*

Have thread, will travel! Is your wardrobe passé and your pocketbook not up to the challenge? Here is a great way to get high-fashion looks at bargain-basement prices if you're willing to put a little time and effort into the process. Anything and everything you need to know about creating your own wardrobe is within these walls. A myriad of classes for every level from beginner on up. You are a phone call away from becoming the next Miuccia Prada. Okay, that might be a stretch, but sewing your own smart little black dress isn't out of the question.

Tequila Ph.D from Tommy's Mexican Restaurant, 5929 Geary St. (@ 24th Ave.), Richmond, (415) 387-4747, *Alternative Painkiller*

Higher education can be a bitch: classes, homework, thesises (or are those theses?). Regardless, after a while your brain hurts—unless, of course, the degree you seek is a Tequila Ph.D. from Tommy's, where 145 pure blue-agave tequilas, the largest selection outside Mexico, make for a unique educational opportunity. After a mere 70 double shots and a written test, you too will be among the few, the proud, the doctors of agave. Bartenders might do well to include this on their résumés. Nuclear physicists and school bus drivers might not.

Tse Chen Ling, Center For Tibetan Buddhist Studies "Book of the Month," 4 Joost Ave. (off Monterey Ave.), Glen Park, (415) 339-8002, *www.tclcenter@aol.com, Nervous Breakdown*

The little voices are telling you to devote your life to the pursuit of truth, beauty and Richard Gere. This book club will help you dig into your Zen self: all selections revolve around Tibetan and Buddhist culture, history and politics. Every third Friday of the month at 7 P.M. You are responsible for the cost of the reading material. Now you just have to get Carrie Lowell out of the way. Open noon–6 P.M., Tues.–Fri.

◊ *Citywide:*

AAA Emergency Road Service, (800 222-4357, *Mercedes Meltdown*

If a picnic on the side of the road sounds less romantic when your car is on fire, then don't neglect to join this reliable cult of grease monkeys. They'll whip you and your ride into shape in no time . . . or at least get you home from the boonies before you are abducted by aliens. Let's face it . . . San Francisco is not the place to run out of brake fluid . . . unless you want to explore the bottom of the Bay in your convertible! Open 24 Hours.

Auto Impound, (415) 553-1235, *Strange Disappearances*

Where Oh Where Has My Miata Gone? Yes, you did leave your car "there," but "there" had a DO NOT PARK sign behind a nearby bush, and so "there" is not the same "there" it used to be. In fact, "there" is most likely "here," also known as the impound. Make sure you have *cash* and ID . . . under the best of circumstances this undertaking will take several hours of waiting and paperwork, and that's on a good day! May we suggest checking the bushes for all hidden, obstructed, or plowed-over parking signs *before* you leave the safety of your vehicle?

Blood Bank, (415) 567-6400, *Nosferatu's Juice Bar*

Not as sexy as a spa for vampires, but more utilitarian. The Red Cross *never* has enough blood to meet demand, so if you are feeling altruistic while on vacation or on your lunch break, feel free to pop in and offer a pint or two. You never know when you might need to be on the receiving end of that IV!

City Box Office, (415) 392-4400, *The Scalper of Seville*

When *Madame Butterfly* means more to you than a low-fat substitute for margarine, you are prone to malapropisms and you can't score tickets through main channels at the Opera House, try City Box Office! Known to take on the most challenging of cases, they might even be able to figure out what the butter analogy is all about . . .

Tix Bay Area, (415) 433-7827, *Cheap Thrills*

From rock-bottom Barney to Beethoven to Baryshnikov. If Bargain Betty is your middle name, and expensive cultural events and performances are your M.O., then this is your one-stop shop for bargain-basement ticket prices to top-tier events in the Bay Area. Symphony, sports, opera, ballet, theater, rock concerts, public executions. Whatever is your artistic passion, they have the cure that makes the best of your time and money.

Good to Know:

Dry cleaners refusing to replace your misplaced Dolce & Gabanna skirt? Call the Better Business Bureau, (415) 243-9999.

Is your white wall driving you up the wall? Seek sanity at the artistic hands of muralist Mirko Hensch, who can brighten a room or create a conversation piece, (415) 440-0535.

Best Place to Grocery Shop Without Leaving Home: its prices rival any supermarket chain's and there's no delivery charge for orders over $50, so why endure the fluorescent lighting? The service *www.webvan.com* will bring almost any food item to your door—including fresh produce, meat, and seafood—as well as your favorite wine, beer, soap, and shampoo. Also, Webvan knows you're a creature of habit, so it keeps a complete history of purchases in your "personal market" to make reordering a no-brainer. The site even offers recipe ideas, seasonal meal suggestions, and the opportunity to buy a BART pass. All you have to do is give the company a day's notice and pick your 15-minute window delivery time.

Treasures

Alexander Book Co., 50 2nd St. (bet. Market & Mission Sts.), (415) 495-2992, *Neighborhood Favorite*

Indie bookstore on three floors in Downtown San Fran; a great children's corner and a bimonthly newsletter featuring upcoming events and critiques are just two of the many perks. Linger in this throwback to another time, before giant literary supermarkets ruled the world. Remember Meg Ryan's store in *You've Got Mail?*

Bell'occhio, 8 Brady St. (@ Market St.), (415) 864-4048, *French Finds*

Parisian beauty and European lifestyle define the atmosphere at this sumptuously girly Downtown haven. Catherine Deneuve would have a nose-powdering heyday amidst the comprehensive collection from powder guru T. Leclerc. Hard-to-find bath products from France and Italy along with hair accessories and silk flowers make it fun to while away the afternoon browsing or playing *Belle de Jour!*

Birkenstock, 42 Stockton St. (@ O'Farrell St.), (415) 989-BIRK, *www.birkenstock.com, Comfy Attire*

Speaking of legendary . . . had a little too much Jimmy Choo? There are over 300 styles and colors of this new standard in comfort now housed in this two-story metropolis complete with café. Wheatgrass, anyone? Fun children's section too! And of course you can still get the original sandal that started the Birk phenomenon. Your feet will thank you!

Books Inc. Outlet, 160 Folson St. (@ Main St.), (415) 442-4830, *Reading Binge*

Expand your book collection without blowing your budget! All leftover and/or slightly damaged books from all nine Books Inc. stores throughout the Bay Area end up here. Save 50–90 percent on great coffee-table books, and a nice array of fiction. Happy hunting. Doesn't it feel good to be thrifty?

Candelier, 33 Maiden Lane (bet. Grant Ave. & Kearny St.), (415) 989-8600, *Candles*

Ode to wax. If mood lighting makes you wax philosophic on the meaning of life, don't go alone . . . you will be mesmerized by the plethora of designs, colors, shapes and sizes of these beautiful candles, meant to enhance your home and hearth. Their wicks are wicked, so don't plan on leaving here without a little wax on your hands . . . so to speak!

Copeland Sports, 901 Market St. (@ 5th St.), (415) 495-0928, *Sporting Goods*

Sports and athletics are a way of life in San Francisco. Join the masses and enjoy the beautiful terrain, weather and naturally challenging hilly streets. These guys are here to make sure you are outfitted properly, with names like Patagonia, North Face, and Adidas. They also carry other useful items like yoga mats, bath sandals for the gym, and windbreakers—which are a must in this city! Everything is stocked in wide variety. Open seven days a week.

Crown Point Press Gallery, 20 Hawthorne St. (bet. Folsom & Howard Sts.), (415) 974-6273, *www.crownpoint.com, Authentic Art*

Artists create here by invitation only, and their works are then printed and sold by the press. Amazing etchings and prints from America's up-and-coming are on display and for sale at this unique setting. Internationally renowned for quality.

Diana Slavin, 3 Claude Lane (bet. Bush & Sutter Sts.), (415) 677-9939, *ds@dianaslavin.com, Women's wear*

Sumptuous fabrics that drape and move in all of the right places. Since 1990, this destination is a must for chic women. Go for simple collections (à la Armani) classically designed and distinctive that will take you from the boardroom to dinner with friends in style. Keeping it all in the family, the beautiful shop was designed by her husband, architect Robert Baum.

Fold Art International Gallery, 140 Maiden Lane (bet. Grant Ave. & Stockton St.), (415) 392-9999, *Art & More*

Tucked away in one of the city's most beloved alleyways is a Frank Lloyd Wright masterpiece housing some of the more interesting objets d'art money can buy. The store itself is elegant (think Guggenheim design) with a tremendous selection of folk art, ceramics, tribal masks, amber jewelry and more. Worth a peek even if you are not in the mood to buy.

Gimme Shoes, 50 Grant Ave. (@ Market St.), (415) 434-9242, *Trendy Shoes*

These folks have been setting the standard for fashion in footwear in San Francisco for over 16 years. Now with three stores, all in tony neighborhoods, they are not only trendsetting but they're the leaders of the pack. Select pieces from seasonal collections like Prada/Miu Miu, Clergiere, Costume National, and several hip Belgian designers, like Dirk "Hardname" Bikkemberg and Ann Demeulemeester. Always one step ahead of the curve, and just the right place for our shoe cravings. Diehards swear by this real San Francisco favorite. See other locations in The Heights and Hayes Valley.

Gumps, 135 Post St. (bet. Grant Ave. & Kearny St.), (415) 982-1616, *www.gumps.com, Neighborhood Favorite*

Started in 1861, Gumps is a genuine SF treasure. After branching out across the nation, sometimes successfully, sometimes not, these guys have stayed true to their roots. Jade, freshwater pearls, antique garden ornaments, Oriental treasures, glassware and other treasures. On the run from your dot-com? This is a perfect place to register for your high society wedding. Just hope your rich uncle is willing to show up or at least send a gift! The huge two-story Buddha in the center of the store is worth the trip alone. We felt like we were in Paris at the Buddha Bar . . . sans the champagne hangover! *Psst . . . on the fifth floor of the store is the Joseph Cozza Salon. A full-service salon offering cuts, manicures, waxing, color and makeup service. By appointment only, Tues.-Sat., 9 A.M. until 7 P.M.*

Jeffrey's Toys, 7 3rd St. (@ Market St.), (415) 243-8697, *www.jeffreys-toys.com, Old-Fashioned Toys*

Looking for an alternative place to get gifts for the special tots in your life? Don't expect the trendy objects they carry at Toys "R" Us and FAO Schwartz . . . or Sony, for that matter. Do expect to find cool classics such as Magic 8 balls that tell fortunes or collapsible push-up puppets and other classics like Slinkys. Owner Mark Luna is committed to his classic mission. In fact, they carry the city's largest selection of stuffed animals, and they are the only toy store with a full-fledged comic book store built inside! We love the fun selection of silly toys with the squirting flowers and whoopee cushions—naturally, flowers and whoopee are our fortes! They have it all with no batteries required.

Jeremy's, 2 South Park (@ 2nd St.), (415) 882-4929, *Designer Discount*

Can't bear the idea of traditional discount shopping with throngs of desperate shoppers poring over the same "good racks" for that perfect find? Owner Jeremy Kidson stocks random designer pieces not scooped up by the biggies. Look for Prada, Alberta Ferretti, and other hot designers to fill the aisles. He also carries many lesser-known but equally stylish designer pieces. The shoe selection is impressive in its own right, so after picking up a delicious Vivienne Tam top for next to nothing, grab a cool pair of Costume National sandals for spring. Looking expensive (for next to nothing) is a girl's best revenge! *Psst . . . check out the second, more collegiate, collection at their Berkeley location.*

Jessica McClintock & Gunne Sax Outlet, 35 Stanford St. (bet. Townsend & Brannan Sts.), (415) 495-3326, *Discounts*

Young romantics discover great finds at this San Fran standard. Jessica, Scott and Gunne all hold court in this comprehensive outlet for young innocents and anyone going for a little Annie-Hall-at-the-Prom chic! Whores look elsewhere—there are no fishnets here.

Jin Wang, 111 Maiden Lane, 3rd fl. (bet. Stockton St. & Grant Ave.), (415) 397-9111, *Bridal Diva*

Yi is the maven for custom wedding dresses in the Golden Gate City! After working for 21 years in the design business, she decided to turn her "hobby" into a bona fide business. Four years later, she is outfitting brides, bridesmaids and mothers of the bride with some of the most graceful dresses available. Her chichi address and lofty space make for the ideal glamorous experience. We bet Doris Day would have bought her wedding dress here! *Psst . . . look for shoes and accessories by designers like Cynthia Rowley, Vanessa Noel (so comfy), and the newest editions by Richard Tyler.*

Joseph Domingo, 808 Post St. (@ Leavenworth), (415) 563-2007, *www.josephdomingo.com, Customs Fashions*

Glamour girl alert: custom gowns from Joseph, the darling of San Francisco's up-and-coming fashion scene when it comes to sexy dresses for special occasions. Visit his small but stylish studio in a blah strip of upper Post for a peek, and prepare to be wowed by his creations. A small collection of clothing is available but we are mad for his couture-touched gowns. Average dress costs around $1,000. By appointment only.

La Bouquetiere, 563 Sutter St. (bet. Powell & Mason Sts.), (415) 248-1120, *www.labouquetiere.com, Body Excelsior & More*

No visit to this neighborhood is complete without a side excursion to this lovely place for pretty things for your home and body. Exquisite candles, exclusive perfumes, soaps, and body sprays are properly displayed among chic décor. Taste à la the stylish French.

Lang Antiques and Estate Jewelry, 323 Sutter St. (bet. Grant Ave. & Stockton St.), (415) 982-2213, *www.langantiques.com, Jewels Abound*

If you love one-of-a-kind antique jewelry this is your one-stop shopping. Rivaled only by Frances Klein in Los Angeles, Lang offers the premier stock of estate jewelry—some call her the ring queen. Your ten digits are destined to leave happily bejeweled! For those looking to get hitched, leave this page open in your house and maybe Mr. Right will get the hint!

Limn Company, 290 Townsend St. (bet. 3rd & 4th Sts.), (415) 543-5466, *Twentieth-Century Housewares*

It's not a museum, it just feels like one. This furniture store is chock-full of gorgeous high-style housewares from names to love like Eames, Noguchi, Stark, and others that should be on the list as modern mavericks. We could spend all afternoon poring over the curvaceous knick-knacks and artistically designed pieces. We may never make it back to the office! Big names demand big prices, be prepared to pay. Open seven days a week.

Liquidators, 2899 Cesar Chavez St. (@ York Ave.), (415) 695-1900.

Industrial chic for the home. If you want to bring a little of the restaurant kitchen into your own, check out these folks. Groovy restaurant, retail and industrial fixtures, revamped and restored, create utilitarian chic in your home; like giant kitchen tables on wheels, converted toasters, and more.

Marc Jacobs, 125 Maiden Lane (bet. Stockton St. & Grant Ave.), (415) 362-6500, *www.marcjacobs.com, Designer Duds*

Our wonder boy does it again! Come here to celebrate fashion and life . . . and leave with anything, from an investment piece, à la "the power suit," to his new, perfectly styled dark denim jeans. This is the designer's first and only location outside of New York City, with 3,000 square feet of pure pleasure to enjoy the minimalist fashions with all of San Francisco's other ultrachic city girls. A definite destination for true fashionistas. *Psst . . . menswear available too.*

Margaret O'Leary, 1 Claude Lane, (@ Sutter St.), (415) 391-1010, *Hand-Knit Sweaters*

Yummy does not begin to describe the delicious knitwear hiding on shelves and hangers inside these walls. Margaret lives by her motto, "a good sweater is like an old friend," so prepare to leave with an entourage of knubby buddies! Chenille, textured yarn and more . . . get cozy and tell her we sent you! Stocking other cool designers as well, like Rozae Nichols and Three Dots. Other locations in Berkeley and Mill Valley.

Metier, 355 Sutter St. (bet. Stockton St. & Grant Ave.), (415) 989-5395, *Women's Boutique*

We left our heart in San Fran but took the wardrobe. Find classic San Francisco here. Remember, it's now all about London Fog, rubber boots and Frank Sinatra. Helpful staff, one-of-a-kind finds (Diana Slavin), and great knock-offs make it a pleasure to blow your wad here. Longtime city-wide favorite of these fashionistas in the know.

Rizzoli Bookstore, 117 Post St. (bet. Grant Ave. & Kearny St.), (415) 984-0225, *Classic Bookshop*

This could be the most visually beautiful bookshop in the city. Lined with dark wood and sumptuous carpets, and rows and rows of pretty books. We love to shop here for art books, coffee-table books (great for gifts), and for handsome, artistic men who are poring over their favorite novel. No Amex. Open seven days a week from 10 A.M. to 7 P.M., 6 P.M. on Sunday.

Rolo, 21 Stockton St. (@ Market St.), (415) 989-7656, *Trendy Girl/Guy*

See details in Castro/Noe Valley.

Salon de Thé, 6 Brady St. (@ Market St.), (415) 863-8391, *Trendy Fashions*

The young, the hip and the newsworthy designers of the world hang their "works" at this cutting-edge fashion find. Come to browse or buy; it's a fresh treat for the eye and the body! One-of-a-kind accessories add flair to any purchase.

Satin Moon, 32 Clement St. (bet. Arguello Blvd. & 2nd Ave.), (415) 668-1623, *Sumptuous Notions*

Best fabrics by the yard for the picky, picky girl. Forget the Pashmina. Chic city girls show up to lop off a couple of yards of fabric and double it to make a lovely wrap. Better yet, the button and ribbon selection is astonishing! Make your last purchase from the '90s look new again with new buttons! Costs for buttons: from cheap to ridiculous.

Six Brady, 6 Brady St. (@ Market St.), (415) 626-6678, *Fun Fashions*

Jonesing for something new, with no room in your new budget for power purchasing? This is an amusing place to get your fix without the damaging repercussions! Opt for the perfectly fitting Katayone Adeli's hip-hugging pants or a cool wrap-style Michael Star tee in a playful color. Jewelry crafted by local designers, cashmere cardigans in crayon shades. Rumor has it that Courtney Cox came into town when she was getting married and brought out most of the store! Never mind the hoighty-toighty Maiden Lane crowd, this is a hidden gem in a sea of big rocks.

Spectacle Shoppe, 177 Maiden Lane (@ Stockton St.), (415) 781-8556, *Sunglasses*

Top brands in the heart of Union Square. Set in a doctor's office-style environment, they carry Gucci, Oliver Peoples, Cartier, Paul Smith, and, more importantly, Cutler & Gross.

Tower Records, 2825 Jones St. (bet. Columbus Ave. & Bay St.), (415) 885-0500, *Chain Gang*

The birth of the legend—1968—the baby Tower was born right here, and baby likes to rock! Visit this now-legendary megastore chain-home for music, videos, books, and magazines. *Psst . . . if you have more patience than cash, the Tower Outlet in Soma, 660 3rd St. (bet. Brannan & Townsend), (415) 957-9660, carries tons of music and videos that you wouldn't pay full price for but would love to have in your collection. Back issues of hip import magazines for about a buck!*

Ultimo, 140 Geary St. (bet. Grant Ave. & Stockton St.), (415) 273-7077, *High-Style Fashions*

If Bluemarine, Dolce & Gabbana, JP Gaultiere and Randolph Duke are names that are as close to you as your family, this is your place! The West Coast offspring of Chicago's hottest (and perhaps its first in the late '70s) designer boutique, a plethora of style awaits you! The space itself is unclut-tered and encourages hassle-free (and *big*) spending. Open seven days a week until 6 P.M. and 5 P.M. on Sunday. *Psst . . . we love the close proximity to Jil Sander, for him and her, on nearby Maiden Lane.*

Wilkes Bashford, 375 Sutter St. (@ Stockton St.), (415) 986-4380, *Neighborhood Favorite*

For 34 years, Wilkes Bashford has brought avant-chic to San Francisco. This true gentleman knows style and how to dress those who want to pos-sess it. Bottom line: you can trust that whatever the pushy-yet-informed staff recommends will be great looking . . . whether you're looking to build a wardrobe or to find a midwinter pick-me-up. As long as price is no issue, they've got you covered. Socialites and secretaries are welcome, just bring your checkbook and some time. There are five floors to ponder. Closed on Thursday.

Yard Art, 2188½ Sutter St. (@ Pierce St.), (415) 346-6002, *Outdoor/In-door Furnishings*

Everything antique and exquisite for "furnishing" the backyard and gar-den. No pink flamingos allowed! High-end objets d'art and collectibles (some from the 16th century) mix with antique country furniture to pro-vide a plethora of outdoor design ideas. They are known for their signature Victorian urns that can be used indoors or out as a functional and artistic statement! Planters, fountainheads and Greek friezes are just some of the one-of-a-kind finds available.

❧ Not to Miss:

Brooks Brothers, 150 Post St. (bet. Grant Ave. & Kenney St.), (415) 397-4500, *Classic Attire*

Loehmann's, 222 Sutter St. (bet. Grant Ave. & Kearny St.), (415) 982-3215, *Designer Discount*

Louis Vuitton, 330 Post St. (@ Stockton St.), (415) 391-6200, *Label Slaves*

Caswell-Massey, 373 Sutter St. (@ Stockton St.), (415) 296-1054, *Historical Elixir*

101 Music, 1414 Grant Ave. (@ Green St.), (415) 392-6369, *Alternative Tunes*

More than just music . . . over 10,000 music-related items; you will find a collection of turntables beyond compare, posters, LPs etc. Browse-o-rama! Anything to create a sonic boom!

AB Fits, 1519 Grant Ave. (bet. Union & Filbert Sts.) (415) 982-5726, *Denim Blues*

Ode to great-fitting jeans. Did you know that Levi's were invented by a man who set out to outfit the hard-working gold diggers? The sturdy fabrics were perfect for sitting on your knees for hours on end while searching for gold . . . mostly fool's gold! You just might strike it rich with the perfect jean too. With over two dozen brands, these folks are committed to outfitting the San Francisco girl in the perfect jeans by Diesel, Replay, and the cool Ranch Market, complete with sterling silver buttons! Whether you want the fit-like-a-glove look or the more subdued classic look, they've got you covered.

Alla Prima, 1420 Grant Ave. (bet. Union & Green Sts.), (415) 397-4077, *Sex Kitten Lingerie*

First things first, girls. Let's start with your panties. Fancy-schmancy, sexy undies are the ticket at this boutique for everything bodacious and beautiful. Every SF man should know about this undergarment haven—if not, educate him about their pretty things to make any girl feel like a million bucks. Colors including pale lime, dusty lavender, and icy blue. From the sublime to the not so subtle, they've got you covered . . . or not covered . . . depending on your mood. Names to know: Chantel Thomas, La Perla, Cosabella, and more. It's a fantasy of yummy "finishings." See other location in Hayes Valley. *Psst . . . don't miss the upstairs section for elegant swimwear.*

Atelier des Modistes, 1903 Hyde St. (@ Green St.), (415) 775-0545, *www.atelierdesmodistes.com, Custom Gowns*

If you are Cinderella without a Fairy Godmother, look no further than Suzanne Hanley to conjure up your fantasy frock. Be forewarned: twenty-first century fairies don't come cheap! If you've got the wallet, she's got the whimsy to make your fashion dreams come true. Her couture line and custom designs with delicate jewelry and other delicacies make this a definite stop whether you are planning a first wedding or a second.

City Lights, 262 Columbus Ave. (bet. Pacific Ave. & Broadway), (415) 362-8193, *Famous Bookstore*
In a world of ever-changing technology, disposable everything and fast-paced living, it's good to know that some things remain constant. Since 1953, this bookshop cofounded by Lawrence Ferlinghetti has focused on all things truly literary. The high road for the higher minded. Exotic poetry shares the shelves with outrageous literature, as well as a hearty selection of the classics.

Couture Recycled, 2060 Polk St. (bet. Pacific Ave. & Broadway), (415) 474-1191, *Budget Princess*
Ouch! We saw the Tosca sweater that we paid full price for last month marked down to a mere $35. Tears will get you nowhere! Just get proactive and grab all of the D&G, Calvin Klein, Geoffery Beene, Fendi, Alaia, and Gigli that your pocketbook will tolerate. At these prices, you might need to make extra room in your closet. Open 11 A.M.–6:30 P.M., closed on Sunday.

Donna, 1424 Grant Ave. (bet. Green & Union Sts.), (415) 397-4447, *Affordable*
The antidesigner designer boutique . . . no names, only chic. Helpful staff will help you build an avant-garde wardrobe and then help you figure out how to afford it. Layaway? No problem! You will recognize nothing other than the artistry of the clothing. Great accessories and bags . . . not to mention sales! Very unassuming environment.

The Enchanted House, 1411 Grant Ave., (bet. Green & Union), (415) 981-5870, *Chinese Collectibles*

Peggy Ling is a neighborhood babe with out-of-sight antiquities. You may recognize her world-renowned Ching Dynasty kingfisher feather royal hair ornaments from Bertolucci's film, *The Last Emperor,* but don't despair; she also stocks affordable collectibles, jewelry, and slippers. Check out the antique cremation jars for your ashen mementos! Closed on Sunday.

Girl Stuff, 2255 Polk St. (@ Green St.), (415) 409-2426, *www.stuff-4-girls.com, Baby Doll Fashions*

Who said it wasn't all about you? A SF trend: more girly stuff for girly girls. This tiny store is packed with treasures like custom jewelry, hip handbags, beaded sandals, T-shirts, and more! You deserve a mid-week pick-me-up. Semiprecious jewels by Erickson Beamon and hot little bags by Amy Chan.

Han Palace Fine Arts, 1165 Powell St. (@ Jackson St.), (415) 788-5338, *Collectibles*

When you finally convince your man that furniture does not all come from Pier One, drag him here. Every chic household needs a bit of the Chinois. This place takes Asian antiquities seriously. A great place to browse among museum-quality pieces like life-size Han Dynasty animals, treasures of the Webster Zhou dynasty, and incredible pre-Communist regime exports. Thanks to walls of glass, this is the window-shopper's wonderland, but bring your Black Amex if you are planning to buy. Prices begin at $1,000 and go much, much higher. *Psst . . . owner Henry Yip has amassed these pieces mostly from private collectors.*

In My Dreams, 1300 Pacific Ave. (@ Leavenworth St.), (415) 885-6696, *Silks & Saris*

After burning a million calories by walking up and down the crazy streets of Nob Hill, stop by for a peek at the impressive collection of new and old chinoiserie. Now treat yourself to a little something authentic . . . who knows who you might want to play "dress up" with one day?

Italian French Bakery, 1501 Grant Ave. (@ Union St.), (415) 421-3796, *Specialty Edibles*

Belia Aparicio's world-famous macaroons have people howling at the moon and buying in bulk. Made from only fresh coconut and water, baked in high-heat bread ovens until the outside crisps around the lusciously chewy center, they're heaven the size of a fist and sometimes dipped in chocolate. . . . Need we say more? The line forms to the left!

Italyhome, 2354 Polk St. (@ Union St.), (415) 563-4341, *www.italyhome.com, Bella Casa*

The finest of home furnishings for the woman seeking the best Italian fare this side of Pisa. Owner Luigi is a hands-on kind of guy who is there to help you find the authentic items to make your home the "villa" of your dreams. View the custom tiles, from Italy of course, and enjoy the best European finds Stateside. No leaning permitted. . . .

The Jug Shop, 1567 Pacific (@ Polk St.), (415) 885-2922, *Vino, Baby!*

Touted by some as the best wine store in San Fran. Enjoy the tasting bar for a small fee and try before you buy! Varietal jug wines along with high-end European vintages make up the comprehensive stock for connoisseurs of any budget. Most major liquor brands available as well. Stock your fridge or your cellar with the friendly advice of this knowledgeable staff.

MAC, 1543 Grant Ave. (bet. Union & Filbert Sts.), (415) 837-1694, *Pretty Clothes*

In a neighborhood overrun with trendy designer-clad people and their pursuits, these guys win big kudos for being perhaps *the* ones to bring cutting-edge fashions to the savvy city girl. We challenge you to leave empty-handed, especially after viewing the handbags . . . be still my heart! When the LVs, "G" belt buckles, and Hermes of the world leave you feeling like one of the pack, and broke to boot, let these pros resuscitate your wardrobe and your bank account.

Molte Cose, 2044 Polk St. (bet. Broadway & Pacific Sts.), (415) 921-5374, *Alternative Gifts*

The name of this fun store means "many things," in Italian. Some things old, some things new, that is what you will find at this treasure trove. Here's to Teresa, the shop's owner, for providing a fun and special place to find that one-of-a-kind something for a hard-to-find gift. Unique picture frames, vintage clothing, and furniture. We love the wide selection of reproductions of French posters. *Psst . . . she recently opened a lingerie store with pretty things to spoil yourself with.*

Old Vogue, 1412 Grant Ave. (bet. Green & Union Sts.), (415) 382-1552, *Vintage Chinoiserie*

Every stylish girl needs something vintage in her wardrobe. This is *the* place to go for vintage Chinese a là *The Last Emperor.* Don't get us wrong, they have other "old vogue" clothes, like Hawaiian shirts and such, but we hit the jackpot with a little white geisha number and two authentic smoking jackets. A perfect wardrobe pick-me-up.

Pesaresi Ceramics/Crocker Gallery, 50 Post St. (@ Kearny St.), (415) 362-4570, *Italian Pottery*

Viva Firenze! Find all things Florentine for table and hearth. Traditional tableware along with Florentine Majolica, tin-glazed earthenware, will send you into Suzy Homemaker heaven! The Pitti Palace doesn't seem so far away now, does it?

Quantity Postcards, 1441 Grant Ave. (bet. Green & Union Sts.), (415) 788-4455, *Write Home*

"Camp" never looked so good! You'll be mesmerized by the sheer visual volume of this famous North Beach card shop, carrying every kind of postcard, both vintage and new, imaginable. Most are humorous, some are borderline lewd, but any way you slice it you'll find something to suit your fancy and your message. *Psst . . . sister store, Tilt, 507 Columbus Ave. (bet. Stockton & Union Sts.), (415) 788-5566, www.tiltpix.com, also stocks movie publicity photos, posters, buttons and hundreds of magnets. It's kitschy fun for the whole family, not to mention the saucy gal on the go!*

Smoke Signals, 2223 Polk St. (bet. Vallejo & Green Sts.), (415) 292-6025, *International Rags*

Need to practice your Italian before your business trip to Milano? Want to be up on current affairs in Russia for your next trip? This place is dedicated to smoking and smoking accessories, but they also have an unbelievable selection of international dailies and magazines from around the world, whether it's *Hola!* from Spain or the *International Herald Tribune.* Always be an international woman of mystery, but don't pick up a bad habit while doing your research! Health alert: smoking is the number one cofactor related to gynecologic cancers . . . now you know.

Suey Chong Co., 900 Grant Ave. (bet. Jackson & Washington Sts.), (415) 982-1010, *Authentic Chinoiserie*

For all things Chinese, go directly to the best source in Chinatown for a nice selection of old and new finds. Musts are the vintage dresses and the vast selection of purses and slippers. Even if it's not the year of the dragon, make a fashion statement at the Bubble Lounge (see Twilight, North Beach/Chinatown) this weekend!

Swallowtail, 2217 Polk St. (bet. Green & Vallejo Sts.), (415) 567-1555, *Antique Finds*

Can't make it to Paris before your best friend's birthday this weekend? This is a small but great place to find French flea-market type goodies, things like Venetian glass, Art Deco etched mirrors, and other glamorous stuff from the 1920s through the '70s. From $150 to $4,000. *Psst . . . too broke to dine properly after picking up a treasure too good to pass up? Za Pizza, 1919 Hyde (@ Green St.), (415) 771-3100, is a small pizzeria with gourmet topping on delish dough.*

Ten Ren Tea Co., 949 Grant Ave. (bet. Washington & Jackson Sts.), (415) 362-0656, *www.tenren.com, Promote Health*

Home of the finest teas in the world, aptly located in Chinatown. Ten Ren was founded in 1953 in Taiwan, and now has over 20 locations in North America and in 5 other countries. This location is a perfect place to consider joining the society of passionate tea lovers. Novices and pros alike will find happiness with the variety and quality available. They have their own manufacturing plants to oversee the processing. Former President Bush enjoyed tea with Barbara from here when in San Francisco! Great prices too.

Zonal, 1942 Fillmore St. (bet. Pine & Bush Sts.), (415) 359-9111, *Art & Antiques*

Antiquing in lower Russian Hill is a blast, if you know the deal: it's posh, so be prepared to drop some serious dough. Zonal is the cream of the crop when it comes to folk art and pure American furniture. The motto of owners Scott Kalmbach and Russel Prittchard is "Always Repair, Never Restore." Distressed furniture, natural woods, and wrought iron are what draw girls who appreciate the natural state of antique furniture. Come in search of lamps and leave with a simple couch or a headboard covered in lambskin. Made to order pieces can be shipped anywhere in the world.

Not to Miss:

Barnes & Noble, 2550 Taylor St. (@ North Point), (415) 292-6762, *Neighborhood Favorite*

Columbine Design, 1541 Grant Ave. (bet. Union & Filbert Sts.), (415) 434-3016, *www.columbinedesign.com, Victorian Home*

Hyde and Seek, 1913 Hyde St. (@ Green St.), (415) 776-8865, *Fine Antiques*

Martini Merchantile, 1453 Grant Ave. (bet. Union & Green Sts.), (415) 362-1944, *Vintage Originals*

Marina/Cos Hollow ···

Bed Of Roses, 2274 Union St. (bet. Steiner & Fillmore Sts.), (415) 922-5150, *Flower Power*

Enter this fantasyland of petals and pistils, and be transported to aromatic heaven. For the upscale and intelligent flower junkie, this place offers the crème de la crème in cut flowers and potted plants (orchids are a house specialty). Not for the long-stem red rose brigade, they specialize in unique arrangements, little esoteric descriptions of which are included with every order for a nice touch. The perfect gift for the flower aficionado in your life. Minimum order is $35 with an 8-dollar charge for delivery in the city, including the West Bay area.

Bella Bridesmaid, 3109 Fillmore St., Suite 201 (@ Filbert St.), (415) 931-5492, *www.bellabridesmaid.com, Custom Gowns*

The recently wed Bridget Wells is the adorable scion of this fashionable and functional bridal attire bungalow—all creations custom-designed with flair and fantasy. From the minute you enter the wood-floored, sunny second-story atelier, you will feel at home. By appointment only. Service and personal attention rule the roost.

Briefs, 2258 Chestnut St. (bet. Pierce & Scott Sts.), (415) 359-1600, *Gifts For Him*

Whether "he" is a boxer, brief or nothing kind of guy, these guys have a top-notch selection of underwear for the man in your life. After picking out the perfect pair of undies, adorn him with new slippers and a robe while you are at it. Not that the robe will stay on for long now that you know what lies beneath . . . hey, get your mind out of the gutter! Hanro of Switzerland, Rips, Sauvage, and more. Let's just hope he reciprocates when it's your turn to be spoiled . . . rotten!

California Wine Merchant, 3237 Pierce St. (@ Chestnut St.), (415) 567-0646, *Reliable Wines*

An ideal place to pick up a bottle of wine in the neighborhood while on the way to a dinner party. Heralded in the Michelin Guide for the past 27 years, they simply offer the best California wines. The place is a bit like a winery in Tuscany, with shelves and shelves of wine to pour. Molto bene vino bianco é rosso! Open 11 A.M.–7 P.M., Mon.– Sat.

Canyon Beachwear, 1728 Union St. (bet. Octavia & Gough Sts.), (415) 885-5070, *Swimsuits*

A year-round destination to buy a swimming suit, no matter what your taste or size. The helpful and friendly sales staff are great at finding the perfect suit to suit your needs, whether it's a luxurious voyage by boat around the Hawaiian Islands or a snorkeling trip to Mexico. They carry Calvin Klein, Cacharel, and Delfina. No need to be embarrassed—they have seen it all, and we mean *all*! They just want to make you look good at the seaside. From $89 to $400.

Cara Mia, 1814 Union St. (bet. Laguna & Octavia Sts.), (415) 922-2272, *Clothes Emporium*

From shearlings to string bikinis, this is *the* place to go hog wild on Cosa Bella lingerie. Bottom line: all-Italian goods showcased in a deliciously artistic environment. Gorgeous custom gift wrap makes this a prime destination for a cashmere sweater for sis or secretary. Don't go on the prowl tonight without stopping here for a sexy thong, because you just never know, you know? *Psst . . . Carrol Sport next door has a pool table that is a great place to plant your man while you shop. He just might pick up a couple of nice items for his wardrobe, and the tab for yours!*

Dosa/Workshop, 2254 Union St. (bet. Webster & Buchanan Sts.), (415) 561-9551, *Neighborhood Favorite*

If dressing is more an adventure than an event to you, then take your spirit to the land of exotic Eastern fabrics mixed with classic designs and an emphasis on high quality. When you feel like walking on the sexy side, grab one of their specialties: a slinky slip dress for your night out at Fleur de Lys. Wardrobe staples are on hand along with the "necessities"—white shirts and cashmere sweater sets—but we go here for the saucy little numbers to add real style to your closet!

The Cottage at Workshop, 2254 Union St. (bet. Webster & Buchanan Sts.), *Lingerie Dreams*

Enter the main door of Workshop, and ask the salesperson to escort you to the very chic and very pretty little lingerie boutique in the rear. Don't be in a rush because you will want to linger over the sexy lacey sets for hours and hours . . . and hours. . . . Designers like Laura Urbinati and Colette Dinnegan send us reeling! We would like to be in overnight, especially in the dressing room where they have a bed and nightstand to make you feel right at home. Hansel and Gretel didn't now what they were missing! Only selling sets.

Dress, 2271 Chest St. (bet. Scott & Pierce Sts.), (415) 440-3737, *Girly Boutique*

Great things come in little packages. This miniboutique specializes in the best of the best, offering exquisite pieces of clothing and jewelry for the discerning woman. The Jeanne Payer jewelry collection is mouthwatering: the little inscriptions from Dante strung on antique French ribbon are a must! For the elegantly expecting, don't miss the stylish maternity section. Open daily.

Fiori, 2314 Chestnut St. (@ Scott St.), (415) 346-1100, *Flower Power*

This is an easy yet elegant place to pick up a beautiful, fragrant bouquet on your way home or back to the hotel after a long week of meetings from #&*%! Each flower is simply displayed in tin urns à la a quiet and elegant European flower shop. It's a cash-and-carry place that delivers results with panache! If you are feeling a bit more "rooted," they have topiaries too!

Gio Cellini, 3108 Fillmore St. (bet. Filbert & Greenwich Sts.), (415) 673-1208, *Milano Peds*

For trendy Cinderellas on a knock-off budget, this is your best bet for getting a high-end copy of that Prada boot you've been craving. Neither exact copies nor exactly cheap, you will still be able to find up-to-the-minute Italian style in a chic environment for less than you would pay from one of the big boys (think Manolo!). Sleek-and-mod mod white interior mixed with friendly service makes for fun foot fantasy. Hit the festive end-of-season sales. Prices range from around $90 to $400.

Girlfriends, 1824 Union St. (bet. Octavia & Laguna Sts.), (415) 673-9544, *www.girlfriendsboutique.com, Sandra Dee Emporium*

Where was this place when we were in high school? Everything delicious and darling that your girly-girl heart desires. If you relate to Gidget and feel like throwing a grown-up gals slumber party, stock up on adorable pajamas, yummy Bliss products and Michael Stars T-shirts. Join in the "girlfest!" Open till 6 P.M. daily. *Psst . . . custom sterling silver luggage tags can be ready in a week for a great gift for your newly married girlfriend.*

House of Magic, 2025 Chestnut St. (@ Fillmore St.), (415) 346-2218, *Party Items*

Bachelorette party central. This place is a blast! Any "tools" your heart desires to make your next party one big laugh! Don't be bothered by the noisy "poot machine" blaring over the speakers. Remember the guys in sixth grade? They grew up and opened this joint. Gag gifts, "over the hill" presents, costumes and anything else you might need to torment your "victim."

Loft, 1823 Union St. (bet. Laguna & Octavia Sts.) (415) 674-0470, *www.loft-sf.com, Unique Houseware*

When visiting the loft, prepare to spend plenty of time to smell, play, touch, cuddle, relax in, and linger over and more. Enter into the double doors of the 5,000 square-foot Victorian building, smell the sweet odors of Feng Shui room spray, and relax over the indoor waterfall. It's all up-hill from there: retro furniture, an entertainment area with feel good music that ranges from Frank to bossa nova to bachelor pad collection, a kitchen area, practice your golf put of the "mat" nearby, play the bongos, read some poetry, cuddle with a stuffed bear, smell the hand dipped soaps, rub the chenille blanket in the home spa area, and then lounge on the bench in the garden. The rest if up to you to discover . . . happy exploring. *Psst . . . metered parking on the street for 2 hours max.*

Minis Kids and Maternity, 2042 Union St. (bet. Buchanan & Webster Sts.), (415) 567-9537, *www.minis-sf.com, Expandable Fashions*

Baby on the way? Shop for yourself and the "mini-me" on the way. All of the clothes are handmade in San Francisco by talented owner/designer Christine. (Support your local artists.) Mostly casual stuff for tots, in fun colors, but be sure to check out little linen dresses ($48) with matching blouses ($39)—perfect for those Sunday-best occasions. The maternity clothes are good too. Offering the popular line of Belly Basics and other handmade items to keep you looking good for nine months!

Nest, 2300 Filmore St. (@ Clay St.), (415) 292-6199, *French Flea Finds*

Rustic French interiors brought to the West Coast! Find delicious country French antiques, kitchenware and bedding at a fraction of the cost of a trip to Paris. Say bye-bye to Crate and Barrel and bring a little of the Loire Valley into your home. Bonne chance and happy hunting. Second location at 2340 Polk St. (bet. Union & Green Sts.) opening soon.

Nida, 2163 Union St. (bet. Fillmore & Webster Sts.), (415) 928-4670, *Euro Designs*

Milan meets the Golden Gate Bridge at this destination spot for Italian couture. Prada, Robert Cavalli and Costume Nationale all fight for center stage on the main floor of this trendy boutique. With an emphasis on casual Italian sportswear you can concoct a wardrobe that would make Mui Mui proud. Open 11–7 P.M. daily.

Oceana Rain, 3024 Fillmore St. (@ Union St.), (415) 326-2797, *Optimum Apparel*

Cow Hollow is filled with treasures to go to debtors' prison over, and Oceana Rain is one of them! Location aside, we would trek from anywhere when we "need" a one-stop boutique fix. Whatever you fancy is somewhere inside this place: glamour, elegance, sophistication with a bit of whimsy. They carry lines we have grown to love and kill for, like Theory, Jill Stuart, Daryl K, Katayone Adeli, William B, and Juicy jeans and tees. Loungewear is pretty and plentiful, and check out the jewelry by Sage: one-of-a-kind pieces that you may have read about in *InStyle* magazine, that all of the celebs are wearing. (God forbid we miss a Hollywood trend!) *Psst . . . the lighting is perfect to mask any imperfections visible in the dressing rooms.*

PlumpJack Wines, 3201 Fillmore St. (@ Greenwich St.), (415) 346-9870, *Affordable Wines*

Known throughout San Francisco for its forward-thinking approach to buying wine, and more importantly, to drinking wine! Not only does this shop house the best California vintages and vineyards, but they are aggressive in discovering and promoting young wineries. Their philosophy is that wine is to be "savored and enjoyed, not put on a pedestal." The shop itself is gorgeous, with custom cabinets and artistic mirrors to make all shoppers feel right at home!

Smash, 2030 Chestnut St. (@ Fillmore St.), (415) 673-4736, *Designer Shoes*

Girls, girls, girls! Take note, this is *the* destination in the area to buy your favorite European designer shoes under one roof. Names we all love and know: Stephan Keilan, Robert Cleigere, Freelance, Patrick Cox, Sigerson & Morrison, and more! We could go on and on, but we will stop wasting your precious shopping time. Our feet are smiling already at how smashing they will look lunching at French Laundry in the wine country. *Psst . . . shopping on a Saturday with your boyfriend in tow? Keep him entertained with their nice selection of men's shoes.*

Solar Light Books, 2068 Union St. (bet. Webster & Buchanan Sts.), (415) 567-6082, *www.solarlightbooks.com, Neighborhood Favorite*

For the past 28 years this charming bookstore has been a destination for those who want to enjoy the experience of book shopping *and* take home something interesting. Situated in a quasi-basement, it is much larger than it looks at first glance. Amanda, the owner for the past 10 years, stocks a fine selection of new books, specializing in fiction and psychology, but also a well-rounded collection of art and occult books. The best thing about this shop is the extremely knowledgeable sales staff. Say hello to Rosy the bookstore cat on your way out, after putting your name on the list for the store's fun newsletter. *Psst . . . rumor has it that last year Borders tried to build a megastore across the street, and the neighborhood fought to keep them away and won. You go, girl!*

Union Street Paperie, 2162 Union St. (bet. Webster & Fillmore Sts.), (415) 563-0200, *Correct Correspondence*

Sick of communication by cell phone or e-mail? This is the place for you. Tucked away on busy Union Street, they carry custom papers of every sort and style for every taste and budget. From simple gift enclosures ($3) to handmade cards ($6 each). Surprise him after a spat with a bedside card just to say "I love you—you little shit!" Special orders for parties, weddings, birth announcements, or corporate events are a specialty here. It is a girl's paper paradise! Prepare to linger.

Warm Things, 3063 Fillmore St. (bet. Union & Filbert Sts.), (415) 931-1660, *www.warmthingsonline.com, Down Comfort*

Brought to your doorstep for the past 27 years by their highly successful mail-order company, Warm Things, this city outpost has the best prices and selections of all things filled with down. You name the feathers and you'll find it here: comforters (up to $399), vests for him ($69), feather beds ($69–120), pillows (up to $98), mattress pads ($20–65), and goose down robes ($89) with matching slippers that are comfy on cold, foggy mornings in the Napa Valley. Sheets and throws available too.

◢ *Not to Miss:*

ATYS, 2149B Union St. (bet. Webster & Fillmore Sts.), (415) 441-9220, www.atysdesign.com, *Contemporary Living*

Luca Delicatessen, 2120 Chestnut St. (bet. Pierce & Steiner Sts.), (415) 921-7873, *Great Sandwiches*

The "Heights" (Pacific/Presidio/Laurel) ....

Annies, 2512 Sacramento St. (bet. Fillmore & Steiner Sts.), (415) 292-7164, *www.anniesclothing.com, Fabulous Fashions*

The New York chicks that run this joint will reinvent your style and spice up your closet with their offbeat selections from hot, hip designers: Chaiken and Capone, William B., Woo, and Furstenberg to name a few. Pick up great evening bags (denim and brocade!) and festive fur wraps to finish off the evening ensemble. Little babes will be overjoyed at the unbelievably large selection of petite day and evening wear. Whether you're dressing down, dressing up or dressing "downtown," there is a unique something for every fashion scene at this darling country-French boutique.

Artisan Cheese, 2413 California St. (@ Fillmore St.), (415) 929-8610, *Fromage Delight*

Step into a delightful cheese shop that could rival any in the south of France. The staff, mostly French (image that!), are eager to help you decide the perfect cheese to serve during cocktails before dinner, at a party for dessert, or just to have in the house to nibble all by yourself. The selection is beyond comprehensive! Linger in the clean, white space and enjoy a sample of the goat- and sheep's-milk cheeses served on white cubes of wax paper while you discuss the beauty of life and . . . well, cheese of course! Prices by the pound.

Bath Sense & More, 3610A Sacramento St. (bet. Locust & Spruce Sts.) (415) 567-2638, (800) 868-2610, *Bathing Beauties*

What better way to spend your Saturday morning than poring over lovely French soaps while deciding to go with all-new white or cream towels. It makes perfect sense to pick up all of your needful things here. Maybe a new shower curtain will bring new life to your tired bathroom. Or a cute linen pajama set to wear in the wine country on vacation with friends? This peaceful store is chock-full of your bathing needs and more. Owner Kimberly Campbell keeps us coming back time and again.

Bee Market, 3030 Fillmore St. (@ Union St.), (415) 292-2910, *Housewares*

This is *the* place to fill your new home with unique one-of-a-kind items that have that Zen feel. If Nagouchi lamps tickle your fancy, then grab your beau and spend your time (and his money!) decking out the palace with peaceful pieces.

Bettina, 3654 Sacramento St. (bet. Spruce & Locust Sts.), (415) 563-8002, *High Style*

European minimalism mixed with Asian flare creates the perfect high-fashion ambiance in this PH fashion destination. Meagen Frederiksen buys unique designs for Thiery Mugler and Kajani, along with pieces from Anna Sui and to-die-for designer lingerie. Owner Doretta Boehm has recently returned to Sacramento St. after a brief stint on Fillmore. And her loyal following has never been happier.

Bloomers, 2975 Washington St. (bet. Broderick & Divisadero Sts.), (415) 563-3286, *Sensory Overload*

A well-stocked and well-organized shop for flowers in the neighborhood. Fresh cuts, orchids and plants, and a staff of designers on hand to create interesting arrangements with branches. The store itself is so lovely that you just might want to stop in, take a peek and get a whiff. Too busy? They deliver in the city for a $7–10 fee. Reliable for all of your floral needs. Closed on Sunday. *Psst . . . don't miss their collection of antique French ribbon. Great to use as soft ties on French cuff shirts!*

Blu, 2259 Fillmore St. (@ Clay St.), (415) 776-0643, *Neighborhood Favorite*

Brought to you by the owners of nearby Cielo, this store is a bit less expensive but no less chic. It's easy to shop here . . . lots of room to breathe while you consider buying the fabulous yet practical Katayone Adell jacket or the sexy NY Industry shirt. The staff is particularly helpful without the threat of the dreadful hard sell. Make a mental note: this airy shop is worth the trek even if you are in Soma for meetings all day. Don't forget to check out the Carshoes, the most comfy shoes for the drive to the Napa Valley that transition fashionably for your lunch at French Laundry!

Brown Eyed Girl, 2999 Washington St. (@ Broderick St.), (415) 409-0215, *Neighborhood Favorite*

Home base for the San Francisco "it girl." You'll feel like you're shopping in your best friend's apartment—assuming your best friend has a gorgeous pad loaded with chic babe attire! A bit off the beaten path in this adorable neighborhood, you should beat a path to check out their nifty designer duds and cute gear! Chic yet functional. Open six days a week until 7 P.M., until 5 P.M. on Sunday.

Cielo, 2225 Fillmore St. (bet. Sacramento & Clay Sts.), (415) 776-0641, *Chic Boutique*

All trendy and chic SF girls know to make Cielo a first-stop destination when looking for something high-style. The industrial loftlike space sets the stage for its ultrachic designs from Dries Van Noten, Piazza Simpeone, or Ann Demulemeister. Cool, cool, cool. Get out your black Amex! Or, practice self-control and skip a few dinners at Plouf to save for one of these timeless creations. Excellent sales if you catch them at the right time, but then, timing is everything, darling!

The Designer Consigner, 3525 Sacramento St. (bet. Laurel & Locust Sts.), (415) 440-8664, *Investment Purchasing*

"Ain't nothin' like the real thing, baby," even if it is gently used. This chichi neighborhood find specializes in ultrahigh-fashion pieces from Chanel, Hermes, Versace, Gucci, Valentino, and more. If you're buying for the Symphony Ball, just make sure that last year's "belle of the ball" didn't consign her smashing number here! Otherwise, this is fine clothing for a fraction of what was paid retail just a season or so ago. Penny-savvy fashionistas will love it! Open seven days. No American Express accepted. *Psst . . .*

they do accept designer *clothes anytime during the week. Just ask any sales clerk to help.*

Dobson Gray, 2506 Sacramento St. (@ Fillmore St.), (415) 346-8850, *Home Gifts*

Need to pick up a gift for the hard-to-please? Here's the perfect tiny store stuffed with all things beautiful. The owners, Mark and Delia, have a great eye for treasures that are sure to please you, me and your mother-in-law! We love the lemon soaps from England ($6) for the kitchen sink, or the more elaborate Asian antique butterfly chest ($1,400). Also, check out the small yet interesting selection of wineglasses that make superlative wedding presents.

Fetish, 344 Presidio Ave. (bet. Sacramento & Clay Sts.), (415) 409-7429, *Pedi-Cares*

Gorgeous people with gorgeous feet buying gorgeous shoes. Seek out unique treats for your toes at this beautiful destination for the foot fetishist! Slinky, strappy, sturdy, sexy . . . you name it, if it's off the beaten path. Owned by Sarah Shaw and Andre Schnitzer, they are ahead of the curve of West Coast fashionistas, bringing the newest and funkiest designs to their "it" girl clientele. No more midnight calls to Bergdorf Goodman in New York City.

Fillamento, 2185 Fillmore St. (@ Sacramento St.), (415) 931-2224, *House Wares*

This place is like the pad we always thought we would have. (Our delusional side thought it would be the first year after college.) Give your abode a facelift with these postmodern treasures. Everything your heart desires can be bought or at least registered for. Tons of soon-to-be-wed Bay Area couples are seen combing the floors for slick possessions. Some furniture can be found on the fifth floor.

George, 2411 California St. (@ Fillmore St.), 441-0564, *www. georgesf.com, Neighborhood Favorite*

Calling all beauties and beasts to this citywide favorite for trend-setting pet owners and their faithful companions. If *Sex and the City* starred Mr. Ed instead of Mr. Big, he would hang here. If Burberry made pet-wear it would be here as well . . . and it probably does, but we got too caught up in the cashmere tennis balls to notice! Fun and functional; chic, not snooty—a perfect afternoon jaunt for you and the pet in your life. All-organic dog treats and custom-engraved food dishes will please even the most finicky pups. *Psst . . . if you happen to bring Spot with you to Japan on business, they have two locations there!*

Gimme Shoes, 2358 Fillmore St. (bet. Washington & Clay Sts.), (415) 441-3040, *Trendy Shoes*

See details in Downtown, other location in Hayes Valley.

GoodByes, 3464 Sacramento St. (bet. Walnut & Laurel Sts.), (415) 346-6388, *Consignment Clothes*

Lucky you. Shopaholics of all sorts, sizes and styles send their designer duds here to dump them at a fraction of the cost they paid down the street "last season" . . . which for some could actually mean three weeks ago! The neighborhood is as pristine as the goods, so grab an early yoga class down the road and then linger over the endless racks of gently used goods. It's a win-win situation. Breathe in, buy out! Open seven days a week, until 8 P.M. on Thursday. No Amex.

Liege, 2991 Sacramento St. (bet. Broderick & Divisadero Sts.), (415) 614-2123, *www.liege-sf.com, Blooming Delights*

Simple, delightful place for flowers. Order a tasteful, naturally arranged bunch to brighten your hotel room or office. Planning a wedding? Whatever your needs, ask Laura Early, the shining star, to design your flowers. She is one of the most talented floral artists in the city. City dwellers should look to owner Daniel to design a pretty garden no matter how small the space. Trust us, he is a real pro and a swell guy too! *Psst . . . Liege is a member of the by-invitation-only society of the Fine Flowers Association.*

Max Furniture, 1633 Fillmore St. (@ Geary St.), (415) 440-9002, *www.maxdsn.com, Chic Furniture*

Owner and designer James Do wins Jane accolades for taste and style. This spacious and airy furniture store is dedicated to bringing high style to your home or office. Sleek, innovative and showcased in a way that is conducive to shopping, whether you have a vision or are looking for direction. Featuring renowned emerging artists in revolving exhibitions. The adventurous and the more classically minded girl will both be satisfied with the selections here.

Mom's the Word, 3385 Sacramento St. (bet. Presidio Ave. & Walnut St.), (415) 441-8261, *Maternity Duds*

Shhh . . . If Moby were pregnant, he would shop here! Rock 'n' roll mamas-to-be will love the "to-birth-for" leather pants along with chic day, night and nightie-night wear. You may have a bun in the oven, but that doesn't mean your buns can't be cool in the meantime!

Next-to-New Shop, 2226 Fillmore St. (bet. Sacramento & Clay Sts.), (415) 567-1627, *www.jlsf.org, Charitable Consignment*

Wealthy volunteer babes will resurrect your wardrobe while you help resurrect the underprivileged of SF. Owned by the Junior League of SF, this well-stocked shop of gently used garments from SF's toniest closets is a treasure trove for the savvy shopper. Grab a Hermes scarf and help the homeless at the same time! What better way to rationalize your shopping binge? *Psst . . . the shop next door is a consignment shop owned by the same people. Call (415) 440-1500 for info.*

Paper Source, 1925 Fillmore St. (bet. Pine & Bush Sts.), (415) 409-7710, *Luscious Paper*

Wrapping, writing and gifting. Don't worry if your gift wrap costs more than your gift, it will make you look like you spent a fortune! We love the alternative gift cards and delicious writing paper and pens. . . .

The Piano Care Company/Music Shop, 2011 Divisadero St. (bet. California & Sacramento Sts.), (415) 567-1800, *Beethoven Babes*

They sell. They buy. They tune. They repair. Your ivories never looked or sounded so good. The best place in the Bay Area to piano shop.

Quatrine, 3235 Sacramento St. (bet. Lyon St. & Presidio Ave.), (415) 345-8590, *www.quatrine.com, Washable Furniture*

This white slip-covered furniture emphasizes quality of craftsmanship and is 100-percent machine washable. Gina and Bill Ellis opened their first shop in Manhattan Beach, California. Since then, they have branched out with locations in Texas, Colorado, Michigan, and Illinois. Pick your style, pick your fabric, and let the magic unfold. Alternative to the beloved Shabby Chic.

Sue Fisher King, 3067 Sacramento St. (bet. Baker & Broderick Sts.), (415) 922-7276, (888) 811-7276, *Gifts Galore*

Everything fine, fluffy and fashionable for the bed, bath and boudoir. Carrying the finest brands of bed linens (including lovely baby sheets), unique glassware, home and garden books, decorative accessories, and towels (even the European waffle style). Sleep, bathe, and lounge in luxury! Wedding registry available. *Psst . . . visit their satellite location at Wilkes Bashford in Soma.*

Surprise Party, 1900A Fillmore St. (@ Bush St.), (415) 771-8550, *Beaded Delights*

This postage stamp-sized store houses beads, beads and more beads, including fabulous one-of-kind finds. Unleash the artistic side of your personality. String these two thoughts together: relaxation with results to enjoy for years to come. Make a special beaded lampshade for your boyfriend's recently renovated office, or how about an ankle bracelet for your best friend's bachelorette party? Prices range from 30¢ to $95.

Susan, 3685 Sacramento St. (@ Spruce St.), (415) 922-3685, *Designer Clothing*

These girls are way ahead of the fashion curve. Owners Susan Foslien and Joyce Gardner are longtime fans of now-hot designers Yamamoto and Comme des Garcons. These collectible clothes are delicious. Not to be overlooked are lovely pieces by Marni (Italian), Dolce & Gabbana, and Helmut Lang. It's of-the-moment style, it's fashion forward and it's a "must-see" for all slaves to fashion. Closed Sunday.

Toujours Lingerie, 2484 Sacramento St. (@ Fillmore St.), (415) 346-3988, *www.toujourslingerie.com, Lingerie Closet*

Delightfully feminine treats that just might delight him too! If you blink you might miss this little shop filled with every surprise your lingerie-filled dreams could conjure. They carry name brands we have come to know and love: Hanro, Cosa Bella (best thong panties), sexy bustiers, white cotton pajamas, and other one-of-a-kind pieces. We prefer shopping by ourselves, for ourselves. Picking out a lavender lace bra and garter to wear under your power suit while giving a presentation to a roomful of boring men . . . fantasy indeed! We dare you to leave without a little something naughty, or nice!

Victorian House, 2033 Fillmore St. (bet. Pine & California Sts.), (415) 567-3149, *Top Consignment*

This is a chichi neighborhood for haute fashions and this is the place where "they" send theirs. Designer labels for a fraction of the price at nearby first-run stores. Be thrifty and help the needy too. All of the proceeds go to a nearby medical center. Open daily from 10 A.M. to 5 P.M. Closed on Saturday.

Zinc Details, 1905 Fillmore St. (bet. Pine & Bush Sts.), (415) 776-2100, *Zen Bazaar*

Ultimate in high design for the home of the high-tech girl! You may have heard about this place in *InStyle.* But don't be scared away by all the hype . . . there is something here for all savvy "Jane" types. Highly elegant Japanese bud vases, colorful Zenlike floating candles, VHS films of Charles and Rae Eames, a tidy backpack for picnics, tasteful paper lamp shades, stylish sushi sets, etc. Schedule a few hours to browse and dream of the possibilities. See especially the sophisticated wineglasses and vodka shot glasses and designer dishware that is to-die-for by local San Franciscan Tom Bonnauro.

✦ *Not to Miss:*

Anderson Antiques, 2799 Bush St. (@ Baker St.), (415) 351-1958. *www.AndersonAntiques.net, Quality Estate/Consigned*
Button Down, 3415 Sacramento St. (@ Walnut St.), (415) 563-1311, *Italian Men's Clothes*
Departures From the Past, 2028 Fillmore St. (@ California St.), (415) 885-3377, *Festive Vintage*
Shabby Chic, 3075 Sacramento St. (bet. Baker & Broderick Sts.), (415) 771-3881, *www.shabbychic.com, Home*
Sarah Shaw, 3095 Sacramento St. (@ Baker St.), (415) 929-2990, *www.shopsarahshaw.com, Woman's Boutique*
Papyrus, 2109 Fillmore St. (bet. California & Sacramento Sts.), (415) 474-1171, *Paper Goods*
Vintage Boutique, 560 Hayes St. (bet. Octavia & Laguna Sts.), (415) 861-7993

Hayes Valley/Civic Center

560 Hayes, 560 Hayes St. (bet. Octavia & Laguna Sts.), (415) 861-7993, *Vintage Boutique*

This place rocks when it comes to the best in vintage finds for us girly-girls. Hit the jackpot in frilly dresses from the 1950s; great handbags and shoes too. It's all special and hand-picked and waiting to find a home in your closet. Be open to the endless opportunities to stand out in unique style. Open noon–7 P.M. weekdays, 11 A.M.–6 P.M. weekends.

Alabaster's, 597 Hayes St. (@ Laguna St.), (415) 558-0482, *www.alabastersf.com, Antique Home*

Paul Davis and Nelson Bloncourt set *the* standard in the Bay Area and beyond when it comes to tasteful home furnishings. The store itself is artistically arranged and is truly a shrine to the good taste of the owners. Treasures from Italy and Paris such as high-end Venetian chandeliers, vintage alabaster lamps, stainless-steel tables custom made exclusively for the store. *Elle Décor* sings their praises, and we are right there with them!

Alla Prima, 539 Hayes St. (bet. Laguna & Octavia Sts.) (415) 864-8180, *Sex Kitten Lingerie*

See details in Nob Hill/Russian Hill/North Beach/Chinatown.

Amphora, 384A Hayes St. (bet. Gough & Franklin Sts.), (415) 863-1104, *www.amphorawine.com, Alternative Grape*

Enter the beautiful wine world of Amphora. This wine emporium carries wines not only from the beloved California region but a nice selection of French, Italian, and Australian wines as well. And for those looking for the rare find, take the Henry Higgins–style library ladder to find the wine of your dreams. Now if there was only a staircase to Mr. Right. . . . We always walk away with something new . . . as well as a minibottle of Pommery champagne complete with its own personal straw. *Psst . . . need a gift for your hard-to-please man? Great gadgets and chic travel wine openers, around $95 or so.*

Bulo, 418 Hayes St. and 437 Hayes St. (bet. Gough & Octavia Sts.), (415) 225-4939, *www.buloshoes.com, Trendy Shoes*

Gap be gone. No need to look like everyone else at the office anymore. Style-mavens and sassy girls know that this is the place in San Francisco to get "boutique" brands of high-fashion quality shoes. Some of the most sought-after brands are Cydqoq (designed by an architect), Aeffe, Roberto Del Carlo, and Camper, a must in every "Jane" girl's wardrobe and the perfect shoes to hit the crazy streets of the city. Let the ultrafriendly staff fit you in the perfect pair to satisfy all of your cravings. High fashion never felt so good, inside and out! Prices range from $150–400. *Psst . . . check out the men's collections across the street!*

Buu, 506 Hayes St. (@ Octavia St.), (415) 626-1503, *Luxurious Spoils*

After a day with the dog in Golden Gate Park, head straight here. All things we love: candles, Fresh products, Barbara Bui clothes, lamps, French perfume. . . .

A Clean Well-Lighted Place For Books, 601 Van Ness Ave. (@ Turk St.), (415) 441-6670, *Neighborhood Favorite*

If San Francisco is a melting pot, then this is a reflection of that stew. Catering to special interests and obscure subjects, this is more than just a world-renowned bookstore—it is a destination in and of itself! Regular reading and discussion groups along with special events round out the fare. Open Sunday–Thursday, 10 A.M.–11 P.M., Friday/Saturday until midnight.

Deborah Hampton, 555 Hayes St. (bet. Laguna & Octavia Sts.), (415) 701-8682, *Neighborhood Favorite*

This British-born fashion designer moved to the Bay Area in 1998 after stints with minimalist gurus Calvin Klein and Michael Kors. Since splashing onto the scene with her own collection, she has become a true SF treasure. Evoking images of her idols, YSL and one of the original "Jane" girls, Coco Chanel, her style is pure, yet innovative. The collections are consistently out of this world! Whether you fancy a feminine, symmetrical little black dress or a classic shirt, you will be the best-dressed girl in the room. The boutique itself is airy and industrial with thrift-shop fixtures. We must stop raving now! Prices range from $190 to $1,300. *Psst . . . her collection can be found at the likes of Henri Bendel in New York City and in small boutiques in Atlanta and Arizona.*

Gimme Shoes, 416 Hayes St. (bet. Gough & Octavia Sts.), (415) 864-0691, *Original Location*

See details in Downtown, other location in The Heights.

Mapuche, 500 Laguna St. (@ Hayes St.), (415) 551-0725, *Leather Lowdown*

Goldie Hawn probably carried a bag like this on the set of *Laugh In,* and we're certain her daughter, Kate Hudson, has one today. A flashback to 1970s leather works, these bags are handcrafted and hip. Embroidered motifs and no-pocket interiors are their signature, and check out the handmade shoes. All can be made to order and to match!

Ms Daisy, 225 Gough St. (bet. Fell & Oak Sts.), (415) 252-9789, *Flower Power*

Owner Maryam Salami has taken her formal training in Ikebana flower arranging and combined it with a bright and sunny garden atmosphere to bring the most hard-to-find and interesting flowers to life in Hayes Valley. Focusing her attention on offering what others can't has given her shop a unique edge for the serious flower aficionado. From wild blossoms to fragile imports, no petal is left unturned. *Psst . . . take a whiff of some fragrant chocolate cosmos and cure that craving before you take a bite of the brownie hidden in your purse!*

Worldware, 336 Hayes St. (bet. Gough & Franklin Sts.), (415) 487-9030, *Home Furnishings*

Reminds us a bit of Carlyle in Santa Monica. This store offers a comprehensive collection of stylishly classic furnishings. Custom club chairs and sofas are their specialty along with a vast array of finishes, fabrics and coverings from which to choose—over 20 types of leather alone. Delivery is speedier than most: four weeks. Gorgeous armoires, buffets, and tables from South Cone and Nusa, the former practicing reforestation and the latter appointing the trendy W hotels with their mahogany-veneered pieces. Great for browsing or seriously redefining your home!

Haight-Ashbury

Amoeba Music, 1855 Haight St., (415) 552-5095, *Killer Tunes*

We thought we'd died and gone to Music Heaven. A bowling alley in years gone by, now this transformed superstore (not the chain type) carries a wide assortment of new and used CDs, tapes, DVDs, and even trusty ol' eight-tracks. If you have been searching for something specific with no luck, we bet they have it here. If not, it most likely never existed. Spooky!

The Booksmith, 1644 Haight St. (@ Clayton St.), (415) 863-8688, *www.booksmith.com, Historic Bookshop*

Booksmith has been a fixture in the neighborhood since 1976, and has hosted some of the city's most impressive author appearances and literary readings. Some will go down in history as "events." Allen Ginsberg, Timothy Leary, and Isabelle Allende are just a few of the names to drop. In fact, science-fiction author Harlan Ellison wrote a short story while sitting in the front window of the store. Staff is ultraknowledgeable and can help find almost any book from its million-plus-title database. Out-of-towners can order via the Web.

Dishes Delmar, 1359 Waller St. (@ Delmar St.), (415) 558-8882) by appointment only, *www.dishesdelmar.com, Play House*

Situated in a lovely 1893 Victorian home, book an appointment to view some of the best collections of dishware from the 1950s and 1960s. We are talking classics like Fiestaware, Russell Wright, Tickled Pink (circa 1955), and more—some of the rarest and most comprehensive collections available in all of California. They boast clients from four continents. Remember, by appointment only. Ask for Burt.

Held Over, 1543 Haight St. (bet. Ashbury & Clayton Sts.), (415) 864-0818, *Vintage T-Shirts*

Stocking excellent vintage women's furs and leather coats, and our favorite, tons of vintage T-shirts covering the '60s, '70s, and '80s. Our picks from one shopping spree: a cool, black Starsky & Hutch; a mint-colored girly shirt with the cheesy saying "lovable" (that goes for all "Jane" girls!); and rocker's delight, a Pat Benatar '80s tour T-shirt. New shipments arrive daily. T-shirts range from $10–25. Serious collectibles could cost more.
Psst . . . they have a fantastic selection of men's suits for the adventurous man in your life. Great for a night on the town swing dancing!

Luichiny, 1529 Haight St. (bet. Ashbury & Clayton Sts.), (415) 252-7065, *www.luichiny.com, Italian Shoes*

Rock stars and girls who wish they were shop here. This groovy shop is as fashion forward as you will find in San Francisco, offering skyscraper platform shoes and boots. Pair them with a micromini, or maybe with "nothing," if you know what we mean. It's sexy, baby, for the young or the brave. *Psst . . . log on the Web site for shots from the latest Luichiny runway fashion show.*

Pipe Dreams, 1376 Haight St. (@ Masonic Ave.), (415) 431-3553, *Head Shop*

So this is what they mean by "hippie era." In Amsterdam, joints like these are a dime a dozen . . . no pun intended. In San Francisco, even for this neighborhood, this is a stretch. Purchase pipes, bongs and other tools to make your . . . smoking experience . . . more "organic." It's worth a trip even if you don't "smoke" to check out the glow-in-the-dark posters. What would this book be without mentioning the occasional subversive underbelly? Visa only. Open seven days a week from 10:00 A.M.–7:00 P.M.

PlaNet Weavers Treasure Store, 1573 Haight St. (@ Clayton St.), (415) 864-4415, *Hippie Stuff*

Let the treasure hunt begin: jump into the wacky world of PlaNet! It's just what you would expect to find in this neighborhood. Incense, wind chimes and all that's needed for your Zen moments. (And we know they are probably few and far between!) Pick up an unusual musical instrument or some of the excellent candles and gift cards. Jerry Garcia would approve! Open seven days a week from 10 A.M.–8 P.M., until 9 P.M. on Friday and Saturday.

Reckless Records, 1401 Haight St. (@ Masonic Ave.), (415) 431-3434, *Used Music*

Step off the beaten path into this nice neighborhood shop that specializes in great used CDs and vinyl. The throngs of tourists in the neighborhood have been known to devour every square inch of this area, but somehow these guys have been left untainted. Their loss is your gain!

Recycled Records, 1377 Haight St. (@ Masonic Ave.), (415) 626-4075, *www.recycled-records.com, Treasure Hunting*

Located in the counter-culture haven, this place is a wacky blast! You never know what might show up on their shelves. Serious collectors and curious visitors will find happiness when visiting this neighborhood fixture. Rare vintage LPs are just the beginning, but don't limit your hunt. How about an album of Art Deco Japanese matchbook covers or vintage Barbies still in their box? Not limited to but including CDs, posters, paper memorabilia, and rare books. It really is a business, not a museum, but their "collection" is amazing!

Revival of the Fittest, 1701 Haight St. (@ Cole St.), (415) 751-8857, *Hippie Loot*

Flower girls and hippie chicks, along with a fair share of the rest of us, can find reasonably priced jewelry, gifts, coats, hosiery, cozy sweaters, and handbags at this eclectically enticing store established in 1977. Pick up a groovy backpack and some delicious candles before you head out into this colorful neighborhood.

Shoe Biz, 1446 Haight St. (bet. Ashbury & Masonic Sts.), (415) 864-0990, *www.shoebizsf.com, Shoe Bonanza*

Talk about cornering the market! These guys have three locations on the same street. Here is the lowdown: store one has been around for 20 years and caters to teenagers and trendsetting twentysomethings, with funky platforms from Spain. Ask for Francesca. The second store, just four doors down on the same side of the street, stocks high-end Italian shoes, not famous lines like Prada or Gucci, but every bit as fashionable and well made. The third store, a block away, 1553 Haight St. (bet. Clayton & Ashbury Sts.), (415) 861-3933, carries nothing but the chicest tennis shoe—not the kind you actually play tennis in, but the latest from Puma and Adidas and more.

Taxi, 1615 Haight St. (@ Clayton St.), (415) 431-9614, *Neighborhood Favorite*

Don't miss this adorable shop with the discrete window and small sign. Be seduced by the selective collection of cool clothes from the likes of Paul & Joe, United Bamboo, Ulla Johnson, Development, Knitware by Liz Collins, Earl Jeans, and Koi Couture. Decorative and functional jewelry too, as well as cool vintage belts and unique antique brooches. A must-stop on a "Jane" shopping binge. Prices range from $50–650. *Psst . . . they share a space with Happy Trails, specializing in '50s-style Roy Rogers regalia!*

Villain's Vault, 1653 Haight St. (@ Belvedere St.), (415) 864-7727, *Sporty Wear*

Soft and pretty separates (for him too) that evoke a casual elegance in true San Francisco style. Featuring hotshot designers Helmut Lang, G-Star and William B, among others. The shoe collection is selective, focusing on chunkier styles from lines like Costume National and Dries Van Noten.

✐ Not to Miss:

Aardvark's Odd Ark, 1501 Haight St. (@ Ashbury St.), (415) 621-3141, *Cheap Vintage*

The Castro/Noe Valley

All American Boy, 463 Castro St. (bet. Market & 18th Sts.), (415) 861-0444, *Gift For Him*

If you are trapped in a *Hawaii Five-O* fantasy, buying a gift for a friend or just ogling the hot gay boys on a fashion binge, this store offers the best of the best in Hawaiian shirts. Paradise Valley will run you around $60. But FYI, don't go looking to get "leied" here . . . most likely you're sporting the wrong equipment!

The Ark, 3845 24th St. (bet. Church & Sanchez Sts.), (415) 821-1257, *www.innerchild.com, Classic Toys*

Move over, Noah! "Where once upon a time is now!" German puppets, wooden toys, fluffy animals, crafts, puzzles and games to entice and entrance your curious and brilliant progeny. A fantasyland for adults and kids alike. Check out the molding beeswax, but remember to mind your own! Open seven days a week.

Bare Necessities Luxurious Bath and Body, 421 Castro St. (@ Market St.), (415) 626-5859, *Buff 'n' Puff*

If you want to pamper yourself, find the product here! Personally, we would never leave if we had a choice. Products from all countries sit next to each other in harmony (if only the seating in the UN could be so easy). Allow plenty of time to drift around. Terax, Phyto, and Dr. Hauschka are all best-sellers, and prices are competitive. Now fill up the tub, light the candles and relax with a magazine. You deserve the best, just don't fall asleep!

Cliff's Variety, 479 Castro St. (bet. Market & 18th Sts.), (415) 431-5365, *Trinkets*

A cyber five & dime for the New Millennium. From killer costumes to comfy towels, it's a little bit of everything rolled up into one. Maybe best known for its selection of Halloween costumes and fabrics, not to mention drag queen attire, you can also find household paints and other sundries while you're at it. Where else can you get wallpaper and feather boas in the same basket?

Crossroads Trading Company, 2231 Market St. (bet. Noe & Sanchez Sts.), (415) 626-8989, *www.crossroadstrading.com, Used Clothing*

All roads lead to this great one-stop-shopping spot if you're looking for that perfect "something" from the past five decades, even the not-so-long-ago 1990s. Take home a '50s fitted dress, a '60s flowery shirt, a '70s patent bag, an '80s denim shirt, or a '90s pair of "gently used" Levi's. They stock a fantastic selection of Levi's. Open 11 A.M.–7 P.M., until 8 P.M. Fri, Sat. *Psst . . . clean out your closet and bring your oldies but goodies here for resale. They buy, sell and trade, all day, for 40 percent in cash on the spot or 50 percent in trade.*

Don't Panic, 541 Castro St. (@ 18th St.), (415) 553-8989, *www.don't-panic.com, Gift Emporium*

It's all the rage, and we wouldn't be caught without one of the fun T-shirts at this emporium. We love the "super concentrated bitch" tee that is screened to look like a Tide box, or "I love being the princess." We could never relate, but appreciate the thought! Gag gifts like penis pasta for bachelorette parties, glow-in-the-dark stuff, alternative CDs, toys, stickers (rainbow peace signs!), and gift cards. It's an entertaining place with plenty of objects to live without, and lots to smile about.

a girl and her dog, 3932 24th St. (bet. Sanchez & Noe Sts.), (415) 643-0346, *Lovely Fashions*

Literally—a girl, Annette, and a dog, Bronte, a Yorkshire Terrier, greet you as you begin your treasure hunt for "of the moment" designs and designers. We love the "one of each size per style" offerings from Chaiken, Theory, Fondu, Jill Stuart, and Catherine Maladrino. From daytime to nightlife you will prowl the city in style. Thanks to fashion advice from man's best friend and his hip diva master!

Harvest Ranch Market, 2285 Market St. (@ Noe St.), (415) 626-0805, *Health Food Shop*

All things organic. Not your run-of-the-mill supermarket; find anything and everything for your healthy lifestyle. Not so healthy? Jump-start your fitness program with their selection of trendy juices, veggies, grains, and salad bar extravaganza. Gourmet millet never looked so good!

Joseph Schmidt Confections, 3489 16th St. (@ Sanchez St.), (415) 861-8682, *Chocolate Dreams*

Eye-catching designs and edible sculpture are Joseph's specialties! Never has chocolate been so artistically designed. European-style hand-made confections for all seasons or any day of the week except Sunday. Delight in the egg-shaped truffles from the finest Belgian chocolate.

Just For Fun & Scribbledoodles, 3982 24th St. (bet. Noe & Sanchez Sts.), (415) 285-4068, *Gifts, Cards & More*

We don't quite know what a scribbledoodle is, but we do know that this place caters to your needs for cards, custom invitations and stationery. Need a gift on the run? They house a great collection of children's books and toys. Have fun and take a stab at your own scribbledoodle!

Rolo, 450 Castro St. (bet. Market & 18th Sts.), (415) 626-7171; 2351 Market St. (bet. Noe & Castro Sts.), (415) 431-4545, *www.rolo.com, Trendy Girl/Guy*

Gift for your oh-so-cool beau? Or maybe you need to liven up your wardrobe now that you have adopted the dot-commer style of dressing down. Street fashions for the twentysomething set who love the idea of wearing cutting-edge British imports, shirts bearing the names of old-fashioned sports clubs like "Havana" (for him) or something new from the fast-selling Nice Collective. While you're at it, pick up a pretty Barbara Bui jacket or some great-fitting jeans by Earl or Daryl K. The women's clothes are a bit more serious and more pricey. It's all in good fun. Open seven days a week until 8 P.M., 7 P.M. on Sunday. See other location in Downtown.

Streetlight Records, 3979 24th St. (@ Noe St.), (415) 282-3550, *www.slrecords.com, Cool Tunes*

The best of all worlds: records bought, sold and traded. Trade in your old, tired Willie Nelson LPs for a new Thievery Corporation disc. One girl's trash is another girl's treasure! Selling? They buy daily until 9 P.M.

The fee depends upon the title and the condition of your goods . . . you will get 25 percent more if you trade versus receive cash. See other location, 2350 Market St. (@ Castro St.), (415) 282-8000.

✦ *Not to Miss:*

Cover to Cover, 3812 24th St. (@ Church St.), *www.covertocoversf.com,* (415) 282-8080, *Read Easy*

Designer's Club, 3899 24th St. (@ Sanchez St.), (415) 648-1057, *Neighborhood Favorite*

Medium Rare Records, 2310 Market St. (@ Noe St.), *www.newcast.com/ mediumrare.com,* (415) 255-7273, *Alternative Recordings*

Mission
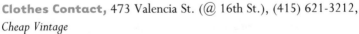

Aquarius Records, 1055 Valencia St. (bet. 21st & 22nd Sts.), (415) 647-2272, *Alternative Tunes*

Don't expect to find Michael Bolton music here. Calling all true record geeks! Think *High Fidelity* but, believe it or not, these sales guys are funnier. Wendy, the "girly" owner, stocks awesome CDs for the alternative cravings of punk, drum'n' bass, rap, and techno, with a bit of regular old music thrown in. Short descriptions of new music will help even a novice decide what to buy.

Borderlands Books, 866 Valencia Street, (888) 893-4008, *www.border-lands-books.com, Specialty Books*

These guys love books, mainly science fiction, fantasy, horror, and some "fringe." Even if you arrive five minutes before closing time, the knowledgeable staff will gladly help you find the book of your fantasy from the cheap paperback to the rarest first edition. Clean and user friendly.

Clothes Contact, 473 Valencia St. (@ 16th St.), (415) 621-3212, *Cheap Vintage*

Here is the fashionable "bag lady" deal: for $8 per pound, take home all the vintage clothing you can carry. This is the premier by-the-pound shop in the Bay Area. Most of the pieces arrive in large crates from around the world, so it really is a hit-or-miss situation. Great for costumes . . . or if you enjoy the hunt! The store plays cool mix tapes while the young, eager and heavily pierced rove the racks. Good luck, my friend.

Currents, 911 Valencia St. (@ 20th St.), (415) 648-2015, *www.currentssf.com, Pamper Central*

Adorable place on the main drag in Mission to buy candles, potpourri, massage oils (not that kind, you naughty girl!), bath tea bags, and organic soaps. It's a peaceful place to drift in and drift out of with no hassle. Ask about the frequent-shopper's card that gives a discount based on your frequency of purchasing different items in the shop. Favorite perk? Make your own lavender sachet.

Dema, 1038 Valencia St. (@ 21st St.), (415) 206-0500, *Neighborhood Favorite*

Betty Boop meets the girl next door in this mod shop for separates and baby doll dresses. Everything for fun, sun, skateboarding and strutting— little tees and beyond. Think Audrey in Capri pants and sweater set on her bicycle. Dema Grim is now a local favorite and a must-go on your shopping spree in San Fran! Open 11 A.M.–7 P.M. daily, until 6 P.M. on Sunday.

Fishbowl, 3253 16th St. (bet. Guerrero & Dolores Sts.), (415) 934-1726, *Trendy Finds*

Hip clothes brought to you by British cool girl Adrian Leong. Housing some of the best up-to-the-minute fashions for the high-fashion edge-seekers. Whatever the hot look of the moment, find it here. In fact, buy it when you see it because it could be out of style by the time you figure out what to wear with it! Dresses, jeans, T-shirts, and some shirts for men too. Continually on the "best of" lists in the city.

Home Remedies, 1026 Valencia St. (bet. 21st & 22nd Sts.), (415) 826-2026, *Home Furnishings*

Presto duomo! Order custom designs and get delivery in less than three weeks! Pottery Barn was never this cool or efficient! Find great furniture and great gifts in this one-of-a-kind neighborhood merchant. Transition is tough, so make your life easier by choosing interior design's equivalent to comfort food. Bridal registry too.

International Market Gallery Home, 819 Valencia St. (bet. 19th & 20th Sts.), (415) 643-5221, *Ethnic Housewares*

Looking to revamp your pad on the cheap? This is a large loftlike space that houses some great pieces of furniture, rugs and large accessories, all from Turkey and India. The Kilim rugs are new but sure to make any drab room come alive with festive style. The prices are astoundingly low for such high-quality goods. The friendly but not overly pushy sales staff makes it even more enjoyable to poke around for hidden bargains. Open six days a week until 8 P.M., 7 P.M. on Sunday.

Laku, 1069 Valencia St. (bet. 21st & 22nd Sts.), (415) 695-1462, *Flirty Clothes*

Girls flock from all over the city for one-of-a-kind pretty things. Little hats, antique jewelry and Yaeko Yamashita's princesslike slippers are in high demand. The store is tiny, and the pale pink walls with painted striped wood floor create an ideal backdrop to fulfill your dreams. *Psst . . . check out the adorable miniature versions of the pointy slippers for children—so cute that they might incite maternal urges!*

Modern Times, 888 Valencia St. (@ 20th St.), (415) 282-9246, *Favorite Books*

This bookstore is worthy of a trip, even from across town. Think the opposite of a chain! Their excellent selection of books will challenge your mind and expand your horizons, including new fiction, cultural theory and revolutionary rhetoric, as well as every imaginable unconventional magazine! As the neighborhood dictates, there is a large selection of Spanish-language offerings. Come relaxed and with plenty of time to explore the possibilities. We would bet our own purchase of a book on the writings of Plato that Che Guevara would approve!

Rayon Vert, 3187 16th St. (bet. Valencia & Guerrero Sts.), (415) 861-3516, *Japanese Memorabilia*

Psycho tchotchkes and antique collectibles board the Orient Express. A cornucopia of unique and arty finds . . . from mint julep cups to paint-by-number still-lifes. No one ever said the Mission District wasn't funky and here's your proof! *Psst . . . write mysterious love notes to your shy guy on the Japanese stationery hiding in the back. . . .*

Retrofit Vintage, 910 Valencia St. (bet. 20th & 21st Sts.), (415) 550-1530, *Retro Clothes*

Watch for the old-fashioned seated hair dryer with leopard upholstery, and you'll know that you have arrived! Find a vintage leather jacket for a great price. The selection is vast, although most "vintage" items tend to run in small to medium sizes. Prices range from $40 to $125. Cool vintage dresses (in very small sizes) too. All credit cards accepted, as well as ATM debit cards.

Schauplatz, 791 Valencia St. (@ 19th St.), (415) 864-5665, *Top Vintage*

It's all cheap and chic, so to speak. This is one of the best places in all of San Francisco to buy killer vintage accessories (a pristine Lucite purse), clothing (a Pucci wrap dress), and furniture (upstairs) that will turn your boring loft into a shagadelic place. Groovy, baby!

Tall Stories, 2141 Mission St., Suite 304 (bet. 17th & 18th Sts.), (415) 255-1951, *Antique Books*

If lingering in big chairs over a serious collection of antique books appeals to you, do we have the scoop! This secret hideaway is on the second floor and doesn't even have much of a sign. Press the buzzer on the ground floor and enter this delightful playland for intellectuals and wannabes. Pore over first editions or an unusual book. Believe it or not, the stock turns over quickly, so be prepared to dish out serious cash on the spot. But remember, there is no charge to look and linger!

Valencia Cyclery, 1077 and 1065 Valencia St. (bet. 21st & 22nd Sts.), (415) 550-6600, *Cycle-Rama*

Every outdoorsy city claims to be the inventor of the mountain bike. But if you hit the trails on Marin's Mount Tam, riding is believing! Stocking the largest selection of bikes and all of the tricks that go along, plus the overall best prices in town. This is *the* one-stop destination if you are looking to get going with your New Year's resolution to "get in shape" . . . again. Open seven days a week, closing at 4 P.M. on Sunday. Prices range from $300 to $1,300.

Not to Miss:

Discolandia, 2964 24th St. (bet. Harrison & Alabama Sts.), (415) 826-9446, *Disco Diva*

Ritmo Latino, 2401 Mission St. (@ 20th St.), (415) 824-8556, *Latin Music*

Other Neighborhoods ....

Beauty Mark, 605 Irving St. (bet. 7th & 8th Aves.), Sunset, (415) 564-9396, *Beauty Supplies*

Since 1989, Beauty Mark has been providing the neighborhood with 4,000 products, including hair dye, shampoo (Paul Mitchell, KMS, Goldwell), gels and stellar, salon-quality flatirons and blow dryers. Worth the investment if you want to recreate that "in" sleek-tressed look on your own! *Psst . . . the salon on premises offers color, highlights and cuts.*

First Chop, 954 Irving St. (@ 11th Ave.), Sunset, (415) 564-7030, *Pre-Owned Bonanza*

Demand first quality at second-rate prices! First Chop, an Anglo-Indian expression coined during the time of the British Colonial Empire, means "first in quality, stature or position." Owner Janet Meinsma seeks out customers to consign the best of the recent past—much of which has never been worn. She will act as your personal shopper and search out the item desired to meet specific tastes and budgets. Your selections will be hanging in the dressing room ready to try on by the time you arrive at the store! Armani, Comme des Garcons, Jil Sander, Yamamoto, Hermes Kelly bags, and much, much more,

Green Apple Books, 506 Clement (@ 6th Ave.), (415) 387-2272, *Heady Pursuits*

Calling all bookworms to the core of the literary apple. Get lost for the day, or the week, in the delightfully mazelike nooks and crannies of this used-book emporium. Voted best and brightest year after year by its loyal San Franciscan clientele, you will be delighted by the overwhelming selection, knowledgeable staff, fantastic bargains and charmingly musty ambiance. New titles also available with handwritten recommendations by the staff! Love it!

Le Video, 1239 9th Ave. (bet. Lincoln Way & Irving St.), Sunset, (415) 566-3606, *Alternative Video*

This is our pick for the greatest indie-owner video store, stocking a notable selection of European, Japanese, and Indian films along with the usual suspects—over 65,000 titles. We dare you not to find what you are looking for, from the bland to the bizarre! Remember *Liquid Sky*? DVDs and LaserDiscs too!

Twilight

Downtown/Soma/Union Square

Azie, 816 Folsom St. (bet. 4th & 5th Sts.), (415) 538-0918, *Trendy*

This is a romantic place to take your honey and neck in privacy behind a curtain that closes around your own booth while a DJ spins sexy tunes. Mostly known for its outstanding French Asian fare, another good reason to book a table at this Soma hot spot. Order a bottle of wine, eat in leisure, and chill out at this red-hot newcomer. *Psst . . . it's situated next door to one of SF's favorite places to dine, Lulu's, 816 Folsom (@ 4th St.), (415) 495-5775, which was one of the first to venture to this seeming culinary wasteland. It is a great alternative if you are not in the mood to romance and rock.*

Bacar, 448 Brannan St. (bet. 3rd & 4th Sts.), (415) 904-4100, *Trendy Eats/Drinks*

Nestled off the beaten path among the high-tech companies, this place knows how to make a killer cocktail. Downstairs is the lounge area, with comfy couches and such. Upstairs, the restaurant serves a seafood-based menu with an extensive wine list. However, downstairs, thanks to the talented bartenders, you can order whatever your heart desires. Ask bartender Tina Wilson to help when you want to get really creative. Of course, she'll make modern-day standards like the Cosmopolitan or Lemon Drop, but try something different, from the early twentieth century, when generations before you developed some of the classics that are still favorites today. Serving food until 1 A.M., drinks until 2 A.M.

Backflip, @ The Phoenix Hotel, 601 Eddy St. (@ Larkin St.), (415) 771-3547, *Beautiful People*

Viva Las Vegas! Think of an Elvis Presley movie set blended with Austin Powers's apartment and that's what you get! The bar/club wraps around one side of the 1950s-style, kitschy Phoenix Hotel (see Tripping, Hayes Valley, Sweet Dreams) and overlooks the swimming pool. Show up at this mod spot and spend happy hour with other stylish locals, grouped around the doughnut-shaped bar in a room that is swathed in sparkly blue everything (Fridays, 5–7 P.M.). Listen to groovy tunes and munch on a few appetizers. Then, hit the dance floor, baby, and work off all the week's frustrations. Sometimes it can be a velvet-rope situation, so make a pretty mouth and use your mojo. Open Tues.–Sat., 7 P.M.–2 A.M. *Psst . . . This is*

151

the somewhat-scary Tenderloin section of town, so be sure to have someone help get a taxi when you leave at night. Preferably the cute guy you met earlier!

Bamboo Hut, 479 Broadway (bet. Kearny & Montgomery Sts.), (415) 989-8555, *Tiki Bar*

Remnants of Trader Vic's, with bamboo lining the walls and a full palapa bar, presided over by a large 1948 tiki-god statue. Tropical cocktails are a must, but don't miss the flaming volcano; it is a mainstay. Super Tiki happy hour is a blast from 5–8 P.M., Thur. and Fri. *Psst . . . private parties are encouraged and offered.*

Cityscape, @ The Hilton San Francisco & Towers, 333 O'Farrell St. (bet. Mason & Taylor Sts.), (415) 923-5002, *Room With A View*

We could argue for days about who has the best rooftop view of the city, but after careful consideration, we deem this place the winner! This rooftop restaurant and bar is situated on the top of the Downtown Hilton, so find the elevator and head up. Go for sunset and sit on the right side (from the entrance) of the room, where the top-to-bottom glass showcases a view that's truly sweeping and breathtaking! After one peek, you too will follow Tony Bennett's adage and leave your heart in San Francisco!

Fifth Floor, @ Hotel Palomar, 12 4th St. (@ Market St.), (415) 348-1555, *Hidden Jewel*

Heavenly French food in a sleek setting for those who want a discreet meeting place for cocktails and appetizers at the end of a rough day. The food is really the focus at the French restaurant that is a foodie dream destination. We love to sit in the front bar and sip incredible wines sold by the half glass, perfect for creating your own wine tasting, and sample an interesting cheese platter. They are actually located on the fifth floor of the hot new Hotel Palomar (see Tripping, Downtown, Sweet Dreams).

Ginger's Trois, 246 Kearny St. (bet. Sutter & Bush Sts.), (415) 989-0282, *Alternative Bar*

Come one, come all to this odd little clubby bar that is squarely out of place among the tall buildings in the Financial District! It's a strange place, with a disco ball and walls covered in Ginger Rogers posters (hence the name). The jukebox is as eclectic as the crowd, a mixed bag of drag queens, gays and financial whiz kids, all looking to drink the night away in a nonintimidating atmosphere. Open 10 A.M.–10 P.M. daily; Sat., 2 P.M.–10 P.M.

Grand Café, 501 Geary St. (@ Taylor St.), (415) 292-0101, *After Dinner*

Who would have known that this bar/café attached to the Hotel Monaco (see Tripping, Downtown, Sweet Dreams) used to be an all-night coffee shop? It is a "grand" art deco/nouveau space, built at the turn of the century, complete with vaulted ceilings, museum-quality original art, and attentive wait staff. Late night is fun for drinks after a show at the nearby historic Fillmore Auditorium (see Tripping). The crowd is a nice mix of local, business travelers, and in-the-know touristas. Either way, it's always a preferred destination. Scarlett would have been right at home, and fellow Southerner Wynonna Judd was spotted sipping margaritas at the bar on our last visit! *Psst . . . Rock n' Roll Hall of Famer Carmine Appice, drummer from Metallica, is a regular, as well as other local luminaries.*

Harry Denton's Starlight Room, 450 Powell St. (@ Sutter St.), (415) 395-8595, *Room With A View*

A glamour-girl haven awaits on the 21st floor of the Sir Francis Drake Hotel! Harry Denton is as much a local icon as the Golden Gate Bridge, and this is his Grand Dame establishment. Equal parts supper club and bar. Wear your prettiest dress and red lipstick, and sip the famous Starlight chocolate martini. Refinement in a neat little package does not come cheap, but the view alone is worth maxing out your Visa for! Don't be surprised if you ride the elevator up with Warren Beatty, who has been spotted cavorting here. Open 4:30 P.M.–2 A.M. daily.

The High Ball Lounge, 473 Broadway (bet. Kearny & Montgomery Sts.), (415) 397-9464, *Retro/Live Music*

A classic alternative to the regular nightclub scene. If you are not looking to hang with the twentysomethings, this is the perfect destination to rock to cool DJs (some from Paris or New York), or just to recorded music.

Hotel Utah Saloon, 500 4th St. (@ Bryant St.), (415) 421-8308, *Unwind*

Time to let your hair down, girlfriend! If you are looking to relax in an old-fashioned two-level bar with a beautiful balcony for sitting and watching local singer/songwriters and other acoustic acts, this is our pick in Soma.

The stage is small but the intentions are pure. Offering standard but good pub fare (go for the veggie chili and a microbrew). Small cover charge, under $5 nightly. *Psst . . . Monday's are open mike night, so bring your guitar and your guts!*

Infusion, 555 2nd St. (bet. Bryant & Brannan Sts.), (415) 543-2282, *After Work/Late Night*

Vodka-infused drinks and bistro fare are enough of a reason for us to go anywhere! But this special Soma hangout is the best place to sip creative concoctions, like watermelon-flavored cocktails, and nibble on mussels and garlic fries or mashed potatoes and roast chicken until 1 A.M. on the weekends. Or, go with a group of friends after work or late at night with a friend. Even if the crowd is dull, after a few of the inventive drinks, everyone seems interesting! Just don't blame us for your hangover—sweet drinks always seem to make your morning a bit foggy!

Le Colonial, 20 Cosmo Place (bet. Post & Taylor Sts.), (415) 931-3600, *Power Scene*

Socialites and dot-commers commune here. Formerly Trader Vic's, they left all of the paper umbrellas behind, but everything else has changed. The second-floor balcony is ideal for holding court, or just holding hands. After work meet the girls if you are in one of "those moods," or meet your beau and nibble on tasty Vietnamese spring rolls and spareribs. Alert: smoking allowed on the outdoor patio. Shocking!

London Wine Bar, 415 Sansome St. (bet. Sacramento & Clay Sts.), (415) 788-4811, *Mingle*

These guys were a wine bar before wine bars were the hot thing. Since 1974, when we were still sipping Shirley Temples with our parents at the club, well-heeled San Franciscan oenophiles have been enjoying fine wine by the glass. Its close proximity to the Financial District keeps it brimming with handsomely dressed men and women, and the set-up encourages privacy and conversation. Now it's up to you to figure out how to meet him. Pricey, but not overly so.

Paradise Lounge, 1501 Folsom St. (@ 11th St.), (415) 621-1912, *Rock Out*

This is a true San Francisco institution when it comes to huge but still cool places to see rock bands from one of the three stages and bars. It is a bit of a crapshoot as to the quality of the group—some can be painful—but rest assured, it is always a good time if you are in the mood.

Blue Lalique @ Shanghai 1930, 133 Steuart St. (bet. Howard & Mission Sts.), (415) 896-5600, *Sexy Cocktails*

Looking for a place to go for a romantic cocktail? This chic bar at this restaurant places you in Shanghai in the 1930s, where authentic glamour meets the New Millennium. Sit at the bar and face the gorgeous turquoise blue backlit wall, or nuzzle in one of the mohair tub chairs with low ceilings and Ella Fitzgerald tunes in the background. The crowd is part Euro, part Chinese, and part those who just want to enjoy the peace and serenity of this chic nightspot. Bear the (unbearable staff's) attitude, it is worth it. *Psst . . . the food is amazing, with a 45-dollar prix-fix menu. Or ask for a peek into the Guanxi Lounge, a private, membership-only, secret section for cigar lovers and a more private bar. For $3,000 you too can join!*

Sno-Drift, 1830 3rd St. (bet. 16th & Mariposa Sts.), (415) 431-4766, *Dance Party*

This place is red-hot, with its finger on the pulse of what's happening downtown right now! This bar/nightclub is modeled after a funky 1960s ski lodge. It truly feels like a big ball of snow that rolled down a hill and, *poof,* turned into a kitschy lodge for après ski cocktails! There are two parts to the somewhat compact club: the front, which is actually the rear because you enter from the back side, is a bar for hanging around a fireplace and chatting. The "back" is a large dance space with backlit walls, raging tunes, and a rocking dance floor. The weekend crowds tend to be a bit bridge and tunnel but it's still a blast. Cover is $20 on weekends. (There's an ATM machine inside in case you need cash!) *Psst . . . be sure to arrange transportation to and from because it is located off the beaten path and could be difficult to get home from without a car.*

Up and Down Club, 1151 Folsom St. (bet. 7th & 8th Sts.), (415) 626-2388, *Live Music*

For the past ten-plus years this has been reliable destination to hear live music. You never know what's happening at this bi-level club. Downstairs, it's all about the candlelit, curved bar and the latest in sophisticated live music; sometimes it's jazz, or maybe a hip hop group, or some vibey soul. Upstairs is a more casual spot, with a DJ spinning loud avant tunes on an oh-so-small dance floor. Open Thurs–Sat., 9–2 P.M. Call for daily listing of who is playing. *Psst . . . rumor has it that supercool supermodel Christy Turlington is part owner and shows up on occasion to check in and check out the scene.*

XYZ, @ The W Hotel, 181 3rd St. (@ Howard St.), (415) 817-7836, *Neighborhood Favorite*

The Downtown/Soma area is crawling with partygoers on any given night, looking for a place to sip cocktails in a mod environment. And the W Hotel restaurant/bar is just the place to park your group. It sets the standard in design and style, attracting the most diverse crowd in Soma. Part Euro, part yuppie, plus random hotel guests. Make this a high priority on your list on any night out. *Psst . . . brides (yes, in white gowns) are continuously seen having a preconsummation cocktail with friends—perhaps for a little liquid ambition before they head to their honeymoon suites!*

Not to Miss:

C Bobby's Owl Tree, 601 Post St. (@ Taylor St.), (415) 776-9344, *Quirky*

Pow!, 101 6th St. (@ Mission St.), (415) 278-0940, *Attention Grabber*

Nob Hill/Russian Hill/North Beach/Chinatown

The Big Four Restaurant, @ The Huntington Hotel, 1075 California St. (@ Taylor St.), (415) 771-1140, *www.big4restaurant.com, Husband Hunting*

This elegant restaurant and bar is situated in the ultrafabulous Huntington Hotel (see Tripping, Nob Hill, Sweet Dreams). Step into a dimly lit room with dark wood paneling and hunter green banquettes, deeply steeped in California history. (Specifically, the "Big 4" was named after four nineteenth-century railroad tycoons: C.P. Huntington, Charles Crocker, Leland Stanford, and Mark Hopkins.) The walls are covered with original artifacts, historical photos and other memorabilia. We prefer to go for cocktail hour at the small bar, and nibble on Tuna Tartare with White Truf-

fle Oil ($13) and sip scotch. You just never know who might sit down next to you. Maybe a Jack Kerouac lookalike or a fat cat millionaire who's migrated from across the street at the all-male members-only Pacific Union Club. Conducive to conversation, or just a quiet drink if you are solo. *Psst . . . in the mood to sit and dine? The restaurant is fabulous, including an award-winning wine list. Reservations recommended.*

Bimbo's 365 Club, 1025 Columbus Ave. (bet. Chestnut & Francisco Sts.), (415) 474-0365, *Live Music*

Dress up and look fabulous at this highbrow nightclub/lounge for girls who are looking for a swanky destination to hear an avant selection of live music while guzzling chilly cocktails. Ranging from rock to soul to R&B, it's always amusing and features rising stars on their path to fame and fortune. This is a family-owned place with a lovely interior: plush red-velvet curtains, oversized candelabra, and what every true bar should have, a mirrored disco ball. When the band takes a break, venture to the separate room where a huge fishbowl awaits. The food is unremarkable; cover varies with the act, and they're open only for performances. *Psst . . . feeling lucky? You just might catch a glimpse of sometime guest appearances of the "Girl in the Fishbowl"—a live mermaid model, mainly for private parties.*

Bix, 56 Gold St. (bet. Jackson & Pacific Sts.), (415) 433-6300, *Sophisticated Supper Club*

"Some enchanted evening, you will meet a stranger," and it could be tonight! Located in a Jackson Square alleyway, this is about as good as it gets when it comes to finding an authentic Art Deco supper club that reeks of history and timeless elegance. The long, dark mahogany bar invites you to sip champagne and relax. Even in a neighborhood known for its strip joints, this place is perfect to take your well-heeled client or your loaded date. The menu is pricey but worth it (try the steak tartare made table-side). *Psst . . . take an original Bix souvenir to your friends back home. Sounds cheesy, but this place is a San Francisco classic.*

Black Cat & Blue Bar, 501 Broadway (@ Kearny St.), (415) 981-2233, *Historic/Live Music*

Owned by famed restaurateur Reed Hearon (of nearby Rose Pistola's), this is a living tribute to the bohemian nightclub lifestyle of San Francisco in its glory years. It's part brasserie, serving classic San Francisco noodle dishes and seafood specialties (thanks to its close proximity to Chinatown and Fisherman's Wharf) in a white-tiled, red-leather setting. Downstairs is the Blue Bar, home to some of the best live jazz, that is brimming with excitement nightly. There are 60 seats and plenty of standing room. It's sleek and swanky, with a blue upholstered bar, blue carpet, and zebrawood tables. Happy hour from 5:30–8:30 P.M. daily. Closed on Sundays. Cover charge varies. *Psst . . . surprise your honey for his birthday with a private party. They happily rent out the space.*

Caffè Proust, 1801 McAllister St. (@ Baker St.), (415) 345-9560, *www.caffeproust.com, Culture Vultures*

Get your culture fix here: if you like a side of literature with your linguine, check out Caffè Proust. Okay, so linguine's not on the menu, but other pastas are. The restaurant is a tribute to the writer, featuring "Proust references everywhere" (to quote its menu), as well as serving as home base for the Marcel Proust Support Group (www.proust.com). CP is also a tribute to cafè living "circa late-century San Francisco" (to quote its Web site), and has the aura of a Parisian café, where stories are shared, ideas are fomented, and wine is drunk. The food is good, the menu is good reading, the service is attentive, and no one rushes you from your table—although the lack of cushioning on the chairs might. We have only one quibble: no tiramisu! (A cannoli just isn't the same.) Cash only.

Cypress Club, 500 Jackson St. (bet. Columbus Ave. & Montgomery St.), (415) 296-8555, *Unique Setting*

Stepping out with your honey tonight, or your boss who just took the company public? This is *the* place to go for cocktails in a luxurious but somewhat Dali-esque 1940s-style supper club. The surreal décor is pretty and sensual in every way, with great jazz in the background to serenade you as you sip an ice-cold "Lucy & Ricky Limon Drop" among others who have good taste, at least when it comes to where to go for a lovely night on the town. Serving high-end entrees until 11 P.M. on weekends, drinks nightly until "after midnight."

Emma, @ The San Remo Hotel, 2237 Mason St. (bet. Chestnut & Francisco Sts.), (415) 673-9090, *Time Travel*

Slip inside this toast to yesteryear and toast anything! The gorgeously restored vintage atmosphere will lure you in and make you lose track of time and space. . . . Then again, maybe that's the Dewar's talking! While away the evening or the entire day at the long wooden bar, watching the sun set through the giant glass windows with a beloved friend, or a beloved, surrounded by stained glass, inlaid tiling, antique posters and streetcar signs. An absolute throwback to another time, when modems weren't à la mode. . . . Guinness, Bass, and Pilsner Urquell (try it!) are all available on tap, or try the house specialty, the perpetually icy-cold and delicious Anna Martini.

Enrico's, 504 Broadway (@ Kearny St.), (415) 982-6223, *People Watching*

San Francisco's best sidewalk scene. Situated in the heart of North Beach, where nightlife is alive and well, this is a fine place to hang out with a group. Best Mojito's in the Bay Area. Jazz enthusiasts will enjoy the occasional live music to set the stage for your big night out. Good thing you bought that new skirt at Loehmann's, now affording eight exotic cocktails doesn't seem to hurt at all. Just don't blame us for your "pleasure" hangover.

Gino & Carlo, 548 Green St. (bet. Grant Ave. & Stockton St.), (415) 421-0896, *Institution*

For 50-plus years this North Beach landmark has been serving the neighborhood proudly. Don't look for Gino or Carlo because they're no longer around, but do expect to find a wide variety of characters holding court at the small wooden bar. Great place to chill out on a weeknight and play a relaxed game of pool on one of the two tables in the rear. It gets superpacked on weekends but we still fight our way in to be part of all that's happening in this true San Francisco treasure. Open daily, 6 P.M.–2 A.M.

Globe, 290 Pacific Ave. (bet. Battery & Front Sts.), (415) 391-4132, *Late Nite*

We love our late-night rendezvous at this ever-so-chic eatery. It feels like a sleek, industrial Manhattan restaurant with exposed brick walls and indirect lighting. Go for the excellent innovative cuisine (reservations recommended), but stay for the late-night action at the bar. It's known for being the hangout for all of the top chefs in the city. We have met a few of the top guys ourselves here! A perfect stopover after a "night in the kitchen" or for a late-night drink after a long plane ride in from the East Coast. No matter who or what or when we are planning a night out, a visit to the Globe always comes up as an option. Open until 1 A.M. nightly. *Psst . . . be sure to arrange for transportation ahead of time because they are on a strangely desolate street. Or just call for a taxi (see Trauma) when you are ready to go.*

The Concession Stand @ Golden Gate Ferry, Ferry Building, (bet. Embarcadero & Market Sts.), (415) 923-2000, *Special Cocktail*

There's nothing particularly special about the Bloody Marys served on the ferryboats that embark, many times a day, for Sausalito and Larkspur. Your basic vodka, tomato juice, and Tabasco in a plastic cup—nothing so captivating as, for instance, the wasabi-and-sake-informed concoction prepared at Ponzu—but the setting can't be beat. There's the salty, briny air; the rhythmic swaying beneath your feet; the wheeling seagulls and the bobbing sailboats and the stiff western breeze. And, at one special confluence, there's the city to your left, Mount Tamalpais to your right, and the Golden Gate Bridge and the Pacific Ocean straight ahead. If you time it so the sun is setting and the lights are coming up at just that moment, you'll agree: no Bloody Mary ever tasted so good.

Hyde-Out, 1068 Hyde St. (@ California St.), (415) 441-1914, *Solo*

The tons of windows at this great neighborhood spot make for great people-watching. Even if you are alone, you won't be afraid to plop yourself at one of the 20 seats at the bar and order one of the 30 beers on tap. Upstairs there is a small space to watch the busy street below or to grab a little kiss in privacy. Cable cars stop right in front, so the crowd is always a nice mix of locals, tourists, and young executives. Take along some single bills because it's impossible to not be inspired by the awesome jukebox, with Nina Simone, Moby, Dean Martin, Beck, and Jeff Beck and more! Open daily 11 A.M.–2 A.M.

Li Po's, 916 Grant Ave. (bet. Washington & Jackson Sts.), (415) 982-0072, *Chinese Classic*

Seeking a weird but authentic place to experience Chinatown by night? Here lies the answer. Largely untouched by yuppies and dot-commers, local barflies hang out in the hip bar. A beaming neon green-and-red sign out front sets the tone for a night of surreal sipping and grooving to out-of-date tunes from the jukebox. It's all happening now; card playing, dice throwing, and strong cocktails. And they would be remiss without a token Buddhist shrine behind the bar.

Moose's, 1652 Stockton St. (bet. Fillbert & Union Sts.), (415) 989-7800, *Husband Hunting*

Live jazz, crowded bar and "suits" are the markings of a place we like to be. Mergers abound, in love and finance, at this San

Francisco sizzling hot spot. Whether it's a wedding or a buyout, magic seems to spread like wildfire here. After nine years, they still offer one of the best schmoozing and boozing scenes for the thirtysomething set in SF. Eat at the bar or in front of the exposed kitchen. No cell phones allowed; all the better to focus on the entertainment and eye candy. The crowd knows how to live and they are enjoying the fruits of their labor! *Psst . . . parking in this neighborhood is a disaster, so plan to walk or take a taxi.*

Rex Café, 2323 Polk St. (bet. Union & Green Sts.), (415) 441-2244, *Pickup Scene*

What a scene it is, especially on the weekends when throngs of young, unmarried types pack the place to eat, drink and be chased. There is a pool table on hand if you want to lure Mr. Right by offering a game. Grab a snack too, so tonight's drinks don't become tomorrow's headache! By day this is a great place for the late-to-rise crowd come to "brunch"; in nice weather, the front windows open and there is sidewalk seating. Open 5:30 P.M.– 11 P.M.

Sushi Groove, 1916 Hyde St. (bet. California & Sacramento Sts.), (415) 440-1905, *Be Seen*

An ideal destination for sake and snacks among the pretty people of SF. The crowd is lively and packed with regulars, who must feel groovy drinking and eating among their trendy and oh-so-fabulous compadres. Both your palate and your rising social status will be satisfied in one fell swoop.

Tonga Room, @ The Fairmont Hotel, 950 Mason St. (bet. California & Sacramento Sts.), (415) 772-5278, *Kitsch Galore*

This is the Grande Dame of all themed bars in San Francisco and beyond. Head to the dark and moody basement of the tony Fairmont Hotel (see Tripping, Nob Hill). Still under thatched hut roofs, fake bamboo trees, and a floating stage where the house band plays a wide variety of tunes for you to boogie the night away! Because this bar is located in a famous hotel, it draws an eclectic crowd of tourists, convention goers, and city dwellers in pursuit of guaranteed fun. Go during happy hour and enjoy the Polynesian buffet for appetizers, or late at night when the crowd gets heavier and more rowdy. Order a coconut-pineapple something topped with paper umbrella, and grab the cute guy from the Tomato Growers Association convention next to you at the bar and go to it! *Psst . . . best-kept secret? Every half hour there is a fake tropical storm complete with rain from the "sky" and huge sounds of thunder and lightning. Nuzzle next to "him" with fear!*

Tonic, 2360 Polk St. (@ Union Sts.), (415) 771-5535, *Neighborhood Hangout*
There are two different ways to enjoy this dimly lit place where locals flock to sip swanky cocktails. First, it's a great low-key destination for drinks before dinner where it's quiet enough to talk. The next reason is the late-night crowd that shows up to party and have fun. Everyone is friendly and we always end up talking to someone interesting.

Top of the Mark, @ The Mark Hopkins Inter-Continental Hotel, 999 California St. (@ Mason St.), (415) 392-3434, *Sunset Cocktails*
It's all about the view at this spectacular rooftop hotel bar. Go for the drinks at sunset, when a piano serenades the hours away. Sip a champagne cocktail, and ooh and ahh at the gorgeous view. Then, at night, a dance floor rises in the center of the room and live music kicks in. It's not cheap but it can be worth your hard-earned pennies—or, better yet, "his!"

Tosca Café, 242 Columbus Ave. (bet. Broadway & Pacific St.), (415) 391-1244, *Local And Legendary*
This just might be the coolest place to sip, sway and hang in all of SF. It is so chic that it looks like a movie setting. Enter into a long, narrow-ish room with a wooden bar complete with stools for the solo experience. If you are meeting friends, go the back, where oversized red covered booths line a square room with ultratall ceilings and perfect dim lighting. Weekdays, it's an ideal place for intimate conversation and opera tunes from the fabulous jukebox. Weekends, it's packed and lively throughout. Cute boys, pretty girls, stellar martinis, and "cappuccinos" (coffee, cream and brandy all in one). *Psst . . . Sean Penn, Sharon Stone, Kid Rock, and other SF celeb sightings.*

Vesuvio, 255 Columbus Ave. (bet. Broadway & Pacific St.), (415) 362-3370, *www.vesuvio.com, Neighborhood Favorite*
This world-renowned watering hole is most famous for its history that is deeply rooted in the Beat poet society who were regulars. Located just across from City Lights Bookstore, it remains a monument to "jazz, poetry, art, and the good life of the off Beat Generation." One peek at the diverse crowd and we were instantly hooked. Taxi drivers sip the Jack Kerouac (rum, tequila, orange-cranberry juice, and

lime served in a bucket glass) shoulder to shoulder with so-cialites, chess players, and gawking European tourists. (Jack used to be a frequent patron, with friends, in the late '50s and early '60s.) It is *the* perfect "Jane" place for a thinking and drink-ing night on the town. Stay awhile and read the clippings that cover the walls. Jazz jams are a must on Sundays from 4–7 P.M.; ongoing art exhibi-tions are always interesting. Open 365 days a year, 6 P.M.–2 A.M.

✐ Not to Miss:

850 Cigar Bar, 850 Montgomery St. (bet. Jackson & Pacific Sts.), (415) 291-0850, *Yuppies*

Bubble Lounge, 714 Montgomery St. (bet. Jackson & Washington Sts.), (415) 434-4204, *Champagne Central*

Buddha Lounge, 901 Grant Ave. (@ Washington St.), (415) 362-1792, *Chinatown Watering Hole*

Club Cocodrie, 1024 Kearny St. (bet. Broadway & Pacific St.), (415) 986-6678, *Dive Bar*

Marina/Cow Hollow

Betelnut Pejiu Wu, 2026 Union St. (@ Buchanan St.), (415) 929-8855, *Happy Hour*

This Pan-Asian scene is great for after-work cocktails and a bit of fresh air on the hustle and bustle of Union Street. People-watch, enjoy the weather, the cocktails and the happening crowd. Hungry girls will enjoy a light bite of creative fusion finger food at the bar. The signature green beans are a must to balance the food-to-alcohol ratio. Open until 11 P.M. daily. Prepare to wait, especially for a table near the open doors that spill onto the streets.

Black Horse London Pub, 1514 Union St. (@ Van Ness Ave.), (415) 928-2414, *London Pub*

Feeling homesick for the motherland? Enter the small, tried-and-true English-style pub serving the best warm ale. According to our English friend Stuart, "warm ale" is not really warm, just not as cold as typical American beer. Open nightly from 7 P.M.–midnight.

Charlie's, 1830 Union St. (bet. Laguna & Octavia Sts.), (415) 474-3773, *Beautiful People*

A chic new neighborhood place that serves dinner, and then they roll up the tablecloths and the good times roll! Owned by Charles Schwab (yes, the son of the famous financial wizard), his recent tasteful renovations make this one of the premiere cool bar cum restaurants to grab a few drinks after dinner. Dark wood, indirect lighting, fresh flowers, and all of the best-looking young people we have seen this side of Manhattan. The weekends can get a bit out of control with singles looking to mingle. Pouring until 2 A.M. *Psst . . . go early for a delicious dinner, or try brunch on Sat. and Sun.*

Comet Club, 3111 Fillmore St. (bet. Filbert & Greenwich Sts.), (415) 567-5589, *Night Fever*

Formerly the Desert Moon, locals and those who love a "scene" congregate at the red formica tables with leather banquettes for a night to remember. The disco balls in this dark and narrow room set the tone for a blast of a night. All that's left is for you to choose your dance partner! Open until 2 A.M.

HiFi Lounge, 2125 Lombard St. (@ Fillmore St.), (415) 345-8663, *www.maximumproductions.com, Live Music*

This place is a collage of styles in appreciation of the past, whatever the era. Sparkling white booths and walls are a big draw for style mavens. The dance floor churns out cutting-edge music. One large booth in the back is *the* place to be with a group of friends.

Marina Lounge, 2138 Chestnut St. (@ Pierce St.), (415) 922-1475, *Local Hang*

Sip at swanky martinis and sway to timeless tunes at this comfortable neighborhood hot spot. We love the dark mahogany bar that seats only 16 people. Perfect for quiet conversation and introspection, from a dive bar with feeeeeling. We need both, you know! Feel free to stand and sway, and when the urge hits, let the music take control. Exposed brick walls and dark wainscoting line the walls, making lovers and loners both feel welcome. Venture to the back for a game of pool or a video game or two, which locals tend to do with frequency.

Pier 23 Café, The Embarcadero (@ Battery St.), (415) 362-5125, *After-Work Escape*

On a sunny day there is no better place to take in the sunset on one of the rare days without rain or wind. Grab a plastic chair, sit on the dock, and watch the clouds roll around the sky. Later in the evening, dancing die-hards show up and rule the place. Live bands play nightly except Monday, and the cover charge is nominal for the huge amounts of fun to be had. Salsa, reggae, jazz—the crowd varies depending on the type of music, so call ahead if, say, R&B is not your thing. Open daily from 4:30 P.M.–2:30 A.M.

Tounge Groove, 2513 Van Ness Ave. (@ Union St.), (415) 928-0404, *Toe Tapping*
It's all good fun, with live music from some wacky cover bands. Come for the groovy drinks and diverse selection of sessions. It can be a pick-up scene so single girls beware . . . unless of course you want to be caught. Cleavage a plus but not required. Cover ranges from $5–12, depending on the performer. Closed on Monday.

"The Heights" (Pacific, Presidio, Laurel)

Balboa Café, 3199 Fillmore St. (@ Greenwich St.), (415) 921-3944, *Happy Hour*
Since 1914, before Prohibition, this place has been alive and rockin', serving loyal patrons delicious cocktails. The long dark wood bar is a perfect place to perch and prowl, whatever you desire. Ella blares in the background early in the day, while the ladies "do lunch"; Tiny gets things rolling around sunset. Be young, be foolish, be proud, just don't show up if you are looking for a quiet drink at the bar with your book.

Boom Boom Room, 1601 Fillmore St. (@ Geary St.), (415) 673-8000, *Live Jazz*
Founded by legendary blues man John Lee Hooker, this is fast becoming one of the best places to hear blues in the East Bay area. Live traditional blues played nightly by some old greats as well as new up-and-coming talents. There is a dance floor, always the great equalizer, where older neighborhood types shake their groove thang next to younger hipsters—all in the name of good music and a good time. Ain't it great to be an American? Open seven days and nights from 2 P.M.–2 A.M.

East Side West, 3154 Fillmore St. (@ Greenwich St.), (415) 885-4000, *Raw Bar*

West Coast girls go East Coast for this wildly popular bar, where you may even see an occasional boy in a blue blazer. (Not done in San Francisco since the Gold Rush.) It may be a meat market but you are bound to run into someone you know . . . even if he's from your alma mater back East. The seafood menu is less focused, but in a pinch, try the lobster bisque or the fondue. *Psst . . . Yankee fans are welcomed. Order a house drink called "the Bronx." Don't ask what's in it. Just enjoy!*

Florio, 1915 Fillmore St. (bet. Bush & Pine Sts.), (415) 775-4300, *Local Hangout*

Retro hang for those looking to chill in a European-style bar/café. The lighting is just right to hide imperfections showing from the past few weeks of exhausting travel. Nestle up to the bar or shimmy into a cozy table near the front for an old-fashioned martini. The lovely sugar bowls create a look to rival any bar in Paris. Nat King Cole wails in the background as you sip, pout, and pose after a week of computer nightmares. You deserve the best and they are ready to deliver. Limited but tasty menu will satisfy the hunger pangs if the vodka didn't do the trick.

G Bar, 488 Presidio St. (@ California St.), (415) 431-4766, *Trendy Scene*

This stylish bar is all the rage in the Presidio Heights, so much so that the word is out and people are flocking to this place. It feels a bit like a late-1940s apartment, Hollywood in its heyday. The tables, accessories and the "woodless" fireplace all set the tone for bottles of French champagne and caviar. The crowd is lovely; even your mother would approve! Open Tues–Sat. 5:30 P.M.–1:30 A.M., Mon. until midnight only. *Psst . . . looking to host a special event? This is an ideal place to be a hostess with the mostest. Available for parties, ask for Liz.*

Perlot, @ Hotel Majestic, 1500 Sutter St. (@ Gough St.), (415) 441-1100, *Romantic Hideaway*

Think Casablanca meets the Bay Area. You'll love the beautiful mahogany bar tucked away in this out-of-the-way location. Indulge your senses in their rare butterfly collection, nightly piano music, and fantastic martinis. An intimate place for a drink with your lover, your daddy, or your sugar daddy! Off the beaten path . . . but seek and ye shall find this little cocktail treasure. Bogie would approve.

Hayes Valley/Civic Center

Absinthe, 398 Hayes St. (@ Gough St.), (415) 551-1590, *Elegant Drinks*

Tres French brasserie with a '20s feel. A jewel of a bistro allusive to Chevalier, Piaf and Sartre, you will be charmed into a Left Bank stupor. The large bar is perfect for sipping vintage-style cocktails, and the yellow walls and Toulouse Lautrec posters make an ideal backdrop for swanky boozing. Nibble on steak frites and "un demi" (half beer/half lemonade) late-night after the ballet or the opera. Just say oui, oui to this upscale hot spot. *Psst . . . prepare your palette for a sensorially indulgent brunch extravaganza! Featuring light, buttery scones; creamy poleta with a dash of maple and mascarpone cheese; granola with fresh berries, papaya and pecans; omelets bursting with delicious Louisiana shrimp and fresh herbs; a croque monsieur layered with Madrange ham, Gruyere cheese, and a hint of Dijon . . . the list goes on!*

Carta, 1760 Market St. (bet. Gough & Octavia Sts.), (415) 863-3516, *Eat/Drink/Be Merry*

This lounge-y hotspot changes its menu every two months. Cocktails and exotic treats prevail; if your palate thrives on surprise then don't miss this culinary world circus, though it can be a bit inconsistent. Something for everybody, some of the time! In spite of the quirks, this is a fun and inventive treat. Will it be appetizers from Mozambique or entrées from Czechoslovakia? Adds new meaning to the idea of "night school." Serving food until midnight.

Hayes and Vine Wine Bar, 377 Hayes St. (bet. Franklin & Gough Sts.), (415) 626-5301, *Pre/Post Opera*

Vino babes, take note! The only problem here is that it is impossible to choose from the 800 different wines by the half glass, glass, flute, or bottle. Stop by for a delicious glass of "something" grape before going to the nearby opera. The knowledgeable bartenders are par excellence! This is a top-of-the-list "Jane" pick for the Golden Gate city. Open till 1 A.M. *Psst . . . this is one of the more "late-night" places in a town that rolls up the streets rather early for "Jane."*

Orbit Room, 1900 Market St. (@ Laguna St.), (415) 252-9525, *Mod Squad*

Where to begin in describing the coolness of this place? An innocent coffee shop by day, this place lets its hair down and becomes a major hip hang by night. The space itself is minimalist meets 007, so we love to stop by for a daytime java pick-me-up and rub elbows with the literary crowd poring over their latest novel or screenplay in the works. By night, we hop on our vintage Vespa and blast into Orbit for their fabulous martinis from the round bar, accompanied by groovy tunes from the stocked jukebox. Live music is featured from time to time, but the jukebox is more festive! No credit cards accepted. Open from 7–2 A.M., Mon.–Sat.; until midnight on Sunday.

Place Pigalle, 520 Hayes St. (bet. Octavia & Laguna Sts.), (415) 552-2671, *Chill Out*

The infamous red-light district of Paris has certainly lent its more arty influence to this funky Hayes Valley wine-and-beer hangout. The couches make it comfy, the crowd makes it chic in a downtown-artsy-scene way. . . . The occasional DJ pops in for an unexpected energy boost to an otherwise perfect chill. Kick back and imbibe with friends and other trendoids!

Stars, 555 Golden Gate Ave. (@ Van Ness St.), (415) 554-0352, *Neighborhood Favorite*

See and be seen at one of the city's most famous scenes! This place still holds the crown as one of the most famous bars in the city. You just may meet a "fat cat" willing to buy those pricey cocktails for you and your girlfriends! If not, surely you will be entertained by the lively crowd of colorful patrons. Food-a-frolics of yesteryear will know this place as one of San Francisco's most treasured dining experiences, thanks to former owner Jeremiah Tower. (Since its sale and remodeling, some argue that it is not as sparkly as it used to be.)

⸎ *Not to Miss:*

Ovations, 333 Fulton St. (@ Franklin St.), (415) 398-1243, *Romantic Rendezvous*

Cha Cha Cha, 1801 Haight St. (@ Shrader St.), (415) 386-5758, *Neighborhood Favorite*

Party like it's 1999 in the New Millenium! Join in the fun for sangria and tapas at this original location. This ever-popular destination is chock-full of twentysomethings, and those who still think that they are! The packed crowd grooves to the Marley-esque beats while waiting . . . waiting . . . waiting for a table. Oh well, who needs a table when you just drank your dinner, much less a week's calories, standing on the sidelines! The décor is Carmen Miranda 2002 and very "cha cha cha!" See other location in Mission.

Club Deluxe, 1511 Haight St. (bet. Ashbury & Clayton Sts.), (415) 552-6949, *Retro Dance / Lounge*

In the mood for ambiance, entertainment and a smooth cocktail all at once? This is the deluxe place for glamorous beverages in a retro setting as you delight in the live musical acts, singing renditions of Frank, Dean, and other beloved crooners. Is it the 1950s or the 1940s? Who cares! It's all presented in good taste with strong drinks to boot! What more could a girl want, besides Tony Bennett himself to join in the fun! *Psst . . . put on that vintage dress you bought on eBay for ten bucks and look like a million in the lounge area that hosts swing bands on occasion.*

Finnegan's Wake, 937 Cole St. (bet. Parnessus & Carl Sts.), (415) 731-6119, *Quasi-Dublin*

A friendly place to plant yourself for a casual beer and a quick game of darts to detox from the stress of the fast lane! The look of the place is less than thrilling, but go for the friendly Generation-X crowd that will leave you feeling on the top of the world. You are, aren't you?

The Golden Cane Cocktail Lounge, 1569 Haight St. (bet. Ashbury & Clayton Sts.), (415) 626-1112, *Neighborhood Favorite*

After 60-plus years this Haight Street rendezvous is still blowing and going. Hipsters, socialites, and punk rockers sit side by side and tell stories of the past and the future! Huge moose heads adorn the walls, along with photos of luminaries such as JFK, who made a dedication of love to this unpretentious venue. *Psst . . . interesting trivia printed on the cocktail napkins makes for many a controversial conversation at the bar!*

Mad Dog in the Fog, 530 Haight St. (@ Fillmore St.), (415) 626-7279, *Sports Enthusiasts*

Euro boys and the girls who love them flock here on special days to watch European football (more fondly referred to as soccer on this side of the pond). It's a popular neighborhood spot with a highly coveted satellite television. Go for the boys, but have fun with your best girl buddies while you're at it!

Nickie's BBQ, 460 Haight St. (bet. Webster & Fillmore Sts.), (415) 621-6508, *Late Night*

The Grateful Dead are not really dead, at least not at Nickie's. Congregate with old-world hippies and those who wish they were hippies and pay homage with new mixes of old favorites to make it all seem like yesterday. World beat and deep funk balance out the play list for a night of authentic entertainment. No tie-dye or bong required for admittance.

Noc Noc, 557 Haight St. (bet. Fillmore & Steiner Sts.), (415) 861-5811, *Groovy Babes*

Designed as if a film animator joined efforts with a Dada artist to create a uniquely artsy-fartsy imaginative place to sip wine and guzzle beer simultaneously. The house music is prone to ambient or goth, so knock yourself out as you "booze cruise" through this hip hangout.

Persian Aub Zam Zam, 1633 Haight St. (bet. Clayton & Belvedere Sts.), (415) 861-2545, *Club Attitude*

A little *Arabian Nights* meets *9½ Weeks*. If you are hell-bent on a strong drink in a dark, windowless place with attitude, then this is your perfect destination. Order a martini (gin, of course) and sip in reverence. There is a classic padded-leather horseshoe-shaped bar on which to drape yourself and drown your sorrows, and tables in the back that are usually kept empty for the "in" clientele, unless you win the favor of Bruno, the owner and keeper of the bar. Open "when he feels like it," but usually starting around 4 P.M. House rules: Only girls get napkins, and no cell phones. No credit cards. *Psst . . . first-timers are usually kicked out, so don't be offended . . . just prepare to be thick-skinned. We "Jane" girls love a challenge, or maybe just a little punishment!*

↓ *Not to Miss:*

The Top, 424 Haight St. (bet. Webster & Fillmore Sts.), (415)
864-7386, *DJs Deluxe*

The Castro/Noe Valley

Café du Nord, 2170 Market St. (bet. Church & Sanchez Sts.), (415) 861-
5016, *Speakeasy*

Live music sets the tone for this rambling-basement, Prohibition era–
style club. Whatever floats your boat: swing bands, cabaret, salsa, soul DJs,
and more. The crowd is fashionable yet nonthreatening, so put on your best
Ungaro floral dress and strut your stuff to tunes that would tantalize the
most "white-bread" girls to cut a rug . . . or at least cut loose on a Friday
night! Costs up to $5, no cover before 8 P.M. *Psst . . . at happy hour, 4–7 P.M.
daily, cocktails are $2! Happy days are here again. . . .*

Lucky 13, 2140 Market St. (bet. Church & Sanchez Sts.), (415) 487-
1313, *Local Hang*

Boys and girls unite! Join the party at this eerie joint lit exclusively by
red bulbs. The name itself, and the black cat above the doors, tip you off
that this place is weird yet wonderful. Taste one or more of the 28 beers on
tap, or the 40 bottled brews, or sample a wide variety of scotches and other
top-drawer alcoholic beverages. The crowd is an unusual mix of locals and
cool types on hand to enjoy the pool table and the coveted one-dollar drafts
during happy hour (until 7 P.M. daily).

Mecca, 2029 Market St. (bet. Dolores & 14th Sts.), (415) 621-7000,
www.sfmecca.com, Neighborhood Favorite

Social girls, take note! There's something for everyone at this restau-
rant/bar that is perfect for cocktails, and dinner too. Pull up a stool or a
plush sofa for a gin martini from one of the ultracool bartenders. Mood
lighting is set by famed designer Celeste Gainey. Gay and straight alike co-
exist in peace while enjoying a night on the town in one of the best-looking
bars in the area. Grab a Manhattan, put on your best Benefit cheek stain and
let the night unfold. *Psst . . . they serve a full menu at the bar, providing access to
ever-changing, often-brilliant seasonal fare. And we love those cool little peephole*

lights that make your drink change colors. Of course, getting a seat at the bar is no picnic. One hint: strike up a conversation with someone who seems about to leave. Another: "Man, this dynamite itches!"

Midnight Sun, 4067 18th St. (bet. Hartford & Castro Sts.), (415) 861-4186, *Gay Times*

Don't expect to find Mr. Right here, but flirting is permitted and encouraged. For an alternative night on the town, try this trendy, up-to-the-minute, happening "guy" bar. The scoop: it's a video bar with dance music, clips of campy films and comedy shows blaring on two huge screens. It's a whole lotta fun. Just don't get too attached to "him," because he's probably not really your type after all. . . .

The Pilsner Inn, 225 Church St. (bet. Market & 15th Sts.), (415) 621-7058, *Afternoon Delight*

This may seem at first like a run-of-the-mill beer joint, but there is a reason to hang out here beyond the 16 beers on hand. The beer garden in back is *the* place to perch on a pretty afternoon and while away the precious off-hours by searching for the Little Dipper with a friend. Or, grab a seat at the long bar or one of the tables in the front for a real cocktail and plan the rest of your evening. Open Mon–Sat., 9 A.M.–2 A.M.

⚘ *Not to Miss:*

The Twin Peaks, 401 Castro St. (bet. 17th & Market Sts.), (415) 864-9470, *Lifestyle Exposed*

Mission ....

Beauty Bar, 2299 Mission St. (@ 19th St.), (415) 285-0323, *Nails and Ales*

Yes, it's the same as in New York. This is a fun place to stop by for a cocktail in a truly kitschy setting. Formerly a 1950s-style beauty shop, it still has its quirky barber chairs and old-fashioned hair dryers, where you can sit and socialize. It's a good time for a while, then we like to head out to some of the other neighborhood joints for live music or quiet conversation. Open 5 P.M.–2 A.M. daily. Happy hour

Mon–Fri., 6–10 P.M. *Psst . . . too busy to book your weekly mani-cure? Try the first-come, first-served manicures offered Wed–Sat., 6–10 P.M. Appointments available for groups of six or more. Ask about the bachelorette party special!*

Blondie's, 540 Valencia St. (@ 16th St.), (415) 864-2419, *Ruby Tuesday*
Ah, the joy of a Tuesday-night aperitif at Blondie's—soft, lilting jazz, an open-air patio, and some of the best (and largest) cocktails in the city. But then: ah, the horror of Blondie's on a weekend, when frat types, suburban-ites—to be honest, we don't know who they are—spill from the patio onto the street, drown out whatever music is playing and make ordering a drink almost impossible. Though this seems to happen everywhere in the Mission on weekends, Blondie's offers the most dramatic example. By the time it's over, it's hard not to exclaim: "Thank God it's Monday!'

Bruno's, 2389 Mission St. (@ 20th St.), (415) 648-7701, *Lounge Deluxe*
It's hard for us not to gloat about all of the reasons we love this place. Recently reopened by Jon Varnedoe (of Foreign Cinema fame), and re-stored to its former glory with red leather booths and a 500-gallon fish tank in the rear near the bar. Lovers and others (namely groups of girls packed tightly in the booths) gather by the baby grand piano and sip, sway, and swing the night away with other lounge lizards like us! Cosmos flow freely. *Psst . . . got the munchies? The menu leans toward Italian with a bit of a flare; if you are trying to entice the boy next to you at the bar, order the Oysters Martini (and slip him a few). After all, you are the Goddess of Love!*

Café Multi-Cultural Valencia, 1109 Valencia St. (@ 22nd St.), (415) 824-7659, *Dive Bar*
Locals and the seriously curious come here if they want know what it feels like to be part of the Mission district pregentrification. The place is the size of a postage stamp and is covered from top to bottom with paintings, posters and other memorabilia paying tribute to heroes that represent the mindset of the crowd; like Einstein, Bo Didley and some lesser-known icons. A Salvador Dali painting greets you at the door and leads you inside, where the mostly Latino crowd drinks coffee and eats cake. They close "when people leave." Occasional spoken-word events add extra cha-cha, to the night. No credit cards.

Cha Cha Cha, 2327 Mission St. (bet. 19th & 20th Sts.), (415) 648-0504, *Caribbean Hangout*

See details in Haight-Ashbury.

Elbo Room, 647 Valencia St. (bet. 17th & 18th Sts.), (415) 552-7788, *www.elbo.com, Boozy Crowd*

You never know what to expect when you enter the doors of this neighborhood hot spot. Dress casual and get ready for an all-out good time. The twentysomething crowd includes everything from prissy sorority girls to tongue-pierced, pigtail-wearing hipsters, hanging out together like peanut butter and jelly! There is a cool formica-topped bar with wooden arches, and candles for perfect lighting. Venture upstairs if you're in the mood for a "jam session" that could be DJs spinning tunes or live jazz-fusion—or something else. Every night has a different musical theme so call ahead! There is usually a five-dollar cover upstairs, but it's worth every last penny if it's your scene. Otherwise, host a game of pool with that cutie in the corner!

El Rio, 3158 Mission St. (bet. Cesar Chavez & Valencia Sts.), (415) 282-3325, *Outdoor Patio*

There is just one thing to do in this neighborhood on a warm night: go directly to this self-proclaimed dive bar and sit in one of the city's most expansive outdoor bars for cheap margaritas ($2 on Tuesday nights). It is covered in tropical plants and little twinkle lights, and they occasionally offer music that could range from salsa to hard rock. You never know what to expect—one "Jane" girlfriend had belly-dancing lessons one night on the patio! Owner Malcolm knows how to throw a party, and we love her for that! Open daily from 3 P.M.–2 A.M. except Monday, when they close at midnight. No credit cards accepted.

Esta Noche, 3079 16th St. (bet. Valencia & Mission Sts.), (415) 861-5757, *Sexy Latino*

Dance fever got you? This is the best gay bar in the neighborhood, drawing a heavy Latino crowd to blow it out to the hippest salsa, '80s disco and wacky stuff from the '90s. Drag shows are a fixture so order a Coca Light (light rum & Diet Coke) and get ready to cha, cha, cha! No Glen Campbell or Carpenters allowed—even though we keep those CDs close by at all times! "We've only just begun . . ."

Firecracker, 1007½ Valencia St. (@ 21st St.), (415) 642-3470, *People Watching*

Excited by the thought of a loud, rambunctious hot spot with innovative and sizzling Chinese food to match? Just like its name, it's hot, hot, hot. . . . Grab your coworker, or your lover, and join in the fun at this sexy destination. It's all in the name of good, clean fun at a place that's bound to stand the test of "trendy" time. *Kabaam!*

Foreign Cinema, 2534 Mission St. (bet. 21st & 22nd Sts.), (415) 648-7600, *First Date*

This is the ultimate cool place for a sexy night with a new crush. Sashay into the barren cinderblock hallway lined with votive candles. A small bar on the left is an inviting place for quiet conversation and an aperitif. Venture back onto the patio, where foreign films and French food are paired like Fred and Ginger. Share a seat outside (complete with heaters on cold nights) at one of the communal tables. Or, slink inside to the fireplace near the exposed kitchen for a martini. Go for the ambiance and stay for the flicks; we bet real sparks will fly.

La Roundalla, 901 Valencia St. (@ 20th St.), (415) 647-7474, *Margarita Bonanza*

We love this place, and you will too if you enjoy smoke, tequila, crowds, jukebox (mostly Mexican CDs) and greasy food. (Are we showing our true colors?) There are two rooms to enjoy: one is a causal diner that serves guacamole, chips, enchiladas, and other Mexican staples in a somewhat serene environment, and the other is a bar divided into two main areas. Choose red pleather banquettes to lounge and gorge in, or the main bar that has fake wood paneling, dim lighting, and Mexican streamers hanging from the walls and ceiling. Either way, it's fun with a group or solo as a voyeur of all the action. An occasional strolling minstrel will wander around and serenade! Open until 3 A.M. daily.

Latin American Club, 3286 22nd St. (bet. Valencia & Mission Sts.), (415) 647-2732, *Hangout*

Calling all slacker wanna-bes to this ultracool divey mainstay in the Mission area. Welcome to Hip Central. Be sure to follow the rule on the front door to be quiet when you leave because the "f**king neighbors are trying to sleep." A pool table greets you, where cute sideburned boys are racking up and setting the tone for a low-key night on the town. Don't let the simple décor fool you; this is a great place for complicated conversation and cool cocktails. Formerly a festive Latino hangout, the walls now display art from future stars in the making and photos from years gone by. There is a sign by the bar in red neon that says SIN. Well, have a good time, you little devil! Open daily from 5 P.M.–2 A.M.

Lone Palm, 3394 22nd St. (@ Guerrero St.), (415) 648-0109, *Neighborhood Favorite*

"We had it all, just like Bogie & Bacall . . ." The night is young and potential abounds here! This is the place to go for classic cocktails in a chick dive with an upscale crowd. Dimly lit by the glow of a neon "lone palm" tree on the back wall, that somehow radiates a glow making pretty people look even prettier. Style abounds in the simple glass-brick entrance, with little round tables with white tablecloths and great glassware for easy toasting. The bartenders are real pros who know how to make a true martini, even misting the glass with vermouth sprayed from a perfume atomizer. Don't dare ask for some girly, sweet cocktail . . . you just might get enough dirty looks to last a lifetime! We love to go early on weeknights, when it's quiet and has an air of mystery, but you can always brave the crowds on weekends when live music (mostly acoustic) and big crowds are certain.

The Make-Out Room, 3225 22nd St. (bet. Mission & Valencia Sts.), (415) 647-2888, *Neighborhood Favorite*

Be young, be foolish, and be seen! Arrive early to avoid the wait and to secure a place in one of the few booths near the front in this perennially hot spot. There's something for everyone in this flea market ode to minimalism, with plenty of pretty people to keep the adrenaline going even if your date is a bore. The bathrooms are tiny, so no "making out" in this ladies' room! Live music on occasion can be a delight or a bummer, depending on the night—it's an eclectic luck of the draw as to who's playing.

Martuni's, 4 Valencia St. (@ Market St.), (415) 241-0205, *Martini Deluxe*

This low-key campy piano bar attracts a great mix of patrons from the young to the old, the straight to the gay and the tipsy to the flat-out drunk! You just never know who might stumble up to the piano for a murderous rendition of "Misty." That being said, you might as well prepare your "chops" in case the mood or the martinis strike and send you into crooning mode! Don't worry, the fun piano player has seen it all! "Some enchanted evening . . ."

Rite Spot Café, 2099 Folsom St. (@ 17th St.), (415) 552-6066, *www.ritespotcafe.com, Hangout*

Sip cocktails among the crowds of SF cool types. Its low-key style proves these folks are definitely not poseurs. The regulars actually debate who is better than whom in the revolving art collection. Go early for quiet conversation. Weekends get a bit rowdy but never out of control. This is the "right spot!" *Psst . . . stop by the ATM before you park or get dropped off in your cab or limo, because they only take cash, and the neighborhood is not great for "Jane" girls strutting about looking perplexed with their pocketbooks open.*

Slim's, 333 11th St. (bet. Folsom & Harrison Sts.), (415) 522-0333, *www.slims-sf.com, Live Music*

This is the most ideal spot in San Francisco to hang your hat if live music is your thing, and what "Jane" girl isn't into music? The best of the best grace the doors of this place at one time or another, including singer Boz Skaggs, who is part owner. Diversity is the word: Super Diamond, Dave Walking (the lead singer of General Public and English Beat), more eclectic country acts like Steve Earle, or bluegrass performers. The acoustics are stellar. *Psst . . . don't miss a minute of Alison Krauss's set by delaying over dinner. Come early and head to the balcony, where you can eat decent bar food and overlook the stage below.*

The Slow Club, 2501 Mariposa St. (@ Hampshire St.), (415) 241-9390, *First Date*

Duck into this intimate restaurant but keep going past the door. . . . Head straight to the back where a chic backlit bar with glowing bottles of vodka awaits you. As the neighborhood dictates, the décor is a bit of a mishmash, combining spare with coziness. The weekends are overrun with a party crowd, but maybe that's just what you're in the mood for. Alternatively, weekdays are pleasant and quasi-peaceful; order some tapas and a well-made Cosmo to wash it back! A very "Jane" place. Open 11 A.M.–11 P.M. Tues., until midnight Wed.–Sat. *Psst . . . brunch is served on Saturday & Sunday, food is Mediterranean-style as well as burgers and fries.*

The Tip Top Inn, 3001 Mission St. (@ 26th St.), (415) 824-6486, *Underground Favorite*

Shhh . . . insiders and those in the know want to keep their secret neighborhood treasure just that—a secret! This is a cool place to hang your hat for a top-shelf drink from a pro bartender who can make any drink your imaginative little heart desires. Put some money in the jukebox and relax! The décor is a mixed bag of velvet paintings of the Virgin Mary and crucifixes.

♪ *Not to Miss:*

Doc's Clock, 2575 Mission St. (bet. 21st & 22nd Sts.), (415) 824-3627, *Locals Galore*

Tripping

⚬ *Time Off*

AMC 1000, 1000 Van Ness Ave. (@ O'Farrell St.), (415) 922-4AMC, *Cineplex*

This is the theatrical equivalent of the *Love Boat!* They have loveseat-style seating that allows cuddlers to pull up the armrests that divide them and nuzzle away! However, they do show the latest and greatest films on 14 screens, so try to pay attention. Beware of the cacophony of cell phones . . . *Psst . . . are you one of the "loser chicks" who always manage to wind up behind a Bigfoot no matter where you sit? Not to worry . . . these rows of seats are at such a steep incline (stadium style), you will have no "blockage" by Big Hair!*

Ansel Adams Center for Photography, 655 Mission St. (bet. New Montgomery & Third Sts.), (415) 495-7000, *Photo Buffs*

The fact that every doctor's office and dorm room has a reprinted poster of one of his classic photos makes it easy to forget the unique artistry and unparalleled brilliance that Ansel Adams brought to the world of black-and-white photography. Adams was the front-runner in the movement to establish cutting-edge photography as an actual art form. This sleek center contains five exhibition halls, one of which is dedicated solely to Adams's works. The other four showcase exhibitions of various artists like Imogene Cunningham, Annie Liebovitz, and other forward-thinking photographers. Open daily from 11 A.M.–5 P.M.; $5 for adults, free for kids under 13.

Cable Car Museum, 1201 Mason St. (@ Washington St.), (415) 474-1887, *Doris Day's Wheels*

"Rice-A-Roni, the San Francisco treat!" This commercial would not have existed as we know it without the cable car. . . . Here you will find everything and anything about the making of the cable car. The museum is actually the original cable car barn and powerhouse, circa 1887. There is a viewing gallery of one-of-a-kind cable cars, historic photos, and cable car artifacts. Put down the Hamburger Helper and see for yourself.

California Historical Society, 678 Mission St. (bet. 3rd & New Montgomery Sts.), (415) 357-1848, *www.calhist.org, History Buff*

"The Way We Were . . . " If you have an hour or so to kill, venture here to find out anything and everything imaginable about the history of San Francisco, as well as other parts of California. Find books on such diverse subjects as the escapades of literary icons Mark Twain and Joan Didion, and the inside scoop on the city's architectural history. It's more educational than entertaining, so don't attempt a visit on days when you are feeling drained or suffering from ADD . . . On the other hand, inquiring minds will find a treasure trove of memorabilia, books and unique gifts. There is one main floor with three small galleries branching out from the center. Open Tues.–Sun., 11 A.M.–5 P.M. Cost is $3.

Cartoon Art Museum, 1017 Market St. (bet. 4th and 5th Sts.), (415) 227-8660, *www.cartoonart.org, Funny Things*

One of the three museums in the country dedicated to the preservation and exhibition of funny things that come in small packages, they have over 11,000 items in the permanent collection and 3,000 in the research library, including an interactive children's section. Let's just hope that Nancy, Cathy, Blondie, Veronica & Betty, and Lucy make it into the Hall of Fame girl greats! Otherwise, see everyone from the superheroes of the 1970s to the Hanna Barbera cartoons that date back to 1965. They are planning to open in a new location in the next few years. Five dollars for adults, two dollars for children.

The Embarcadero Center Cinema, 1 Embarcadero Center (@ Clay & Battery Sts.), (415) 352-0810, *Art House*

This groovy art house complex shows first-run foreign films like *Butterfly,* and occasionally blockbuster American titles such as *The Talented Mr. Ripley,* but overall it's all about the art of filmmaking in a festive environment. Take a postfilm walk near the Bay by the Ferry Building for stunning views of the water. Maybe he will propose after a romantic viewing of *La Dolce Vita.* Also within sight are San Francisco's most coveted sights: Coit Tower and the ever scary Alcatraz Island . . . Breathe in, breathe out, and realize how short life really is.

Folk Art International, Xanadu Tribal Arts, Boretti Amber & Design, 140 Maiden Ln. (bet.Grant & Stockton Sts.), (415) 392-9999, *www.folkartintl.com, Antiquities*

This original Frank Lloyd Wright–designed building (circa 1949) is an architectural oasis housing three upscale

galleries that carry mostly museum-quality artifacts. The
Folk Art International Gallery was established in 1979, to
house antiquities and collectibles from around the world.
Would you not love to see an ivory horn from West Africa, or a vase from
the Han Dynasty, circa 200 A.D.? Or, if you are interested in artifacts from
indigenous peoples, the Xanadu Gallery offers serious tribal art. This landmark setting is the perfect backdrop to house icons, textiles, artworks and
jewelry from Asia, Latin America, and Africa. The structure itself is outrageously stunning. Open Mon.–Sat. 10 A.M.–6 P.M.

Lumiere Theatre, 1572 California St. (@ Polk St.), (415) 352-0810,
Alternative Films

Ruling the alternative movie scene since the 1960s, this is a mecca for
San Francisco's indie film junkies and aficionados! One large theater seats
300, and two smaller screens each seat 100. Shows can run a week to six
months, depending on popularity. Blink and they might be gone . . . or
maybe not. . . .

Mechanic's Institute Library, 57 Post St. (@ Market), (415) 421-
1750, *Private Bookworm*

This private library stands head and shoulders above its competition.
Whether you want to chill out amidst an incredible collection of books or
look for specific information, this is THE one-stop destination. Take time
to browse the open stacks or use the simple computer database that makes
finding anything specific a breeze. The staff is unbelievably helpful and
knowledgeable. Annual membership is $60 but well worth it in a city that
seems to be lacking in the public and private library arena.

Pacific Bell Park, 24 Willie Mays Plaza (@ The Embarcadero), (415)
227-8660, *www.sfgiants.com, Play Ball*

A sight to behold . . . an affair to remember . . . a baseball game in a
stadium where the game is treated like a religious experience. The park
opened to the public on April 11, 2000, when the SF Giants christened the
place against the rival LA Dodgers. They lost by one, but the fans' enthusi-
asm never wanes! Plan to go waaaaay in advance—tickets are hard to come
by. If you lose interest in the game (you heathen!), you can always cast your
eyes to the sea and watch passing sailboats. Hot guys in baggy tights or sailboats . . . pick your poison!

San Francisco Museum of Modern Art, 151 3rd St. (bet. Mission & Howard Sts.), (415) 357-4000, *www.sfmoma.com, Modern Mecca*

This is the granddaddy of all venues for modern art in the Bay Area. The menu of things to see, do and taste is really too much to consume under one roof. But if we must, the structure itself was designed by the internationally acclaimed Swiss architect Mario Botta and houses over 17,000 masterpieces by names we know and love: Matisse, Pollock, Warhol, Klee, Picasso, Lichtenstein, Rivera, Duchamp, Giacometti, Mondrian, Rauschenberg. We could go on and on, or focus on the stunning structure itself, equally impressive in its own artistic way. Natural light via circular skylighting illuminates the main area. Strategically, the light bleeds to several of the attached galleries. The "West Wing" has become home to many cutting-edge temporary installations, ranging from a genius exhibition by American photographer Walker Evans to a show on Rene Magritte. The bookstore alone is worth a trip. Open daily except Wed., 11 A.M.–6 P.M. On Thurs. evenings, go for the music and art in tandem programs, where live jazz and blues serenade the art lovers. *Psst . . . they offer an outstanding series of lectures by a group called Art Sandwiched In. The most popular program is an annual forum named Design Lecture Series, which presents a different topic each year depending on the installations. Membership not required but it is worth it if you are a patron of the arts. Call (415) 357-4125 for information.*

♂ *Sweet Dreams*

Hotel Rex, 562 Sutter St. (bet. Mason & Powell Sts.), (415) 433-4434, www.sftrips.com, *Hip Boutique*

Owned and operated by the highly specialized San Francisco–based small hotel group Joie de Vivre, this hotel is designed after its East Coast "sister," the Algonquin, legendary haunt of Dorothy Parker and other high-rolling literary giants. The prime location is just one of the many reasons to stay at the Hotel Rex. There is a library with leather-bound first editions beckoning from solid mahogany cabinets, along with miles and miles of other books. We take great comfort in knowing they are there, even if we are too busy to actually read them! In the evening, groups of literary types gather to drink scotch and enjoy the impressive collection of 1930s art. The

 rooms are uniquely masculine with dark carpets, bedspreads and appointments, all chosen with an angle toward the bookish type, and overwhelmingly romantic for the rest of us regular "Janes." Rates start at $160.

Psst . . . lunchtime readings occur frequently so check it out before checking in.

Mandarin Oriental, 222 Sansome St. (bet. California & Pine Sts.), (415) 885-0999, *www.mandarinoriental.com, Expense Account*

An Asian-inspired oasis in the heart of the Financial District, yet close to Union Square, this world-class hotel is fit for a Hong Kong princess! The sweeping view is not to be outdone by the huge marble bathrooms, some of which even have views from the tub! Rest assured, everyone has a view because the hotel occupies floors 38 to 48 of the city's third-tallest building. Every room comes equipped with a pair of binoculars for spying . . . *not!* The service passes our white-glove "Jane" inspection, making sure that your every need is met. The one problem with staying here is that you may never want to leave, and there is so much to do and see in the "real world!" But then again, maybe you'll stay in and order from the room service that is available 24 hours a day. . . . You only live once! Rates are $475–785.

Hotel Monaco, 501 Geary St. (@ Taylor St.), (415) 292-0100, *www.hotelmonaco.com, Trendy*

Whether you are shopping for the weekend or hitting it hard for work, this is one of the best centrally located downtown hotels. The lobby is grand and historic-feeling, with modern touches added. There is a massive fireplace, with a sitting area to chat and sip coffee in between the lobby and the Grand Café (see Twilight, Downtown). The 201 rooms are tiny but well proportioned, and appointed with bold colors and stripes that are the stuff of fairy tales, complete with canopied beds! It is somewhat girly yet not too feminine for men. RobinWright Penn recommends this place to her out-of-town guests. Web TV, full spa (Equilibrium; see Treats, Downtown), and afternoon cookies are just a few of the services we love. Room service is available until midnight from the yummy Grand Café. Rates start at $250 and go up to $519 for a luxury suite. *Psst . . . can't bear to leave home without Fido? This hotel is pet friendly. Traveling solo? Ask for a complimentary goldfish to be delivered to your room before you arrive.*

Nikko Hotel, 222 Mason St. (@ O'Farrell St.), (415) 394-1111, *www.nikkohotels.com, Absolute Efficiency*

This is a great business hotel if you need to make efficient use of your time and energies in a clutter-free environment. The amenities are sleek, with large desks for working in your room in the morning before meetings.

The staff is friendly and well equipped. The restaurant serves fabulous sushi for late-night, low-cal nibbles after a long day! Rates start at $325. *Psst . . . save the boss some cash and ask for "super discounts" on less busy times, when rates can drop as much as $100.*

Palace Hotel, 2 New Montgomery St. (@ Market St.), (415) 512-1111 or (800) 325-3535, *www.sfpalace.com, Historic Hideout*

In 1997 this magnificent hotel closed its doors and renovated to the tune of $170 million to restore it to its original grandeur. Luminaries such as Winston Churchill, Thomas Edison and Amelia Earhart have graced the premises, as well as royalty. Listed in the National Register of Historic Places, the rooms are well furnished with antiques, and they all vary in size, so ask ahead if size matters. Don't miss the Maxfield Parrish painting in the Pied Piper Lounge. Afternoon tea is served in the Garden Court, which has a stunning stained-glass ceiling. All are welcome: the business traveler, families, and, of course, locals, who come for the opulent Sunday brunch. Rates start at $500. *Psst . . . Michael Douglas crashed through the ceiling of the Garden Court Restaurant in the movie* The Game. *And, the rooftop pool is a great place to stroke your way out of a midweek fit of utter exhaustion. Don't forget your swim cap especially if you are an enhanced blonde!*

Palomar Hotel, 12 4th St. (@ Market St.), (415) 348-1111, *www.hotel palomar.com, Tres Chic*

This newcomer in the heart of downtown has just the kind of welcoming vibe and décor that make us happy after long journeys. The lobby is small and sleek, with designer accessories, chic appointments and our favorite— leopard-print rugs. Enter the sexy elevator and transcend the noise of the loud neighborhood—no earplugs needed, they have soundproofed all of the rooms. Great artwork and well-lit hallways are as inviting as the rooms, which have stereo systems, in-room fax machines, desks, plush robes, Aveda bath products, down comforters, and great pillows for a lovely experience all around. In-room spa services are available on request. Rates range from $195–340. Five luxury suites are available for those high-maintenance moments—and you know what we are talking about! *Psst . . . if you are planning to bring your boyfriend or husband on your business trip with you, choose this place. He will find lots to do in the neighborhood while you are at meetings.*

W San Francisco, 181 3rd St. (@ Howard St.), (415) 777-5300, *www.whotels.com, Neighborhood Favorite*

Situated next door to the SF MoMA, the W lobby is always jumping with traveling hipsters and locals who want to be in on the action. Although these hotels are spreading faster than wheat grass, this particular "abode" is wildly popular. The appointments are tremendous: window seats in the rooms, CD players, Aveda bath products, and deluxe linens make us very happy. The highspeed modems are a big help if you are doing business out of your room, and we love the "Whatever, Whenever" button on the phone. If we could just get our lover to understand that concept. . . . Don't forget the trendy XYZ (see Twilight, Downtown) located in the hotel. Rates start at $460.

✎ Not to Miss:

Cliff Hotel, 495 Geary St. (@ Taylor St.), (415) 775-4700, *Ian Schrager Takeover*

Westin St. Francis, 355 Powell St. (bet. Geary & Post Sts.), (415) 397-7000, *Classic*

Nob Hill/Russian Hill/North Beach/Chinatown

✎ Time Off

Alcatraz Island Ferry, Pier 41 (@ Fisherman's Wharf), (415) 705-5555, *Lock Up*

Take the 20-minute ferry ride from Pier 41 to Alcatraz and you will never take the sun for granted again. Enter the prison and feel the chill even on a warm day, listen to the intense noise level due to the all-steel building, see the small cells that residents lived in. Alcatraz, which has housed some of America's worst criminals, most notably Al Capone and the "Birdman," is a never-ending source of controversy and subject of movies and documentaries. Never again will you ponder the idea that you will do "anything" for those Sergio Rossi shoes. Tours run hourly and cost $14.50; reservations are recommended for the Blue & Gold fleet. Just don't try to swim back; the word is still out as to whether you can make it or not, you bad girl! *Psst . . . in 1973, long after the prison had closed, Native American Indians claimed the island as their own for a period of time.*

Angel Island, Pier 41 (@ Fisherman's Wharf), (415) 456-1286, *Daytime Exploration*

Considered the Ellis Island of the West, this was once a detainment center for Chinese immigrants seeking refuge and a new life in San Francisco. Some gained entry, and some did not. Today, it is 758 acres of gorgeous views and hiking heaven! The island's fort is fun to explore after the gourmet picnic that you brought along for the ride.

Coit Tower, 1 Telegraph Hill (@ Greenwich St.), (415) 362-0808, *Great View*

The jury is still out, but until Perry Mason tells us differently, we think Coit Tower has *the best view* of the Bay. Completed in 1933 from funds left to the city by an original "Jane" girl, Lillie Hitchcock Coit, who always had a thing for firemen after they saved her life as a child. (What girl in her right mind doesn't have a thing for those who ride big red trucks with giant hoses?) No need for the Firefighter Workout though—getting to the tower situated at the top of Telegraph Hill is a workout in and of itself . . . we stopped counting after 300 steps! But if you've already done your six-mile run and cardio kick class, feel free to drive or hop a Muni bus to the summit. Open daily, 10 A.M.–7 P.M. Rates $3 for adults. *Psst . . . don't miss the murals at the top of the tower that were painted in the 1930s using the view itself as inspiration!*

Pacific Heritage Museum, 608 Commercial St. (@ Montgomery St.), (415) 362-4100, *Cold Cash*

What would life be without the green bills we have come to know and love as . . . money? Situated near several other small Chinatown museums and galleries, this facility is most notably the site of the U.S. Subtreasury, established in 1852, when the huge westward migration called the Gold Rush took place. If you look hard, you can see some of the coin vaults from strategically placed windows. Also, it is a great place to view ancient Chinese pottery, ceremonial objects and old photos that tie the culture of San Francisco to the Pacific Rim, evident in everyday life in this city on the Bay.

San Francisco Helicopter Tours, Pier 39 (@ Fisherman's Wharf), (800) 400-2404, *Fly Away*

The Little Prince isn't the only one who likes to see the

world from above. San Francisco Helicopter Tours will show you the sights of San Francisco and the other Bay areas such as Marin, Sausalito and the Pacific Coastline.  Should you wish to plan a romantic day, why not try a lunch in the wine country while catching all the views from above along the way! Rates: wine country, $300 per person; standard tours start at $140. *Psst . . . while you're there, check out the 600 sea lions that have made their homes at Pier 39 since 1989.*

Transamerica Pyramid, 600 Montgomery St. (bet. Clay & Washington Sts.), (415) 355-9657, *Egyptian Influence*

Remember the song "Walk Like an Egyptian"? This architectural inspiration brings the mysteries of Egyptian design to the West. Let's face it, every city worth its salt needs a pyramid. Unfortunately, the observation deck that gave fantastic views of the city is now closed to visitors.

⌖ Sweet Dreams

Fairmont Hotel, 950 Mason St. (@ California St.), (415) 772-5000, *www.fairmont.com, Grand Dame*

If the walls of this most golden treasure could speak, they would convey a story worthy of a whole book in its own right! Born out of a gold-rush fortune, they were days away from the grand opening when the earthquake of 1906 struck. The structure made it, but the interior was gutted by fire. Since then, this is where the United Nations charter was drafted, and in the 1980s it was the inspiration for the television show *Hotel*. Now, after an 85-million-dollar face-lift in 1999, it's been restored to its ultimate glory. The lobby is to die for, and the domed ceiling and mosaic tile floored restaurant/bar are fit for a queen. The staff is not quite up to the level of the décor, though they do try. All roads lead us to the Karachi Suite, with a full balcony that is perfect for al fresco dining or dozing on a warm night! Rates start at $189 for a room and $700 for a suite. *Psst . . . the penthouse is a whopping $8,000 a night, mostly inhabited by heads of state, presidents and other overpaid celebrities.*

Hotel Boheme, 444 Columbus Ave. (bet. Green & Vallejo Sts.), (415) 433-9111, *www.hotelboheme.com, Boutique*

A small but sexy hotel to hang your wig in the heart of San Francisco's "Beatnik-gone-chichi" neighborhood. With only 15 rooms, this adorable inn is hard to find, with only an awning over a door that is squeezed tightly between a café and a bakery. Arty black-and-white photos line the hallways to the rooms, which are uniquely romantic with armoires, canopies, and Picasso prints. The rooms all have queen-size beds and are surprisingly quiet, with modern-day amenities like cable television. Cafés and bakeries dominate the surrounding blocks in the Little Italy of San Francisco, and this charming and hospitable place is in the heart of all the action. Rates from $165 to $195.

Huntington Hotel, 1075 California St. (bet. Taylor & Mason Sts.), (415) 474-5400, *www.huntingtonhotel.com, Big Spender*
    Situated in a superglam neighborhood, this hotel seems more like a private club . . . one that we would like to join! Celebrate life and treat yourself to the "country club" of hotels. Built in 1924, some say it could use a bit of modernizing, but we love it just as it is—plush sofas, a mix of lovely European antiques, and *objets d'art,* some of which are museum-quality pieces. Celebrities and diplomats love it for its discrete approach and security . . . or at least the illusion of them! The rooms are lavishly decorated with silks, ornate fringe, antiques, marble bears, and original artwork, some dating back to the seventeenth century. Be sure to come out for afternoon tea and sherry. The views are stunning, and the staff welcomes you as if you were a regular from the moment you arrive. Business center, and day passes to the nearby Huntington Spa, are available. Rates start at $300.

Mark Hopkins Inter-Continental, 1 Nob Hill (@ California St.), (415) 392-3434, *www.markhopkins.com, International Favorite*
    This could be the most historic and renowned hotel in all of San Francisco. During WW II, faithful U.S. troops would spend their last night with their sweethearts here before going into the wild blue. The next day, their loyal and devoted girls would go to the top-floor bar to watch them sail away! Built in 1926 on the site of the former mansion of railroad tycoon Mark Hopkins, noted architects pronounced the structure "perfect" upon completion. Partly French chateau and part Spanish Renaissance embellished with elaborate terra-cotta ornament, the views are outstanding, and the various rooms are spacious and perfect for every kind of visitor. High rollers will find happiness in the opulent suites, the business traveler will be satisfied with mid-priced rooms and, not forgetting those who are on somewhat of a budget, the

basic room fits the bill. The cable car line out front takes you to Chinatown and the Financial District. Rates from $220–$1,500. *Psst . . . take a peek at the Room of the Dons—one of the hidden treasures in the hotel, housing nine seven-foot murals depicting life in California in the early years.*

Ritz-Carlton, 600 Stockton St. (bet. Pine & California Sts.), (415) 296-7465, *www.ritzcarlton.com, World Class*

In a city that boasts of mystery, opulence, and history, this hotel is all of these in one location on the slope of Nob Hill. Certainly it's deliciously self-indulgent, a shrine to architecture, elegance, service and style. . . . The impossibly excellent location (near the shopping mecca known as Union Station) and antique-filled hallways make for a world-class hotel that outshines the competition with little or no contest. The concierges are fast on the uptake, meeting all demands, small or large. Afternoon tea is a must—where the old-moneyed hobnob with the other high rollers. Celebrities, dignitaries, princesses, and random "Jane" girls collide in the elevators . . . at least for a few nights a year! Rates start at $325. *Psst . . . the Sunday brunch is unparalleled (the Terrace, see Eats, Nob Hill). And the Dining Room's gourmet cuisine is one step short of perfection. The chefs are formerly of the fabulous Le Cirque, NYC.*

Washington Square Inn, 1660 Stockton St. (bet. Union & Filbert Sts.), (415) 981-4220, *www.wsissf.com, Non-Chain Delight*

This is a European-style B&B situated directly on Washington Square Park amid popular tourist attractions like Fisherman's Wharf, the Embarcadero, Chinatown, and more. The façade is somewhat unremarkable, but inside it's hard to resist the charming manner of this delightful inn. The rooms are modest but, for the price, hard to beat. Each of the 15 rooms is decorated differently, but all contain antiques, floral prints, down pillows, and vases of fresh flowers, making you feel like you are in an elegant but comfy country house. In true European fashion, a simple Continental breakfast is included in the room fee, and can be ordered to your room or eaten in front of the fireplace downstairs. In the afternoon, informal snacks are provided, like cucumber sandwiches, homemade cookies and tea, and in the evening they offer wine and hors d'oeuvres. Parking is scarce in the neighborhood, so take advantage of the valet parking. Rates are $145–245. *Psst . . . skip the freebie breakfast one day and mosey over to one of the many Italian sidewalk cafés in North Beach.*

White Swan Inn, 845 Bush St. (bet. Mason & Taylor Sts.), (415) 775-1755, *www.foursisters.com, B&B*

One of the best bed and breakfasts in the city, built circa 1908, this charming hotel with cozy fireplaces in every room feels more like an English lodge than a trendy hotel. Afternoons bring about hors d'oeuvres—veggies, cheeses, and cakes—accompanied by wine, sherry, or cocktails. The rooms are painted hunter green and burgundy, and seem more informal than the lobby. All are decorated with four-poster beds, wing-back chairs, and floral wallpaper. Four of the rooms have bay windows, and two of the "romance suites" have canopy beds, VCRs, and complimentary chocolates! All major amenities are available, like valet parking ($25 per day), minibar, and full breakfast, which is included in the price of the room. Rates from $180–275.

York Hotel, 940 Sutter St. (bet. Leavenworth & Hyde Sts.), (415) 885-6800, *www.yorkhotel.com, Affordable*

Movie aficionados will be happy to recognize this as the primary setting for Alfred Hitchcock's classic film *Vertigo*. All "scare" tactics aside, it was renovated in 1995; a sunlit, peaceful lobby and a long string of modern amenities and services make this one of the city's most reasonable and elegant places for "Jane" girls to rest—in peace! Of special note is the Plush Room, meeting room by day and cabaret by night. During the height of Prohibition, this hotel quietly (and illegally) opened this now-famous room for events and live cabaret. Make your way through the maze of hidden passageways to reach this "den of sin" gone Junior League. Valet parking available. Rates start at $159. *Psst . . . celebrating something? Ask about the Champagne Cabaret Package: includes a deluxe room, chilled champagne, Continental breakfast, two show tickets, preferred seating, and valet parking, for around $199 plus tax.*

Good to Know:

It's dusk . . . where do you go if you are lovers in search of a place to take in the moonrise experience? Go to the corner of Broadway (bet. Jones & Taylor Sts.). High upon a perch in Russian Hill is the perfect place to experience the whole event in all its grandeur. North Beach in general glistens on clear nights at sunset.

Marina/Cow Hollow

✦ Time Off

Crissy Field, Golden Gate National Recreation Area, north of the Presidio, *Surfing*

For 200 years this property next to the Golden Gate Bridge was a military base. In fact, more then one million servicemen passed through its gates on their way to the Pacific after the attack on Pearl Harbor. Take in the military memorials as you walk along the Bay, spy on the cute windsurfer "dudes" that hang out here . . . It's actually one step above the supermarket for fruitful pursuits of the opposite sex! Bring your in-line skates and feign a sprained ankle . . .

Exploratorium, @ Palace of Fine Arts, 3601 Lyon St. (@ Bay St.), (415) 563-7337, *www.exploratorium.edu, Interactive Science*

The Exploratorium was named one of the best science museums in the world by *Scientific American,* and was originally conceived to "explore" the secrets of heat, light, electricity, electronics, temperature, touch, vision, waves, language, and color through hands-on exhibits. Kids (and adults who never paid attention in school) have a chance to experience science in an interactive setting. We love the weekend seminars on crazy subjects like bubble blowing. Grab an espresso from the Angel Café, on the premises, and explore the afternoon away! Costs $9 for adults and $5 for children aged 6–17, $2.50 for three- to five-year-olds. *Psst . . . make reservations for a special night with the little ones, and check out the Tactile Dome, an enclosed crawl space of textural adventures. It is completely black inside and you crawl, walk, and bounce your way through the darkness trying to identify household objects. Sometimes vertigo can set in, so go before dinner. Adults love it as much as kids.*

Marina Green Park, Marina Blvd. @ Fillmore St., *Walkabout*

A park is a park is a park . . . but when you're in the mood for a nice sunny-day stroll with your pooch or smooch, there's no better place to be! Relax, play a little baseball on one of the fields, roller-blade, picnic, or play Frisbee. And speaking of pooches, San Fran is such a pet-friendly city, you and Rover will have a lot of company on your walk!

The Octagon House, 2645 Gough St. (@ Union St.), (415) 441-7512, *Eight Is Enough*

Let's all salute our historical and "hysterical" Colonial American Dames. What? This is the home to the National Society of Colonial Dames of America of California. It dates back to 1861, and was designed in the belief that this type of house was healthier due to the sunlight streaming through the windows. Most recently, the house was uplifted and moved cross the street from its original location, but it has remained intact and brings us colonial-period treasures. "The House" displays early American furniture, silver, pewter, and extraordinary documents, like the signatures of 54 of the 56 signers of the Declaration of Independence. Admission is free. Open only on the second Sunday and second and fourth Thursdays of each month from noon to 3 P.M. Closed in Jan.

Palace of Fine Arts, 3601 Lyon St. (@ Bay St.), (415) 561-0360, *Romantic Setting*

As poet laureate Herb Caen said more than 50 years ago, San Francisco is Baghdad by the Bay! Built in 1915 for the Pacific International Exposition, to celebrate the opening of the Panama Canal, this was the only structure to survive the celebration, which lasted 288 days. Ironically, it was modeled after Greek ruins. During WW II it housed ammunition. In 1962 wealthy local resident Walter Johnson helped to restore this Beaux Arts beauty to its original grandeur by matching government funds. This site is often called the most romantic destination for picnics, parties and proposals. Wander past the reflecting pool and take a few moments to do just that—reflect.

St. Francis Yacht Club, 700 Marina Blvd., (415) 563-6363, *Boat Yard*

Social high jinks on the high seas . . . Want to join in the fun? If you are a member of any yacht club worldwide, thanks to San Fran hospitality and reciprocity you can spend your days at the St. Francis sailing, having a drink, and dreaming of how great your boat would look on the Bay. Not that it doesn't look good in St. Tropez where you left it . . . right?

✵ Sweet Dreams

The Art Center Bed & Breakfast, 1902 Filbert St. (@ Laguna St.), (415) 567-1526, *www.artcenterbb.citysearch.com, Artists' Haven*

Calling all artists seeking a refuge in San Francisco. There is no sign outside this lovely 1857 French Provincial–style apartment building, so be sure to bring the exact address with you. The whole inn is dedicated to art and culture, so it's not uncommon to find yourself engaged in salon-style discussions, if you're in the mood. Otherwise, it is quite private and peaceful. Choose from five different living spaces: two small studios with fireplaces, two large suites with private street entrances, and one three-room apartment that is perfect to spread out in. There is a sky-lit garden that's a great place to get out your canvas and paint the afternoon away! Rates are $155–265.

Marina Inn, 3110 Octavia St. (@ Lombard St.), (800) 274-1420, *Self-Employed*

Situated on the famous crooked street, this 1924 four-story Victorian home is an ideal place to stay for the "Jane" girl who wants style and plush amenities without having to break her Prada piggybank to do it! Who would expect these special touches: nightly turn downs with chocolates on the pillows, remote-control televisions (hidden in pinewood cabinets), four-poster beds, pretty wallpaper, and full bathtubs with showers. Not forgetting the Continental breakfast and predinner sherry! Convenient to Union Street and directly on the bus route to downtown. Think of all the things you could do with the extra cash that was saved on hotel bills. . . . Rates start at $65.

Union Street Inn, 2229 Union St. (bet. Steiner & Fillmore Sts.), (415) 346-0424, *www.unionstreetinn.com, Home Sweet Home*

Smack-dab in the heart of one of the best shopping and dining "hoods" in the whole Bay Area, if you are tired of large hotels with long elevator waits and corporate blah-ness, this is *the* place to stay. Hosts Jane Berteorelli and David Coyle are eager to help with any of your needs at this home away from home. Step off the street and up the steep stairs, ring the bell, and enter this Edwardian refuge. Each room is furnished beautifully. There are five large guestrooms and a huge deluxe carriage house across the garden—all with private baths, some with Jacuzzis! The parlor downstairs is enchanting, with a fireplace, period furniture, and 24-hour coffee/tea service. In the evening, they serve complimentary wine and cheese. Best of all: the full breakfast served in the lovely private English garden. They book out well in advance, so plan ahead. Rates are $150–$250. Parking nearby for a mere $12.

✎ Not to Miss:

Comfort Inn, 2775 Van Ness Ave. (@ Lombard St.), (415) 928-5000, *Reliable*

"The Heights" (Pacific, Presidio, Laurel) ....

✎ Time Off

Haas-Lilienthal House, 2007 Franklin St. (bet. Washington & Jackson Sts.), (415) 441-3004, *www.sfheritage.org, Architectural Delight*

No visitor or local can call their San Francisco experience complete without a peek at this classic 1886 Victorian house, the city's only historic house that is open to the public as a museum. This is a prime example of a Queen Anne Victorian home; it was built for William Haas, whose descendants went on to own Levi Strauss and the Oakland As. It is now owned by the city, and hour-long docent-led tours are operated by the Foundation for San Francisco's Architectural Heritage. Open Wed., noon to 3 P.M., Sun until 4 P.M. No reservations required. Costs $5.

Presidio Golf Course, 300 Finley Rd. (@ Arguello Gate), (415) 561-4653, *www.presidiogolf.com, Tee Time*

Golfers can stop daydreaming and hit this course just 10 minutes from downtown. This Arnold Palmer Management course has a long history attached to it: presidents Teddy Roosevelt and Dwight Eisenhower played here regularly, and since the course went public in 1995, so can you! The greens overlook the city, the San Francisco Bay and the Pacific. After nine holes it may be time to hit the clubhouse, or have a salad at the café in front of the massive stone fireplace. Should you aspire to be a successful "Jane" girl, plan a corporate meeting here and you will be sure to close the deal. Tee times 6 A.M.–6:30 P.M. seven days a week. Rates $63 weekdays and $93 on weekends.

St. Mary's Cathedral, 1111 Gough St. (@ Geary St.), (415) 567-2020, *Heavenly Glance*

Architects and design freaks flock to this imposing example of modern architecture. Notice how the roof soars toward heaven, recreating a cross. Step inside and even the design layman will be impressed by the massive marble altar, 190-foot stained-glass cross, and oversized organ pipes. Don't miss this opportunity to appreciate an early 1970s structure that skillfully combines Christianity with modern-day architecture.

❧ *Sweet Dreams*

El Drisco Hotel, 2901 Pacific Ave. (@ Broderick St.), (415) 346-2880, *www.eldriscohotel.com, Neighborhood Favorite*

Situated in the ultratony residential area of Pacific Heights, this small ultrachic hotel is nestled among multimillion dollar homes. It's *the* ideal home away from home for the international jet-set girl! The six-story structure was completely renovated in 1997 and is a welcome addition to the city. Business travelers will enjoy the free morning shuttle downtown to the Financial District. "Jane" touristas will find that personal touches make all the difference. There is a small, somewhat depressing gym in the basement, but it is sufficient in a pinch. We prefer to take a brisk hike of the neighborhood, dreaming about which house we'd buy if we hit the jackpot. The steep hills help stimulate your appetite in the morning before the lavish continental breakfast. The rooms are light and airy, and most have sweeping views of the cityscape. Nonmetered parking is available in the area. Bonus: nightly wine receptions are perfect opportunities to chat with other guests before heading out for a night on the town! Rates start at $245.

Hotel Majestic, 1500 Sutter St. (@ Gough St.), (415) 444-1100, *One of a Kind*

European elegance abounds at this unique Pacific Heights hotel. One step into the lobby of this lovely, recently renovated hotel and you too will be convinced that the Gold Rush was real and not just a history-book tale. Built in 1902, back when San Francisco was still the wild, wild West, the hotel played home to actress Olivia de Havilland, who lived here in the 1930s. To this day it is still all about civilization with its fine linens, down comforters, claw-foot tubs, and plump feather pillows. Good for a romantic night with your overworked honey, or to celebrate your parents' anniversary with a weekend away. The service is outstanding . . . making us all feel more like houseguests than hotel guests. Cocktails can be consumed at the authentic nincteenth-century French bar, which boasts of one of the rarest butterfly collections in the world. Rates from $150–450. *Psst . . . Sunday brunch is a must.*

Laurel Inn, 444 Presidio Ave. (@ California St.), (415) 567-8467, *www.thelaurelinn.com, Mod Squad*

This is a great neighborhood hotel for extended visits. Formerly a 1960s motor inn, redone in stylish mid-century-modern décor. All of the 49 rooms are spacious, with CD players, VCRs, irons, hairdryers, voice mail, data ports, and writing desks (including a nice CD and film lending library). A good majority of the rooms have kitchenettes for those who travel with a personal chef (not!) or at least a Martha Stewart cookbook. We were ready to relocate permanently after a brief stay that included free indoor parking, afternoon lemonade and cookie service, and a pet-friendly policy. Only mom has treated us so well! Rates are $145–165 and include Continental breakfast.

Sherman House, 2160 Green St. (bet. Webster & Fillmore Sts.), (415) 563-3600, *www.theshermanhouse.com, Out of this World*

This is the ultimate "Jane" place! An 1876 mansion that feels more like your rich aunt's home than a hotel, this four-and-a-half-story Victorian luxury hotel was renovated and "designed" by William Gaylord, a veteran resident and arts enthusiast. There are two ways to enjoy this marvelous hotel. The main house includes a wide variety of rooms, some with views of the formal gardens, and Biedermeier accents. (Room 103 has its own garden entrance from a slanted walkway; room 203 is the only room in the main house with a fireplace.) There are also suites, like the Sherman Suite, offering a world-famous view of the whole city, from the Golden Gate Bridge to Alcatraz Island, from a brick-floored terrace that could hold up to 30 people . . . not to mention the elegant Roman-style tub in the bath. Or book the Carriage House, which has several high-priced, highly styled rooms. Honeymooners, take note: the Thomas Church Garden Suite (#501) has two rooms and one-and-a-half baths, a fireplace, French-paned windows that overlook the private gardens, Chinese slate floors, a four-poster bed, and, best of all, it leads to a sunken garden terrace with a gazebo and pond. Rates from $485–$1,200.

✦ Not to Miss:

Queen Anne Hotel, 1590 Sutter St. (@ Octavia St.), (415) 441-2828, *www.queenanne.com, Reliable Favorite*

Hayes Valley/Civic Center

✦ Time Off

Farmers Market, @ United Nations Plaza, Market St. (bet. 7th & 8th Sts.), (415) 558-9455, *Fresh Air*

All sorts of delicious produce from all over sunny California is here for you to browse through and choose from for culinary wizardry in the kitchen tonight! They also sell fish and gardening products. This market is in an area that is frequented by many homeless people, so it can be a little scary to buy food without a pang of guilt, but do understand: San Francisco is the most tolerant state in the Union. Open Sundays and Wednesdays from 7 A.M.–5 P.M.

San Francisco Ballet, @ War Memorial Opera House, 401 Van Ness Ave. (bet. Fulton & Grove Sts.) (415) 865-2000, *www.sfballet.org, Cultural Enclave*

America's oldest ballet company is in the hands of Helgi Tomasson, the current darling of the ballet world. Formerly a principal dancer with the New York City Ballet, he worked closely with the legendary Balanchine. Under his guidance, this San Francisco troupe has matured into a world-class classical company. If you're planning to be in town around the Christmas season, plan ahead to see *The Nutcracker.* Tickets can be purchased on-line or via the Ballet Ticket Services office . . . or pick them up at the Civic Center itself.

San Francisco Opera, @ War Memorial Opera House, 401 Van Ness Ave. (bet. Fulton & Grove Sts.), (415) 864-3330, *Figaro*

"Oh, there's a band?" are the exact words of Julia Roberts's character in *Pretty Woman,* upon arriving at the opera for the first time via Leer jet with the *gorgeous* Richard Gere in tow . . . What "Jane" in her right mind would pay attention to the opera when she could be flirting madly with Richard? The SF Opera performs in the opulent 1932 War Memorial Opera House, and is second only to the Met in size and rank. The facility has been updated to house state-of-the-art lighting and computerized scenery equipment necessary for their artistically open-minded interpretations of the classics. Be blasted into the Golden Age, sitting in brocade chairs in your "box" draped with velvet curtains. Tickets are scarce so plan ahead; wear your best black dress and bring your tiara! *Psst . . . bigger bathrooms for women! Hurray! Want to be a part of the scene but don't sing a note? Join Encore, a cool group of opera enthusiasts who raise money via cocktail receptions and other social events. Membership is $60, and it is a great way to meet new people!*

✒ Sweet Dreams

Archbishop's Mansion, 1000 Fulton St. (@ Steiner St.) (415) 563-7872, *www.archbishopsmansion.com, Romantic*

Built in 1904 as the archbishop's residence, this out-of-the-way Alamo Square Park mansion was converted into one of the premier bed and breakfasts in San Francisco. With only 15 rooms (5 are suites) it provides the lap of luxury for those seeking privacy and intimacy. As you ascend the sweeping three-story staircase, you'll have plenty of time to anticipate the much-talked-about pleasures that await you in the Gypsy Baron's Room, bedecked with a sunken hot tub. Crisp linens, VCRs, and spa robes are just the tip of the iceberg when it comes to amenities. We particularly love the bathroom sofas that are perfect for lolling about au naturel postbath! Rates start at $200.

Cathedral Hill Hotel, 1101 Van Ness Ave. (@ Geary St.), (415) 776-8200, *Working Girl*

You over there! Need a functional place to stay while on a business trip? Girls who love the theater, opera and ballet will find this hotel's location ideal, but tourists will find it too far from the city's other major attractions. Never heeding the voice of reason, we naturally prefer to stay near the beloved "arts" center and travel by taxi or cable car to our meetings. They have a nice garden for an afternoon off; otherwise the spacious rooms can seem a bit tired. Bop across the street to steal a peak at the magnificent City Hall. The room service is speedy when rushing out in the morning to a meeting. Fitness center too. Rates start at $109.

Hayes Valley Inn, 417 Gough St. (bet. Ivy & Hayes Sts.), (415) 431-9131 or (800) 930-7999, *www.hayesvalleyinn.com, Euro-Style B&B*

So maybe the thought of a shared-tub-and-toilet situation is scary. Never fear, this place is so darn clean, charming and overall superwelcoming that we just might want to sacrifice a little privacy! Artfully positioned in the heart of the Civic Center, this 32-room European-style hotel has a vanity in every room, cable TV and private phone lines. Breakfast is served in a lovely communal kitchen aptly named the Ivy Room. The halls are brightly lit, with wainscoting and happy colors. Smokers and nonsmokers are welcome and, if you're traveling with Pooch, let them know ahead of time, and they will prepare for the two of you! This truly is one of the best places to park if you are on a budget, or for long-term stays with easy access, without compromising safety, style and comfort. Rates start at $58 for a single, up to $99. *Psst . . . the San Francisco Furniture Mart is nearby, as well as other places to shop. Grab a famous burger at Flippers Gourmet Burgers, a must, 482 Hayes St. (bet. Gough & Octavia Sts.), (415) 552-8880.*

Inn at the Opera, 333 Fulton St. (bet. Franklin & Gough Sts.), (415) 863-8400, *www.innattheopera.com, Old-School Elegance*

Rest your pretty little head at this elegant, small hotel located a stone's throw from the city's Performing Arts Center. Maybe that's why Tony Bennett and other operatic stars love this place. Although some of the 47 rooms are now owned by time-share, it is a genius discovery if you are looking for more than a traditional hotel room. All regular rooms are equipped with small kitchens, complete with microwave, refrigerator, and coffeemaker. Many small touches make it all so lovely. Notice when you enter the room that classical music is playing on the bedside stereo . . . No, the maid did not leave it on by mistake—it's for you, to get you "in the mood" for music! The restaurant in the back of the lobby has a lovely dark bar that is ideal for a pre/post performance cocktail and hors d'oeuvres. Valet parking available. Rooms start at $195. *Psst . . . ask for a suite when you are checking in; you just might get lucky if one of the owners has left it available!*

Phoenix Hotel, 601 Eddy St. (bet. Larkin & Post Sts.), (415) 776-1380, *Retro Chic*

Rock stars and the girls who love them feel at home at this 1950s-style hotel. It may seem deserted, but appearances can be deceiving . . . the majority of the hotel guests are still sleeping at 4 in the afternoon! The 44 rooms are decorated in a "tropical bungalow" style. Although they're nothing like the bungalows at the Beverly Hills Hotel, they will fulfill any tropicana-kitsch fantasy: imported bamboo furniture, gigantic birds of paradise, flowering plants, and various other island-style furnishings create an idyllic backdrop for all of your quirky California dreamin'. Beach boys, Clairol girls, and those of us who "love the night life and like to boogie" will find this the ideal place to park for a weekend and hang out poolside in exotic private cabanas. Forward your calls and pretend that life on the road is dreadful! We love the original art by emerging artists that shower the whole place with extra personality. Pearl Jam, Johnny Depp, and Linda Ronstadt have slept here . . . Abe Lincoln has not, but you can visit him at the Wax Museum. Rates are $129–145, deluxe suites are $205. *Psst . . . the glamorous swimming pool showcases the painting entitled* My Fifteen Minutes—Tumbling Waves.

Warwick Regis Hotel, 490 Geary St. (@ Taylor St.), (415) 928-7900, (800) 827-3447, *www.warwickhotels.com, Business Headquarters*

Yearning for a European experience, but have to come to San Fran on biz so you can't hop the Concorde for Paris? Opt to stay at this intimate hotel filled with one-of-a-kind antiques. The rooms are well appointed, with four-poster beds, marble baths and cushy towels. For the ultimate in luxury, stay in one of the Executive Suites and have dinner in front of the fireplace. The small café and bar, La Scene Café, is usually packed before and after the theater. Chat with a stranger about *Madame Butterfly* or about how in love Onassis was with Callas before Jackie O stole him out from under her. It's all about the arts and the love of the arts. On a less lofty note: twenty-four-hour room service and valet parking available. Rooms start at $215, plus tax. *Psst . . . need to work out the frustration of the week? They sell passes for $10 per visit to a health club that's a hop, skip and grunt away!*

Haight-Ashbury

⚘ Time Off

California Academy of Sciences, @ Golden Gate Park, off Middle Dr. E. (bet. John F. Kennedy & Martin Luther King, Jr. Drs.), (415) 750-7145, *Citywide Favorite*

All things Earth, Ocean, and Space since 1853. The "academy" was established to explore and explain the natural world and was the first of its kind in the West. If the

1989 earthquake wasn't enough for you, try out the Earthquake Theater for a little reality check in sensaround. The
exhibit on Native American culture is amazing. There is
a hall devoted entirely to the natural wonders and history of California,
including life-size exhibits of wildlife from when the West was indeed
wild. Check out the actual size of your run-of-the-mill giraffe in the Africa
Hall . . . unbelievable, baby. Catch one of the daily "sky shows" in the gorgeous planetarium . . . and don't miss the aquarium across the courtyard
that hosts all sorts of reptiles in its "swamp," plus oodles of salt and freshwater fish. And for little wanna-be-married mermaids: the gem and mineral
hall is great for scoping out the rock or boulder of your dreams . . . "Hi, I'm
looking for an emerald-cut Everest . . ." Costs: Aquarium & Natural History
Museum: $8.50, adults; $5.50, students & seniors; free on the first Wed. of
each month. Planetarium/Laserium shows are $2.50, $1.50 for children.

Golden Gate Park Stables, John F. Kennedy Drive (@ 36th Ave.),
(415) 668-7360, *Riding*

Jonesing for Mr. Ed? A horse is a horse is a horse of course, so whether
you're a pro or a beginner gallop on over to the Golden Gate and take a les-
son or a guided tour in the park or along Ocean Beach. Reservations required.

Golden Gate Park, bet. Great Highway, Lincoln Way, Stanyan St., &
Fulton St., (415) 831-2700, *City Escape*

Over 1,000 green acres of outdoor playpen to inspire and exhaust! Bike,
roller-blade, walk, jog, ride horseback, see buffaloes, play baseball, basket-
ball or volleyball, sunbathe, picnic, dance at the bandstand or soak in culture at the museums. If you can't find something fun to do here then we are
plain out of suggestions. . . . Spend time absorbing knowledge at the California Academy of Sciences Museum, and then walk through the park and
catch a glimpse of the roaming buffaloes. Continue a little further, and
you'll see the ocean. Lewis and Clark never had it so good! For little ex-
plorers . . . the children's playground has a magical carousel! *Psst . . . don't
miss the annual Shakespeare Festival held during the summer.*

Japanese Tea Garden, @ Golden Gate Park, (@ Lincoln St. Entrance),
(415) 752-1171, *Outdoor Zen*

Four acres of Zen. Bring your stress, bring your mother-in-law, bring
your pals to this delightfully pastoral tribute to the East. Next door to the

California Academy of Sciences, peaceful gardens and a Japanese hut with walkways are the perfect setting to help melt away modern-day stresses. Wander aimlessly through the romantic tea garden until you happen upon the eighteenth-century Buddha, then stroll over the moon bridge, making sure to stop halfway across to gaze at your reflection in the koi pond before making a wish and tossing the inflationary dime or quarter into the drink. Isn't your wish worth a few extra pennies? Experience a traditional Japanese tea ceremony in the Tea House and pick up some unique gifts and notepaper in the gift shop. . . . Best on a sunny day. You wouldn't want to drag your kimono through the mud now, would you? Cost: $3.50.

The Red Vic 1727 Haight St. (bet. Cole & Schadder Sts.), (415) 668-3994, *Classic Films*

There is nothing like the Golden Age of Hollywood, and you can catch some of her classics at this home for indie entertainment. People-watch from your padded bench while you nibble on scrumptious homemade goodies from the concession stand. Why can't AMC bake brownies this good? Just goes to show that bigger is not always better—even when it comes to a movie screen. We'll take a smaller screen and better snacks any day!

Skates on Haight, 1818 Haight St. (@ Stanyan St.) (415) 752-8375, *www.skates.com, Roller Derby*

If you get to Golden Gate Park and have a burning desire to skate off into the sunset, but forgot your blades, have no fear. These folks sell, rent, and repair skates, roller blades, and skateboards, and for the enthusiastic novice they have lessons available! Skate Golden Gate Park on a Sunday when it is closed to "vehicular competition." Mon.–Fri., 11 A.M.–7 P.M., Sat. & Sun. 10 A.M.–6 P.M. *Psst . . . check out their other location, 1219 Polk St. (bet. Bush & Sutter Sts.), (415) 447-1800, Mon–Fri., 11 A.M.–7 P.M., Sat. 10 A.M.–6 P.M.*

⚜ *Not to Miss:*

AIDS Memorial Grove, Golden Gate Park (at the corner of Middle East & Bowling Green Drs.), (415) 750-8340, *Pay Tribute*

Asian Art Museum of San Francisco, 75 Tea Garden Drive (in Golden Gate Park), (415) 379-8800, *www.asianart.org, Renovation Central Until Fall 2002*

Haight-Ashbury walking tour, (415) 863-1621, *Flower Power*

Sweet Dreams

The Metro Hotel, 319 Divisadero St. (bet. Page & Oak Sts.), (415) 861-5364, *Affordable*

Situated in the heart of Haight-Ashbury, this place is pretty bare bones in terms of furnishings, but adequate for the girl on the go! The halls are wide and lined with some nice antiques. The rooms themselves are brightly lit and clean, and it's comforting to look out the window and see the hustle and bustle on the action-packed street below. It is easy to check in and out, and you will always feel right at home in this neighborhood. More money to save for your shopping spree in Union Square. Rates are $66–120. *Psst . . . the café next door is adorable, with a charming garden that is great for sitting outside in nice weather for brunch, and to relax over the Sunday* Chronicle.

The Red Victorian, 1665 Haight St. (bet. Belvedere & Cole Sts.), (415) 864-1978, *www.redvic.com, Hippie Chicks*

This place is a real blast from the 1960s that is way more than a not-for-profit hotel. Get the true sense that you lived through the era of peace, love, and patchouli in the center of where it all happened, on Haight Street. Here's the deal: it's part inn, part peace center, part gift shop, part community center, and part art gallery. Owner Sami Sunchild is quite a character, and her devotion to spreading peace, love, and happiness is truly admirable. This is *the* place to go if you are in search of more than a room. Prepare to "get the fever" while you are there. Between the inspirational psychedelic lettering ("visual poetry") saying things like "be somebody magnificent," and the meditation space, there is no room for negativity here. There are 18 spacious rooms with different names and themes. We love the "Summer of Love" room. The family-style breakfast downstairs is a nice time to mingle, especially if you're alone and seeking conversation. Rates from $86–200.

Victorian Inn on the Park, 301 Lyon St. (@ Fell St.), (415) 931-1830, *Historic B&B*

There is something special about this centrally located grand historic home, originally constructed in 1897, and restored with modern amenities less than 20 years ago. The inn proprietors are on hand to make sure that your every need is attended to. It is an elegant place to stay in a mostly residential neighborhood, no matter what your purpose. All rooms have private baths and lovely antiques, and one lucky room overlooks the panhandle of Golden Gate Park. Mornings are lovely with a newspaper, juice, seasonal read. Sherry and wine are served in the afternoons. owing of repeat visitors and, after one stay, we were rt at $159, $199 w/fireplace.

Noe Valley

☙ Time Off

Castro Theatre, 429 Castro St. (@ Market St.), (415) 621-6120, *Glamour Filmhouse*

Situated in an ornate Spanish Renaissance–style landmark building, this is undeniably the best "restoration" that manages to seat 1,600 for movies. There is a charming Wurlitzer organ that plays "San Francisco Open Your Golden Gate" before each show and then magically sinks into the floor by way of a modern hydraulic lift. Last fall we felt as if we died and went to heaven at the fantastic Dive e Divine series—Divas: The Divine Women of the Italian Silent Cinema, with live musical accompaniment by Sodo and Laurent. Costs $7.50 for adults and $4.50 for seniors and children. *Psst . . . hop one of the unique imported vintage streetcars that run the old-time Muni F line from here to lower Market Street. The streetcars were imported from Lisbon, Milan, and Beijing, and add a nostalgic touch to the neighborhood, or if the movie you're seeing is popular, go early and dine at Marcello's across the street. It's fast, and innovative pizza is served.*

Randall Museum, 199 Museum Way (bet. 14th & 17th Sts.), (415) 554-9600, *With Kids*

This is a fantastic place to bring the kids for educational entertainment! This museum is geared to children: there is a petting zoo with chickens, ducks, and guinea pigs, and a "look but don't touch" section with snakes, fish, turtles, and owls! They have all sorts of free classes during the week, including art and ceramic, for which reservations are suggested. Saturday class is "drop in" and costs $3.

☙ Sweet Dreams

Noe's Nest, 3973 23rd St. (bet. Sanchez & Noe Sts.), (415) 821-0751, *www.noesnest.com, Neighborhood Favorite*

This neighborhood is a wasteland when it comes to hotels of any sort, and null and void of any large "business" facilities, but if you're in dire need of a place to "store" your mother or brother visiting from Iowa, this is an excellent option. Established in 1988 with the idea of creating a unique home-away-from-home near downtown, this twist on the B&B concept has six rooms named according their décors. Our favorite is the Treehouse ($150), located in the garden next to the hot tub. . . . A pine tree actually winds its way through a room that includes a queen-size bed and fireplace. The other favorite is the Garden Suite ($160), which has a redwood deck and is steps away from the landscaped garden and hot tub. We absolutely adore the shower with a garden view! Indulge in the Brooklyn Breakfast: bagels, lox, and cream cheese included.

The Willows Inn, 710 14th St., (bet. Church & Sanchez Sts.), (415) 431-4770, *www.willowssf.com, Cheap Sleepover*

Largely undiscovered, this inexpensive B&B has the charm of a European inn and is highly popular with the gay or lesbian looking for a quiet, affordable place to rest. There are 12 rooms available, decorated with California Gypsy Willow furniture that lends an extra-special twist to the individuality of the inn. Brush your teeth in privacy with the in-room sinks; otherwise, it's a share kind of thing when you need to bathe or tinkle. Cable TV and mini-bars available by request, and expect to pay more. Rates start at $90–120.

Not to Miss:

Inn on Castro, 321 Castro St. (bet. Market & 16th St.), (415) 861-0321, *www.innoncastro.com, Neighborhood Favorite*

Mission

Time Off

Mission Dolores, 3321 16th St. (@ Dolores St.), (415) 621-8203, *History Buff*

Hailed as the oldest building in San Francisco, this authentic Catholic mission (the actual namesake of the neighborhood!) was designed by Father

Francis Palou and constructed in 1776—supposedly completed four days before the signing of the Declaration of Independence! The forefathers would have been proud! Built mostly by the blood, sweat, and tears of Native Americans, the purpose of the "mission" was to "Christianize" their pagan souls. . . . The structure itself is made of four-foot-thick adobe walls and redwood beams, and has an amazing altar that was brought from Mexico in 1796. Enjoy the peaceful garden, with fragrant roses, redwood trees, and native plants. And don't miss the cemetery where Mexicans, American Indians, and prominent San Franciscans rest in peace—except during the occasional quake! Maybe you will recognize it from the famous Alfred Hitchcock film *Vertigo,* starring Kim Novak and Jimmy Stewart. *Psst . . . religious services are offered daily at noon in Spanish, and two services Sunday mornings in English.*

Precita Eyes Mural Center, 2981 24th St. (bet. Harrison & Alabama Sts.), (415) 285-2287, *Outsider Art*

In case you haven't noticed, the city is home to over 200 public murals. In particular, this neighborhood is home to more than 60 fabulous murals. Dig deep into the mostly Mexican pictures, steeped in color, depicting the lives and history of this Latino community. Some are politically motivated and others are homages to Bay Are pop-culture icons like Carlos Santana. This center offers walking tours of the Mission District every Saturday from 11 A.M.–1:30 P.M. The guides are fun and quite informative. Bike tours are fun as well and are offered on Sundays. Cost: $10 for adults, $2 under 18. *Psst . . . we particularly love the Balmy Alley, where almost every passageway and blank cement wall is covered with amazing urban art. May is Mural Awareness Month . . . Muy caliente, baby.*

The Roxie Cinema, 3117 16th St. (bet. Gurrero & Valencia Sts.), (415) 863-1087, *Eclectic Film*

Another great art house dedicated to seasonal scheduling and multigenre listings: film noir, Japanese à la King Kong, Kung Fu, and pre-Code Hollywood melodrama . . . Get a schedule and bring your giant Gucci tote filled with Diet Coke and air-popped popcorn. Call for show times. Costs $7.

Yerba Buena Center for the Arts, 701 Mission St. (@ Third St.), (415) 978-2787, *www.yerbabuenaarts.org, Citywide Favorite*

Sitting in the shadows of the SF Moma, this is most definitely the center of all things cultural in San Francisco. Designed by famed Japanese architect Fumihiko Maki, the center includes five acres of parks, galleries and community centers . . . a true urban cultural oasis! There are several ways to enjoy this ode-to-the-arts shrine. Hang out in the sun on the large grassy lawn, taking in the gorgeous sculptures. Next, spend some time in front of the Martin Luther King, Jr., Memorial waterfall and fountain, where large panels of etched glass are the backdrop to cascades of water. Then, venture inside to check out the diverse exhibitions, ranging from outlandish video installations to more traditional shows like eighteenth-century Impressionism. And finish the afternoon with a late lunch in the gardens. Open 11 A.M.–8 P.M. Tues–Sun. Admission $5, free the first Thurs. of each month from 5–8 P.M.

Metreon, @ Yerba Buena Gardens, 701 Mission St. (@ Third St.), (415) 543-1275, *Kids Delight*

This is a megaplex entertainment center for little ones who seek the highest form of entertainment and excellence. There are two special parts for the children, housing 15 cinemas including the largest IMAX screen in North America, and then there is the Rooftop at Yerba Buena, which is devoted solely to the entertainment of "youth." Housing an indoor ice skating rink, a children's museum, a bowling alley, a kid-run garden, and the secret treasure, a 93-year-old hand-carved carousel. Originally perched in the Playland at the Beach, it now graces us with it's playful presence! *Psst . . . tours of the YB Gardens are available by appointment for a nominal fee; call (415) 541-0312.*

Sweet Dreams

Andora Inn, 2434 Mission St. (bet. 20th & 21st Sts.), (415) 282-0337, *www.andorainn.citysearch.com, Victorian Charmer*

In a neighborhood with the most happening nightlife, this is a great place to get your beauty rest at the heart of all of the action! Amenities include Internet access, Serta mattresses, bathrobes, and five-star service. Deluxe rooms and suites have even more added attractions and personal touches, with fresh flowers, in-room coffee service, ironing boards, and a fine video library to entertain during attacks of insomnia. Note: there is no 24-hour front desk, so to be safe, have someone walk you to the gated front entrance. From $79 to $119 for European-style (shared baths); deluxe rooms and suites are $119 to $269, which includes a Continental breakfast and wine & cheese in the evenings. *Psst . . . this is a nonsmoking hotel, but feel free to go to the sunny deck and puff, puff, puff away to your heart's content . . . apologize to your lungs later.*

Dolores Park Inn, 3641 17th St. (bet. Church & Dolores Sts.), (415) 621-0482, *Intimate Affair*

Tom Cruise slept here . . . with or without Nicole? We'll never tell! There are only three rooms, one carriage house and one suite at this low-key neighborhood hidden jewel. Situated behind the main house is the carriage house, which has a 12-foot fireplace, a full kitchen, and a massive whirlpool bath that could easily fit eight people. Other rooms include a small room for singles or a suite that comes with a 20-foot deck, a kitchen, a marble bathroom, and a fab view of Twin Peaks. Another has a Louis XVI bedroom set! Some rooms have shared baths, so do inquire if you are a privacy freak. No smoking allowed, two-night minimum required, three nights for the carriage house. Some parking is available on the street. Rates from $89–325.

Inn San Francisco, 943 South Van Ness Ave. (bet. 20th & 21st Sts.), (415) 641-0188, *Charming B&B*

We never expected to find such a lovely, romantic place to stay in the heart of the Mission, but we are proud to proclaim this a tiny gem worthy of serious consideration! Located on a mostly residential street, it's a delightful 1872 Victorian home with a full garden in the back. The backyard gazebo shelters a hot tub, available 24-hours a day for guests to unwind in a little urban oasis. A peaceful, elegant parlor welcomes you "home" in the classic Victorian style, but isn't overdone, with forest green walls, stained glass, tapestries, velvet side chairs, and other British and American antiques. The rooms are unique, but do count on feather beds and chocolate truffles no matter which room you are in. Some even have fireplaces and whirlpools! There is something for everyone here: families, lovers, or solo travelers looking for shelter. Pamper yourself in room 11, on the first floor, that opens onto a patio with its own redwood hot tub . . . very romantic! Full breakfast is included and served buffet-style with juice, fruit, cheeses, quiche, and homemade breads. Coffee, tea, and sherry are available all day long. Rates from $95 to $250. *Psst . . . as if we are not spoiled enough, there is a secret spiral staircase leading to a rooftop patio with an outrageous panoramic view of the city—incomparable to anything we encountered in the whole Bay Area.*

Other Neighborhoods

Guaymas, 5 Main St. (@ the Ferry), Tiburon, (415) 435-6300, *Sunset View*

This is one of the most enjoyable things to do on a sunny afternoon. Take the Blue & Gold Ferry from Fisherman's Wharf, and in 20 minutes you will be sipping margaritas at sunset and snacking on delicious Mexican food. Sit on the deck and enjoy the gorgeous view of the San Francisco Bay. It is always packed and just think, you don't have to drive home. Ain't life grand!

Palace of the Legion of Honor, 34th Ave. & Clement St. (right after the golf course in Lincoln Park), Richmond, (415) 863-3330, *Ancient Art*

Designed after its counterpart in Paris, and dedicated to the soldiers killed in France during WWI, the museum houses works by Rodin, Rubens, Rembrandt, Monet, Manet, Cezanne, and El Greco. Perhaps the most controversial piece is George Segal's Holocaust statue on the lawn, that depicts white plaster figures lying on the ground in anguish while a lone figure watches from behind barbed wire. After you recover from the shock of the statue, visit the garden café with great views of the Golden Gate Bridge. Cost $8.

Pez Museum, 214 California Dr. (bet. Burlingame & Howard Aves.), Burlingame, (650) 347-2301, *www.burlingamepezmuseum.com, I Want Candy*

If your passion is Pez, you will be in weird-fetish-collector heaven at the homage to the little candy dispensers that captured the hearts of millions. Located 15 minutes south of San Francisco, this museum houses nearly 300 "styles" of dispenser, including Tweetie Bird, Batman . . . even some one-of-a-kind Japanese characters. You get the picture? Now pass the candy! Closed on Sun. and Mon. *Psst . . . Pez is and has always been a fat-free food.*

Whitewater Adventures, Napa Valley, (800) 977-4837, *www.whitewater-adv.com, Adventure*

Come whoosh your way to wet and wild oblivion on this secluded (remote, baby!) Class 3 stretch on the Upper Cache Creek in Northern California, just two hours north of San Francisco. It's a whitewater wonder world! Be prepared to work hard as you cascade, but don't forget to take in the beauty that surrounds you. At night you'll bunk under the stars and experience nature at close range . . . and we don't mean your screen saver. You'll feel safe knowing the company has been in business for 20 years and takes pride in making your experience as pleasurable as possible. Adventure "Janes" will find this a great way to spend a spring afternoon or weekend. It encompasses the outdoors, it's active and it's social—all the things we love. Day trips cost $45. Two-day overnight rafting in the remote Colusa mountain range costs $89, May–June, $129 June–September.

◢ *Not to Miss:*

San Francisco Zoo, Sloat Blvd. (@ 45th Ave.) (415) 733-7080, *With Kids*

Getaways

Double Eagle Resort and Spa, 5587 Highway 158, June Lake, (760) 648-7004, *www.double-eagle-resort.com, Fly Away*

Calling all Yosemite freaks for a spa adventure at this best-kept secret of the Eastern Sierras! Where rusticity and luxury collide, you'll find this full-service spa/resort ready to pamper and entertain you to your heart's content no matter the season. Winter months bring snow sports, while the summer allows for horseback riding, hiking, mountain biking, and boating. Fantastic fly-fishing and ski-snowboarding packages are available for the outdoor gal, or maybe just send "him" off into the wilds while you spend the day being treated like the mountain princess you are! The stone-tiled pool and Jacuzzi area lets you soak as you stare out the wall of windows at the beautiful mountain peaks. Their state-of-the-art fitness facility boasts every kind of machine and class known to mankind: EFX, Stairmasters, Olympic free-weight gym, cardio kickboxing, step, yoga . . . A personal fitness evaluation is available to jumpstart your "hot body" program ($80). After exhausting yourself, slip into the saloon-style juice bar for a smoothie or a light lunch! Spa cuisine, along with critically acclaimed fare, is offered at Eagles Landing, their cozy restaurant with panoramic views of the mountains and waterfall. The eight-million-dollar renovation left no detail to chance as the fourteen comfy cabins were spiffed up to include fireplaces, full kitchens, wood-burning stoves, cable TV/VCR, and decks. Whether it's a fitness kick in the pants or a romantic weekend you seek (or perhaps

both!), this is an all-in-one destination! From San Francisco: either go through Yosemite (Hwy 120) or take the Sonora Pass to 395 South, go five miles to June Lake Loop (Hwy 158), and it's eight miles to the spa. Rooms are $153–236.

Harbin Hot Springs Retreat, Middletown, (707) 987-2477, *www. harbin.org, Clothing Optional*

Okay granola gals and freethinkers, this spa's for you! Owned and operated by the Heart Consciousness Church, one wonders whether this is more a commune than a spa getaway, but for those of you who enjoy a laid-back approach to health and beauty it provides the perfect retreat for your world-weary psyche. Come with an open mind to enjoy sunbathing *au naturel* on the beautiful sprawling redwood sundecks; hop into one of the natural hot springs or cold plunge pools for a delicious stress-relieving soak before you head to your deep-tissue massage and aromatherapy facial appointment! Seventeen hundred gorgeous acres spread out before you as you set out on a day hike . . . or maybe you'd like to try Watsu, the unique concept of Zen Shiatsu massage combined with a warm-water pool that was developed here at Harbin. They also host interesting workshops and speakers on a regular basis. If you are a health nut, you'll love that no chlorine is used in the waters here, thanks to their revolutionary filtration system, and that this area has been rated as having the cleanest air in California. They also try to use only organic foods in their restaurants whenever possible: the Storefront Restaurant ($5–15), Blue Room Café, Poolside Café, and Health Food Store. The Victorian-style buildings are charming and comfortable if not luxurious—the basic rooms have European-style shared bathrooms. For babes on a budget, bring your own bedding or sleeping bag and use the dorms, or the sundecks to sleep under the stars! Campers can buy a day pass to the facility for $30 on weekends. Memberships are also available from $10 to $300 for "lifetime." Visit the Web site for in-depth explanations of services. Devotees swear that you will not have a more unique retreat and rejuvenation vacation anywhere else on the planet! *Psst . . . 12-step meetings are held here on a regular basis.*

Directions from SF: Take 101N through Santa Rosa to the Calistoga/ River Road exit. Go east for five miles on the Mark West Road, that then becomes Porter Creek Road. Go another five miles to the flashing red light and turn left on Petrified Forest. Take a left on Foothill Blvd., then right on Tubbs Lane. At the dead end, go left over the mountain on Hwy. 29, then it's left into Middletown and the Harbin Hot Springs Retreat. (It's actually only a 90-minute trip from San Fran. Or take a Greyhound bus to Middle-town, (800) 231-2222.)

Hotel Duchamp, 421 Foss Street, Healdsburg, (707) 431-1300 or (800) 431-9341, *www.duchamphotel.com, Big Spender*

If you're not exactly into the "wild bush" scene, but you're not really a "chintz and lace" B&B gal either, meet in the middle at Sonoma's version of SoHo style: hip gals will enjoy this hotel located in the ultrahip Sonoma town of Healdsburg. Coowner Pat Lenz brought her own artistic sensibility as a sculptor to the design of this ten-cottage newcomer to the wine country "inn" scene. Done in Euro-style meets industrial chic, each cottage is luxuriously appointed with de rigueur stainless-steel fixtures, mod furnishings, and all the latest amenities—CD players, data ports, and portable phones—this is a feasible getaway for workaholics too. The six "villas" have high ceilings, beautiful blond wood floors, fireplaces, and French doors that open onto a lovely courtyard; the other four "cottages" are named after painters Man Ray, Warhol, Miro, and Picasso, and decorated accordingly. These original four structures have exposed ceilings and their own outdoor decks and porches, but never plunge entirely into the bucolic thanks to touches like the neon lips in the Man Ray unit! Enjoy Continental breakfast "en plein air" by the lap pool (weather permitting) or in the attractive reception area. The hotel is within walking distance of the town square, where there is a great selection of adorable cafés and restaurants. Playing hooky during the week was never so easy—just bring your laptop and cell phone! Cottages average $295 per night on weekends/$250 per night during the week. *Psst . . . Peter Lenz oversees their family vineyard nearby. . . . Maybe a little wine tasting is in order!*

Osmosis Enzyme Bath and Massage, 209 Bohemian Hwy, Freestone, (707) 823-8231, *www.osmosis.com, Turning Japanese*

For the more "foo foo" among us, there is one of *Travel and Leisure*'s Top Ten Day Spas waiting patiently for you in Sonoma County's first historic district, Freestone. Just one hour north of San Francisco, find this five-acre key to salvation . . . or at least relaxation! Osmosis Enzyme Bath and Massage is itself a rejuvenating heat treatment bath from Japan, using fragrant cedar, rice bran, and 600 enzymes to naturally break down toxins and relax the body, as well as increase metabolism and circulation. Your bath is then followed by a yummy 75-minute massage ($150 for 2½ hours, including Japanese Tea service). You can even opt for the slightly more expensive but heavenly Outdoor Pagoda Massage, performed behind the pagoda's shoji doors surrounded by the pepperwoods, bamboo, and bonsai gardens along Salmon Creek (add $45). Try the Enzyme Bath à la carte for $75, $65 each for two or more people. The aromatherapy facials, using Australian products with exotic herbs and flowers, are equally magnificent ($90 for 75 min.) and include a footbath, shoulder massage, and hydrating hand treatment. While you can't spend the night at this gorgeous Japanese-style retreat (unless you hide in the pagoda), there is an adorable B&B run by Rosemary Hoffman within walking distance: Green Apple Inn, (707) 874-2526. Don't miss Rosemary's homemade bread! We love the ambiance at Osmosis . . . it is lovely yet relaxed. . . . Summer breeze in a bottle! FYI—if you have ever been to Santa Fe, you may have visited their equally acclaimed sister spa, Ten Thousand Waves.

Safari West, 3115 Porter Creek Road, Santa Rosa, (707) 579-2551, *www.safariwest.com, Out of Africa*

Have you always yearned to take a walk on the wild side but were too afraid of malaria to try? Peter and Nancy Lang have the solution: "Tent Camp" at their exclusive African wildlife reserve, situated on 400 gorgeous acres in the heart of the wine country. As one of only 14 accredited private institutions belonging to the American Zoo and Aquarium Association, the Lang's focus remains on conservation and research, but they hope that by sharing the exotic beauty of these creatures with the public it will heighten global awareness of the many species on the verge of extinction. In order to bring these "wildebeests" to the attention of you "wildebabes," in 1992 they created an authentic safari experience with equally authentic yet luxurious accommodations to entice you into their world, filled with over 350 beasts and birds including giraffe, zebra, antelope, gazelle, and lemur, not to mention the queen of them all, Delilah, the extremely exotic and colorful great Indian hornbill who rules the roost around here! And, do not be surprised if you get the chance to witness baby zebras coming into the world, and then, five minutes later, a baby giraffe—naturalists report that there are sometimes as many as three births a day here. The "tents," designed by a team of South African tent-cabin architects (talk about niche marketing!), come complete with gorgeous hardwood floors, sumptuous king-size beds, and private bathroom with a shower. You will feel like you've been halfway around the globe without the mandatory vaccinations! All jokes aside, Safari

West is "dedicated to wildlife research aimed at sustaining and increasing populations of endangered wildlife while providing extensive and in-depth educational programs on conservation to the public," and your groovy vacation helps fund this noble cause! March–December (weather permitting), cabins start at $200 per night (including food and 2½ hour safari). *Psst . . . have no fear, while you can see the wildlife from your tents, they are safely separated so that there is no chance you'll wake up with a giraffe in your bed!*

Silverado Resort, 1600 Atlas Peak Road, Napa, (800) 532-0500, *www.silveradoresort.com, Full Service*

Built at the turn of the Millennium, this gorgeous European-style spa is the jewel in the crown of the 1870s landmark formerly known as the Napa Valley Resort, located across the street. Unfortunately, you must be a resort guest in order to use the spa, but it is well worth an overnight jaunt to do so! A mere 90-minute drive from the city, you'll find 17 plexipaved tennis courts surrounded by flower gardens, ten pools, and two superb golf courses to while away the weekend. . . . Or, just flat-out indulge your senses with the spa's signature "Silverado" treatment ($195): a stimulating citrus body scrub and buff, followed by a delicious clay mask and 20-minute detoxifying body wrap that is sure to pull out any "urban poisons" lurking on a cellular level! You'll be blissfully ready for an in-suite Couples Massage ($170) by the fire, to end the day on a sensuously relaxed note. Private cottage suites are clustered around hidden courtyards and secluded swimming pools surrounding the main white-pillared mansion. Interiors are airy and spacious—most with fireplaces, kitchen, wet bar, and patio—modern, yet romantic! The restaurant boasts an award-winning chef, but in-room dining is equally delicious and twice as cozy. Rooms $270–1,405 with a two-night weekend minimum April to October. *Psst . . . if water-skiing is your thing, check nearby Lake Berryessa!*

Sonoma Mission Inn & Spa, 18140 Sonoma Highway 12, (707) 938-9000 or (800) 862-4945 for reservations, *www.sonomamissioninn.com, Rest and Relaxation*

You might have left your heart in San Francisco, but there is no better place to leave the rest of you than Sonoma . . . even if it's just for the weekend! Overworked executives, health enthusiasts and couples in love have been flocking to this spa haven since the late 1920s to indulge and self-medicate with their legendary natural mineral waters—glamorously labeled "san-

itas per aquas," aka "healing through water." This is a full-service European health spa done California-style—high on service and aesthetics, but maintaining a laid-back atmosphere. . . . All the amenities of a four-star hotel with two award-winning restaurants. The grounds are lovely and the rooms range from the original design circa 1927 to suites added during their massive Millennium renovation. Forty thousand square feet of spa and exercise facilities, hiking and biking trails, and a championship golf course designed by Whiting and Watson, make for the perfect escape. All roads lead to the Bathing Ritual, a cornerstone of their "program" thanks to the divine hot mineral water 1,100 feet below the Earth's surface: you will be escorted through rooms and dunked in pools of the aforementioned liquid at successively higher temperatures before being cooled off in the shower and sent to the steam room and sauna, before waddling to your next treatment or back to your cozy room for a rare and blissful good night's sleep! And have no fear—if New Age music stresses you out, they have a complete musical library from which to choose your accompanying treatment tunes. . . . There are over 50 specialized spa treatments available, and all are offered à la carte; however, we suggest you try their nifty two- and four-day "immersion" package ($569–1,689), that leave you feeling like you've been on an island for three months staring into space . . . and this island has room service! *Psst . . . the inn's kitchen and restaurants have both regular and spa menus to keep you on track when French fries start calling!*

Ventana Inn & Spa, Highway 1, Big Sur, (800) 628-6500, *www.ventana-inn.com, Couples Getaway*

This is the perfect destination for a spontaneous getaway with Mr. Right. The Pacific views alone will make you swoon, but the deliciously romantic rooms, restaurant and spa make for a weekend to remember! After 25 years as a top-rated resort, the recent addition of the Allegria spa leaves nothing to be desired. . . . Allegria literally means "happiness" and accurately describes the state of body and soul after the Ultimate Spa Experience ($200), a two-hour wrap and massage combo that will send you to nirvana and back in time for dinner at the four-star Cielo, where you can enjoy the best in California cuisine on the patio overlooking the Pacific. The restaurant is reachable by shuttle or a fifteen-minute walk via lighted trail from the rooms, for added privacy. They use vegetables from Ventana's gardens and bake their breads and pastries on-site. Or indulge in the magic Ultimate Couples Experience (2 hours for $425), where your choice of aromatherapeutic bath is drawn while you are both massaged or herbally wrapped in tandem in your candle-lit private room before you are led weak-kneed to the tub and left in peace for a little "hydrotherapy," or just plain old hanky-panky! Both the pools and the Japanese Hot Baths offer "clothing optional" areas. There are 56 enchantingly romantic rooms with ocean or mountain views, and three townhouse suites with the added amenities of fireplace, wet bar and hot tub. Activity mongers will enjoy the local hiking and horseback riding available . . . or just hop back in the car and head 2 hours up the coast to the Hearst Castle in San Simeon before heading back in time for the complimentary wine and cheese served in the gorgeous glass-and-cedar lobby. Rooms are $300–1,575. *Psst . . . the spa also offers unique services like astrology readings and "color/aura analysis," which includes a personalized watercolor of your "light body" ($100).*